Transforming with Water

CW01017616

IFLA 2008 ~ Proceedings of the 45t

of the International Federation of Landscape Architects

30th June – 3rd July 2008, Orpheus Congress Centre

Apeldoorn, The Netherlands

~ Edited by Wybe Kuitert

~ Published by Blauwdruk / Techne Press ~ The Netherlands

IFLA 2008 ~ Proceedings of the 45th World Congress
of the International Federation of Landscape Architects
Transforming with Water

Edited by Wybe Kuitert
Published by Blauwdruk and Techne Press

ISBN 978-90-8594-021-0
Wageningen, The Netherlands
www.uitgeverijblauwdruk.nl
www.technepress.nl
June, 2008

This publication was made possible
by the financial support of

 Nieuwland, Wageningen, The Netherlands
www.nieuwland.nl, www.nieuwlandadvies.nl

and
  MTD landscape architects, 's Hertogenbosch, The
Netherlands
www.mtd@mtdlandschapsarchitecten.nl

We greatefully acknowledge the support of
authors, sponsors and anyone else who has
made the production of this book possible.

  Wybe Kuitert
  Harry Harsema

Foreword

Water: the critical resource

~ **Diane Menzies** ~ President International Federation of Landscape Architects

People ,plants and animals need water to live and flourish. No city can exist without water. Water can also be used to enhance the liveability of cities and towns such as in fountains and ponds. But water, whether in streams or lakes, or used in canals for transport is also a natural element and requires careful management. Too much water or water in the wrong place or condition can be catastrophic. Floods, mud slides, silted, polluted and poisoned water, are all examples of problems which can affect cities and communities. In addition droughts can destroy life and water is being increasingly fought over as a scarce resource. Careful harvesting, cleaning, use and re-use are also a focus. Climate change, with unpredictable rainfall and sea level rise introduces additional problems to address.

This is not news, and attention has been increasingly directed to water and water sensitive management each year recently. Technology and science are now enabling better planning and design skills to be applied, and sharing this information benefits our landscape architecture profession.

Therefore the IFLA World Congress theme 'Transformations with Water' is extremely timely. Experience from around the world will be shared with those who face challenges: academic knowledge will help us and the landscape architecture profession will be in a better position to respond.

I welcome participants to a stimulating and insightful IFLA World Congress in Apeldoorn, Netherlands, and thank our hosts NVTL for their foresight and leadership.

LANDSCAPE ARCHITECTS

MTD Landschapsarchitecten | Zuid-Willemsvaart 142 | PO Box 5225 | 5201 GE 's-Hertogenbosch | The Netherlands
T 0031(0)73-6125033 | **F** 0031(0)73-6136665 | **E** mtd@mtdlandschapsarchitecten.nl | **I** www.mtdlandschapsarchitecten.nl

LANDSCAPE HISTORY

CULTURAL LANDSCAPES

LANDSCAPE PLANNING

LANDSCAPE ECOLOGY

LANDSCAPE AND LEISURE

INFRASTRUCTURES AND LANDSCAPE

HISTORICAL CENTRE DORDRECHT HOLLAND — 08

WATERFRONT HANGZHOU CHINA — 08

TOWNPLAN JUMILLA SPAIN — 08

WATERFRONT RAVENSTEIN HOLLAND — 08

LANDSCAPEPLAN CASTRICUM AT SEA HOLLAND — 08

GENIEPARK STELLING VAN AMSTERDAM HOLLAND — 08

Transforming with Water

45th IFLA World Congress 2008

The congress is jointly organized by
- Stichting IFLA 2008 foundation, in cooperation with
- Netherlands Association for Landscape Architecture NVTL, and
- International Federation of Landscape Architects, IFLA Headquarters

Stichting IFLA 2008 foundation
Founding / acting members:
Charlotte Buys - President
John Boon - Secretary
Michael Reijn - Finances
Frank Lewis - Public Relations
Wybe Kuitert - Program
Michaël van Buuren - Program Coordinator

Program Committee
Wybe Kuitert - President
Natascha van den Ban
Tom Brekelmans
Marlies Brinkhuijsen
Michaël van Buuren
Femke Haccoû
Kasper Klap
Mark Niesten
Jacco Schuurkamp
Wiwi Tjiook

Organization, Project Team
Xander de Bruine – Manager

Contact information
IFLA 2008, Project Team
P.O. BOX 37756
1030 BJ Amsterdam
THE NETHERLANDS
www.nvtl.nl

Table of Contents

Intentions

~ **Wybe Kuitert** ~ President of the Program Committee

Landscapes Work with Water

Without water there is no mankind; no landscape that evolves. For ages man has lived together with water - water which has supported the landscapes of our civilizations. It is with water that the outward appearance, the face of the earth originated, has grown, evolved, and was transformed when man entered on the scene. Of course, landscape architects, planners and designers do understand - and want to understand even better - the fundamentals of water and the power it has in transforming our landscapes.

The transforming forces of water are the common theme on which we create our landscapes: that is why water is our destiny, our fate or fortune. And it is together with the changing forms of water that we ourselves in the end also transform - transform our education, practice, business and profession.

An Epoch-making Opportunity

So, it is water that transforms and presents an opportunity to reaffirm our commitments to landscape. At present the opportunities are epoch-making. Changing weather conditions present an urgent and demanding task to humankind all over the world. The great Tsunami, Hurricane Katrina, melting glaciers, and the extreme drought in many parts of the world show the dramatic forces of water, whether we get too much or too little. Agricultural systems will have to be adapted, our leisure behaviour will change with popular holiday destinations becoming too wet, too hot and dry, or lacking the required snow. Other areas perhaps will prosper from an improving climate. Urban structures will have to be rethought in order to cope with extreme peaks in precipitation, or to manipulate scarce fresh water through smart retention planning for surface and subsoil water.

Transforming with Water

The primary focus of the congress is to facilitate a full discussion on the possibilities of designing with water, whether it is not enough or, on the contrary, too much. In a juxtaposition of water as either friend or foe the congress wants to extend the debate to facilitate the discovery of new ways of living together with water's transforming power. But strictly and honestly speaking, water is never friend, nor foe. When water seems to be a foe, as in the Netherlands, it is rather an indispensable inevitability; nasty perhaps, but it can't be helped. It is something like a chronic disease inside one's body not to be denied, but only to be accepted and accounted for. It is only possible to deal with water with detailed strategies and an intricate landscape planning; it means that we have to understand water as much as possible. As our understanding increases, our approach can develop. It would be naive to say that we understand water completely, that we know what we are doing, and that there is no need to develop thinking further.

On the other hand, when water seems to be a welcome, needed ally, it will never be a reliable friend. Water is so different in character from us. When we want more water in landscapes of scarcity, it is water that sinks away and simply withdraws. We want to see water as a benign, loyal, and always present friend, but it will never be a trustworthy partner. Rather it invokes greediness within ourselves. We shower, swim, and wash our cars. Water just makes us lose control, and landscapes will not reach maturity. Fickle friend or friendly foe. Transforming with the will of water requires our best understanding.

Wisdom with Water – Landscape Wisdom: The Congress

The confidence that wealthier countries have developed when relying on classical paradigms of science and technology as the ultimate solutions to whatever problem seems to be no longer tenable. In the best case a solution works for a limited period of time in a limited part of the world. Now, with the increasing exchange of information, and our increasing awareness of being part of a global community, care should also be taken of other parts of the world that do not profit from science and technology. It is actually the same global awareness that proves the impossibility of a bare technical solution that works globally. Solutions that would satisfy the entire world require resources far above what the earth can provide and are simply not available for all humankind.

In our handling of the world's water, such problems have become most evident and clear. After centuries of living with water, it are the non-developed cultures, in particular, which have developed the wisdom and experience to exploit nature and construct a landscape as a solution with the often limited blessings that nature offers in itself. This kind of landscape makes a culture sustainable in the long run. And when you think of it, this is also true for developed countries as well. No landscape, no culture.

What about landscape architecture? In its innate character it is landscape architecture that is integral and interdisciplinary. It is landscape architecture that can understand the complicated workings of the environment, the interdependence of man and nature, or man and water. It is landscape architecture that can present solutions on ways of shaping this interdependence into a new environment that works. Landscape architecture can create an awareness that transcends the traditional technology-oriented manipulations of water in the landscape.

The small-scale garden or park is the most comprehensive form of man-made landscape. It shows us the pertinence of paradigms, and of ways to understand how landscape works. The garden is the scientific test tube which teaches us how to tackle more extensive, vaster landscapes with more complex requirements from the human side, and more complex and demanding structures as regards topography and ecology.

Without any line of division between developed or underdeveloped, and without a segregation between the garden and regional landscape planning, the aim of the Congress is to learn from other parts of the world, learn from other scales of thinking, and to reflect from a global perspective on wisdom, experience, and universally sound knowledge when it comes to transforming with water.

1

Living with Water

No life without water. A definite truth that keeps landscape architects at work all over the world. We design systems to irrigate in places where water is scarce or we invent landscapes to drain and control a surplus of water. Agriculture, leisure, cityscape: the water system comes to support a complex system of living, working, and loving, a system that we call the human settlement, although it may even include nature conservation aims. Living with scarce water requires contrivance and understanding, as can be understood from case studies presented in this chapter.

Landscape planning in an arid climate requires utmost concern for the use of precious water. Whether used as a means to improve the climate and enlarge possibilities for extensive forestry, finally facilitating human occupation (Gobi); or as an indicator for wisdom of aboriginals from whom, and with whom we must learn to be able to teach again about water's primordial values (Alice Springs). Or we may discover design strategies mitigating the use of water as an opportunity for landscape architecture (Kansas).

But also an abundance of rain transforms our thinking about landscape architecture as a tool to develop strategies for our environment. Living with an excess of water asks for measures and strategies to cope with it, as shown with cases from Malaysia, Vietnam, or Holland.

Well over 5000 mm of yearly rainfall gives extreme problems with flash floods, but also extreme opportunities to beautify the landscape of Malaysia through brilliant design with water. Coping with, and adapting to extreme flooding, generated different urban design strategies in ancient China that hold value for urban development today. Urban wastewater systems are a basis for green infrastructure, where landscape architecture comes to provide viable solutions for sustainable urban design, rather than mitigate or camouflage waste-water. How water was, is and will remain the driving force behind landscape, society, and policy making in the Netherlands is subject of the last paper of this set.

1.1 Living with Water ~ Papers of Morning Sessions

(Image Essay) A Blue Lagoon for the Netherlands
~ Adriaan Geuze, landscape architect, West 8, Netherlands

(Abstract) Facing Urban Water Stress – Robust Findings, Key Uncertainties, and some Ideas
~ Chris Zevenbergen, Professor Urban Water Management and Sanitation for UNESCO-IHE, Netherlands

Creating an Oasis in the Gobi: Water Oriented Network Development in Oasis City
~ Binyi Liu, Professor and Chairman Department of Landscape Studies, College of Architecture and Urban Planning, Tongji University, Shanghai, China

Water and Desert, Alice Springs
~ Judith van Gelderen, Landscape Architect, Director KIAH Infranet, Sydney

Sustainable Design Concepts for Building a Scarce-Watercity
~ Melanie Klein, Professor, Kansas State University, US

Water Purificative Landscapes . Constructed Ecologies and Contemporary Urbanism
~ Antje Stokman, Professor, Faculty of Architecture and Landscape Sciences, Leibniz University Hannover, Germany

Water in Malaysian Landscape Architecture
   ~ Rotina Mohd Daik, Landscape Architect, National Landscape Department, Malaysia, and Mustafa Kamal Bin Mohd Shariff, Professor and Dean, Faculty of Design and Architecture, Universiti Putra Malaysia, Malaysia

The Water Adaptive Landscapes in Ancient Chinese Cities
~ Kongjian Yu, Dihua Li, and Zhang Lei, The Graduate School of Landscape Architecture, Peking University, China

Water and Space in the Netherlands, Living with Water in the 21th Century
~ Renske Peters, Michelle Hendriks, Directorate-General Water, Ministry of Transport and Infrastructure, Netherlands

Project map of the Blue Isles, January 2008. The islands are from 5 to 25 kilometres off the existing shore. The construction of these Blue Isles can neutralise the rising sea level for the coming century.

A Blue Lagoon for the Netherlands

~ **Adriaan Geuze** ~ Professor landscape architecture Harvard University. USA ~

Sander Lap (**image essay**) ~ landscape architects West 8

The Delta Metropolis (the conglomerate of cities in the west of the Low Countries) is one of the most densely populated areas in the world. Contrary to cities like Paris and London, the Delta Metropolis has developed into a zone that is hard to define; Both the Dutch Randstad and the Belgian Vlaamse Ruit are conurbations without a beginning or an end: a disorderly district with outskirts and suburbs, industrial sites, retail parks, ports and infrastructure laced with scraps of authentic, historical scenery. Because of the rising sea level and the steady reduction of open space and nature areas, the Delta Metropolis is loosing its popularity.

The Blue Isles Consortium drew up a plan which combines an agenda for safety and the necessity of new land. The participants offer the metropolis new perspective by proposing a series of sprayed-up islands off the coast of Belgium and the Netherlands. These dune islands, measuring up to 150.000 hectares, will brake the increasing waves. Also, thanks to ingenious engineering of the gullies, the

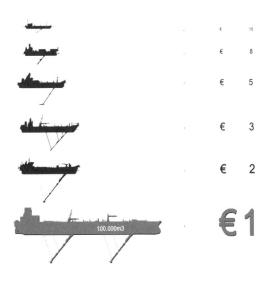

The use of bigger ships, like other innovative solutions lead to higher efficiency, lower costs and new perspectives.

Cross-section of the trough from which the sand is won. The troughs turn into special habitats with new resting areas and spawning grounds for different fish species.

The first island could be built in front of the mouth of the Westerschelde. Here, the new island could lower the sea level by 50 cm during storm surge.

The total area of the Blue Isles will be once or twice as big as the province Flevoland, adding up to more than 150.000 hectares of new land.

■ Landfill en aanplempin

The techniques of reclaiming land above sea level are not new. The Netherlands already has more than 23.000 hectares of landfill.

off-shore under tow will cause the sea level to drop during north-western storms.

The islands, with their extended beaches, dunes and mud-flats, will have softly undulating inner dunes, where one million lots for small estates will be issued. On the biggest island Hollandsoog, a broad representation of the community will be able to obtain a lease. The economy of this island will be based on leisure and nature experience. The Old Country will remain the place for daily traffic, work and schools. The construction of these islands can also benefit the fishing-industry. The sand winning will cause deep troughs. Within this special habitat, resting areas and spawning grounds will develop, causing an increase in the number of species. By combining these different interests, the islands form a sustainable gift for future generations.

Source: *Het Landelijk Dagblad* Designing with Water. *Het Landelijk Dagblad* is published by NVTL. Free copies available at the IFLA-congress.

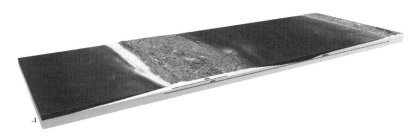

7. Cross section of a Blue Isle. The islands do not consist of the low, reclaimed bottom of the sea, but will be sprayed up to a safe level above the sea.

The biggest island, Hollandsoog, off the coast from the Randstad, will be approximately the size of Long Island, New York.

Scale reference: Reclaimed land off the coast of Dubai, projected off the coast of the Netherlands

Facing Urban Water Stress

Robust Findings, Key Uncertainties, and some Ideas

~ Chris Zevenbergen ~ Professor UrbanWater Management and Sanitation for UNESCO-IHE, Netherlands ~ abstract

Cities are evolving systems. We have little understanding on their behaviour. What we do know, is that they are highly dynamic and complex, in that they face changing environments and inputs, and adapt to these changes. Over a longer, historical time frame cities have always successfully adapted to changing environmental conditions and thus have been extremely resilient. From 1100 to 1800 only 42 cities worldwide were abandoned after their first construction. The year 2007 marks a turning point in history: half of the world population lives in a city. Moreover, the trend of rapid urban growth through the mid-20th century in the developed world has now shifted to the developing regions of Asia and Africa. Urbanisation has lead to an increase of economic and social wealth in some places but also to a continuing poverty of others. The urban population is expected to double from 2 billion to 4 billion in the next 30 to 35 years. These growth rates imply that every week one city of 1 mln inhabitants will be built for the next four decades. It appears that cities have a limited capacity to adapt proactively to these rapid changes and are losing the ability to anticipate and deal with natural hazards such as floods and droughts. It is evident that changes in climate will likely have major implications for the future design of the layout of cities and of their individual buildings. This presentation elaborates on water related impacts that urbanisation and climate change impose on cities, such as a reduction on available water resources and increased flooding. It completes with examples of front runner cities that appear to be successful in responding to these changes, and in steering the process of expansion and redevelopment in the right direction, through integrated planning and action at local level.

Creating an Oasis in the Gobi

Water Oriented Network Development in Oasis City

~ **Binyi Liu** ~ Professor and Chairman Department of Landscape Studies,

College of Architecture and Urban Planning, Tongji University, Shanghai,

China

Introduction

This article describes a landscape planning project that uses water in innovative ways and incorporates extensive forestry plantings in Aksu City, Xinjiang Province, China. Aksu is located in the arid Gobi region of China. The project serves as an example, of the key role that water plays in planning and design for the development of a city in an arid region like Gobi. It is a comprehensive project occupying 11,660 square kilometers and includes the planning of a water system, a forestry system, an urban master plan and the urban design for the development of a new downtown area of the city.

First, the project is based on discovering an active relationship between the urban water network and forestry in an arid region. A construction strategy was used that combines a water network and forestry network. It includes the following steps: step 1 is making a water network (using water) – making a forestry network (media) – anti-desertification-resulting in usable land. Step 2 is circulation of water in a network in an ecologically balanced manner by holding water and extending water-shed – extending forestry by extending ecological community – enlarging oasis area by reducing the desert area and providing green land.

Second, based on conclusions drawn from local practice and experiences with

Figure 1. Project location and context

Figure 2. The landscape of Kekeya forestry construction project

water system construction in the Gobi region, the basic procedure for water network planning was provided and applied: connecting each channel, ditch, and trench to form a water network; adding on to the water area to enlarge the capability of water; combining the water network with forestry by planting more trees along ditches and trenches so that water and trees can help each other in terms of growing more trees and holding more water; combining water front construction with the development of a new downtown area of the city.

Finally, based on the discovery of an active relationship between urban water network and urban development patterns and new developments in the downtown section of this arid region, a new urban development pattern and construction layout based on the water network was proposed.

Project background

Aksu is a place where once the Silk Road passed by. Its urban administration area occupies 11,660 square kilometers with currently a population of nearly 600 thousands. It is one of the world's main arid regions, located in the south of Xinjiang Uighur Autonomous Region, adjacent to the Taklimakan desert.

Since the 18th century, Aksu people struggled against the drought and desert environment using the abundant water resources, getting successful experiences and achievements, especially through the more than 50 years of construction since the founding of the People's Republic of China. The name "Aksu" means "white water", and water resources are distributed abundantly in Aksu region. There are six rivers that flow through this region, their annual runoff is up to

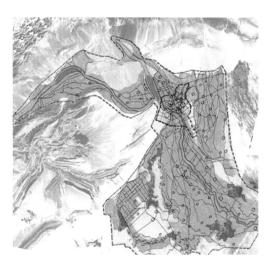

Figure 3. Existing situation of water system and forest in urban administration controlling area of Aksu

Figure 4. Planning of water system and forest in urban administration controlling area of Aksu

11.4 billion cubic meters. After years of agriculture production, the area of arable land of Aksu has increased greatly, giving priority to planting rice, cotton, and fruits. Particularly because of water utilization and irrigation systems, it has been worthy of the phrases "southern part of China in frontier area"; "a land flowing with milk and honey"; "city of melons and fruits". In recent years, taking "Kekeya Greenery Project" (Figure 2.) as representative, the following words are most apt: "forest construction based on water and protecting water resources by forest; circulating construction and improving the ecological environment."

This project has perfected the urban environment: increased precipitation and reduced evaporation improved the quality of the downtown environment and has provided experiences on urban greening construction for the whole Xinjiang region. This Project was evaluated as one of the "Global 500 excellent environments" in 1996 by the UN Food and Agriculture Organization.

On this basis, the municipal government proposed the urban development strategic goal of building Aksu into a "city of water charm; excellent human settlement environment; the pearl of the West Part of China" in 2005. This attempts to solve the human settlement problem of "water–city–desert" following the basic solution of "water–agriculture–desert" for human survival. Therefore, at the beginning of 2005, three projects were established: "urban water system planning", "urban forestry planning", and "urban master planning", and a new idea of urban development guided by a water system and based on forestry was put forward.

Figure 5. Existing situation of water system in urban district area of Aksu

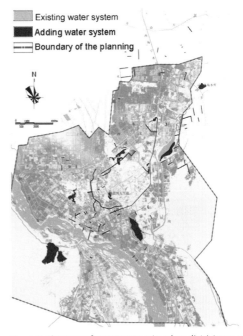

Figure 6. Planning of water system in urban district area of Aksu

Guiding ideology

Aksu urban administration controlling area (city territory) is located in an arid region with rare rainfall, also a fatal problem is that the precipitation is far less than the evaporation. The interaction of arid climate and great evaporation causes deteriorating vicious circles and has further aggravated problems. In the macroscopic regional scale, geographical features in arid district are hard to change. Drought will always be accompanying human's existence. From the macroscopic regional scale to a lodgeable city (Fig.3 and 4.), the positive activities people can do, are to increase forest vegetation and to adjust agricultural industrial structures through forestry planning to protect water resources, conserve water bodies, and decrease water evaporation, and realize water saving.

The urban district area (city district) of Aksu is located in the oasis with relatively rich water resources, so its agriculture could be developed. However, due to unreasonable agriculture industrial development, especially in recent 50 years, the naturally-formed oasis environment deteriorated rapidly. Rice cultivation and large-scale water usage proved unsuitable, resulting in a great evaporation of the ground surface water, so it is imperative that rice cultivation should be changed to economic forestry such as fruits planting. Meanwhile, extensive afforestation along rivers, canales and roads is proved by practice to be active and effective for improving the oasis environment: it conserves the water body; it decreases water evaporation; it reduces sand-dust; it protects the water banks; it prevents loss of water and erosion of soil. This kind of afforestation needs further generalization and implementation. In the city district, opposite to the course of agricultural reclamation and the destruction of natural forest vegetation in the last 100 years, it is a long-term

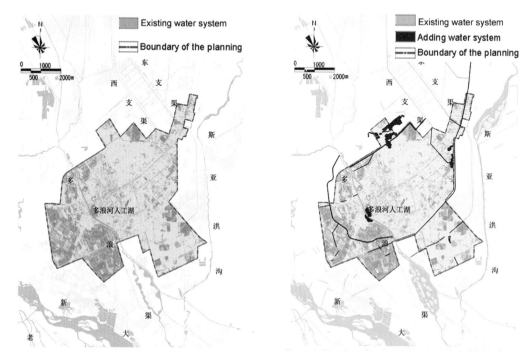

Figure 7. Existing situation of water system in central district of Aksu

Figure 8. planning of water system in central district of Aksu strategic objective to restore the original oasis by the reverse process of non-agri-culturalization, afforestation, conservation of water and soil (Figure 5 and 6).

The central city (city build area) of Aksu is an emerging downtown area. The city was established after the county was canceled in 1983 because of weak municipal infrastructure and lack of urban water system and waterfront area construction. Besides the only one waterfront park, there were dirty ditches, most of which ran through the city. Domestic refuse and sewage were discharged into some ditches, the water quality was so poor that these had become a landfill by people. And such a vicious circle made a city of drought. The traditional oasis habitant environment deteriorated to such an extent that it should be taken into consideration immediately. Meanwhile, as an important tourism city of the Southern Part of Xinjiang on the Silk Road, it is urgent to improve and construct water system, purify and beautify the city. Finally, with the improvement of peo-ple's living standard, the environmental consciousness of all people from the mayor to the citizens is increasing. In the course of a new round of urban plan-ning, expanding, and constructing, it has been the mutual recognition that we should regard the promotion of the urban environment as the moving force, urban forestry construction as a basis, and water system construction as the guide (Figure 7 and 8).

Planning

The framework of the Aksu water system landscape planning shows in Table 1.
The basic evaluation criteria for this planning sytem are threefold: Water secu-rity, water ecology (i.e. water ecosystem / aquatic ecosystem), and water related human activities. These three criteria measure the success or failure for the plan-ning system.

Water security
Water security includes three aspects: economizing and increasing water resource; protecting and promoting the environment of water; flood prevention.
a. Organizing integrated water system and circular network for cyclic usage; combining water and greening to decrease evaporation of the ground surface water, including choosing trees which are of less evaporation such as Xinjiang poplars to limit evaporation of the surface water.
b. Constructing artificial wetland, combined with flood control. Aksu has ever suffered from flood disaster and the downtown district has been flooded. The artificial wetland is drowned in high-flow period, forming water surfaces of vari-able size in drought period. It has solved the problem of flood prevention in the urban, and purified the water used for irrigation.
c. Technical application of collecting and preserving water. Rainwater is a most important resource in arid region. In the aspect of rainwater utilization, people in Southern Part of Xinjiang have rich experiences and the typical example is Karez. Aksu has great potential in utilization of rainwater resources, the evapora-tion and permeating time can be extended with settling reservoirs. The artificial wetland can also play the role of collecting and preserving water.

d. Technical application of agricultural water saving. The agriculture accounts for 85%-90% of the overall water consumption in Aksu. Currently the utilizing rate of irrigation water is 0.47, and if that can be raised by 10%, 1.5 billion cubic meters of water can be saved annually. Agricultural water saving can be realized through multiple means such as anti-seepage of channels, efficient sprinkling irrigation and drip irrigation.

Water ecology

Water ecosystem includes three aspects as improved quality of the water environment; protection of banks or sides of rivers and lakes; conservation of bio-communities:

a. Setting sedimentation tanks in rivers and reducing sediment to improve the quality of water.

b. Applying ecological treatment to waterfront design and enlarging the greening area. There are currently two variations of banks in Aksu: natural earth canals and man-made cement channels. The former is weak in seepage-prevention but is beneficial to the vegetation and the enhancement of waterfront eco-

	Objectives and tasks	Problems to be solved
urban administration controlling area (city territory)	1. protecting the existing natural and artificial rivers and waters 2. protecting the natural forest and artificial greening 3. protecting the eco-environment of oasis	Preserving water through forest
urban districted area (city district)	1. extending rivers and connecting the main and branch canals, increasing wetland and enhancing water circulation	1. organizing water system and form network ;increasing the area of wate conservation
	2 .enlarging forest and economic forest	2. carrying out afforestation and buil green belt
	3. balancing agricultural development and natural environment protection	3. adjusting agriculture industrial str and improving the efficiency of wate in agriculture
The central city (city build area)	1. increasing branch canals and connecting water system, enhancing circulation and forming a high-density water network	1. connecting urban water system an enlarging water area in the city
	2. increasing urban greening	2. increasing the greening of the urba waterfront
	3. developing waterfront area and belt to promote city exploitation and development	3. providing recreational area in the u waterfront to promote city exploitati and development

Table 1. Framework of Aksu landscape water system planning

logical environment; the latter has a good anti-seepage effect, but is unfavorable to the development of bio-communities. The planning advocates a limitation of the latter one, and wants to increase the ecological bank belt.

c. Increasing (Enriching) aquatic plant communities with the basic varieties such as aquatic reeds, Acorus calamus, etc.

Water-related activities

Water-related activities include the following three aspects: constructing the activity fields of urban waterfront; establishing the landscape image of urban waterfront; developing various types of land estate in urban waterfront area.

a. To construct the activity fields of urban waterfront. Exploiting public recreational spaces in waterfront areas along the main rivers and canals of the city, combined with greening.

b. To establish the landscape image of urban waterfront. Making the rivers and riverbanks become the main urban landscape visual corridor by exploiting activity places, streets and greenery to create the image of the city with water charm.

c. To develop various types of land estates in urban waterfront area. Improving

Implementation approaches	Implementation alternatives relating to water	
	Scale	Implementation schemes
1. Circulating water to conserve soil and water& expanding water area		Increasing the main irrigational cooperating
2. Building forest network to extend forest eco-community and improving	Fig.3	with regional forest construction
the potential of storing water 11660 km^2	Fig.4	
1.1. connecting main canals and water system;	498 km^2	Preserving 5 main canals in north-south
1.2. making cyclic use of water and decreasing evaporation of the surface water;	Fig. 5	direction(Total length 104 km);
1.3. constructing artificial lakes and wetland combined with flood control;	Fig. 6	Increasing some branch channels, the total
2. choosing local trees for economic forest;		length is 377.6 km
3.1. Increasing fruit trees and orchards; decreasing the production of crops;		Preserving 1 main canal in east-west direction:
3.2. applying anti-seepage and efficient drip irrigation to agriculture.		Geming big water channel (17km-22m)
		Building 8 new lakes with total area of 345ha.
		Extension of 1 artificial lake of 2.6ha
		Protecting two natural lakes (59 ha).
1.1. connecting main canals and water system ; Making cyclic use of water	36.9km^2	Adding 1 main canal in north-south direction:
1.2. constructing artificial lakes and wetland combined with flood control	Fig. 7	Water channel of Jiangsu Road (4.3km 30m)
1.3. applying ecological treatment to waterfront design	Fig. 8	Adding 3 main canals in east-west
1.4.setting sedimentation tank in rivers	Fig. 9	direction (31 km)
2.1. widening the green belt of waterfront and increasing bio-species		Increasing some branch channels(total length
2.2. increasing water plants		is 6.4 km)
3.1. building waterfront area for recreation		Building 4 new artificial lakes (area 52.9ha)
3.2. constructing the framework for new urban development by the space		1. artificial lake in Huyang park
of waterfront landscape		(lake shoreline 1716m area 5.4ha)
		2. Youyi lake (lake shoreline 1181m area 2.9ha)
		3. Moon lake(lake shoreline 9139m area 42ha)
		4. Yingbin lake (lake shoreline 1147m area
		2.6ha) Extension of 1 artificial lake:
		1. artificial lake in Duolang park (lake shore-
		line is increased by 573m to 2279m,the area
		is increased by 6.1ha to 11ha. Waterfront
		construction: Duolang River 6km.

the quality of environment and promoting the land price at the waterfront by water ecology and water-related activities, thus it can attract land estates such as commerce, office and residence to the waterfront area, and making this area the framework of urban development.

Planning achievement

Planning achievement is shown in detail in Table.1, "Implementation alternatives" and in Table 2 and 3. Besides the planning, many concepts and tentative ideas mentioned above are being realized by the construction of waterfront landscape and urban design projects along Duolang River which extends for 6 km in this district. Duolang River is the mother river of Aksu which provides water resources and symbolizes the culture of the city. This area will become the new down town section area integrating recreation, tourism, commerce, offices, and residence after comprehensive development (Figure 9).

Combining planning of the water system, the planning of forestry system and urban master planning were proposed (Figure 10 and 11).

Figure 9. Urban planning and design of Duolang waterfront

	Length of rivers and trenches (km)	The length of branch channels (km)	Area of rivers and trenches (km²)	Length of lake shoreline (km)	Total area of lakes (km²)
Existing situation	129.3	380	3211.9	15.7	64.28
After planning	131.5	413.7	3524.09	49.4	415.58
Increased ratio	1.7%	8.9%	9.7%	215%	547%

Table 2. Water system changes in urban district area (city district) (498 km)

	Length of rivers and trenches (km)	The length of branch channels (km)	Area of rivers and trenches (km²)	Length of lake shoreline (km)	Total area of lakes (km²)
Existing situation	2.4	22.8	1.2	1.7	4.9
After planning	23.4	29.2	81.7	15.4	63.9
Increased ratio	875%	28%	6808%	806%	1204%

Table 3. Water system changes in the central city (city build area) (36.9 km²)

Figure 10. Planning of water and forest system in urban district of Aksu

Figure 11. Master planning of urban district of Aksu

Water and Desert, Alice Springs

~ **Judith van Gelderen** ~ Landscape Architect, Director KIAH Infranet, Sydney, Australia

Background and Site

We are currently working on a challenging project -Desert Knowledge Precinct - in the central Australian desert, in Alice Springs. The project is a collaboration of education, alternative technology, research, and an environment centre for aboriginal people. We are undertaking the landscape masterplan and documentation for stage one. We are demonstrating water conservation in an arid environment, symbolism of 'water holes' for aboriginal culture- as their essential daily life need, and reflecting the surrounding pattern of the landscape

The site is in the arid zone of the Australian Desert where rainfall is 200 millimeters per year. River basins are the catchment areas of major rivers of which there are 39. They are grouped to form drainage divisions based on rivers flowing into a particular sea, or inland. Much of the water is supplied through ground water.

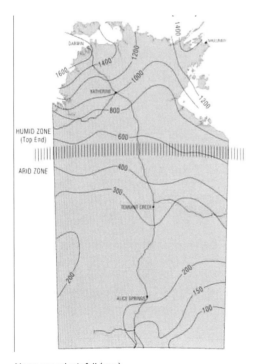

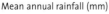

Mean annual rainfall (mm)

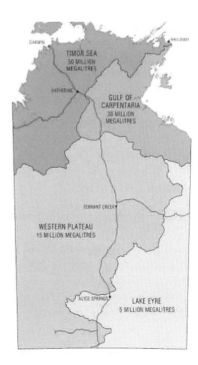

Average annual stream flow

The Project

The Desert Knowledge Precinct will be a local, national and international focal point for desert knowledge activities.

The 73ha core site will initially contain the Desert Peoples Centre and headquarters for Desert Knowledge Australia and the Desert Knowledge Cooperative Research Centre (CRC), while creating stronger linkages between existing facilities of CSIRO, Yirara College and the Northern Territory (NT) Government Departments in the Arid Zone Research Institute. As a large capital investment by the Northern Territory Government in Central Australia, the Desert Knowledge Precinct will protect and enhance the attractive natural environment during development and will have a strong visual connection with the iconic MacDonnell Ranges in Alice Springs.

Objectives

The Precinct will provide a focus for engagement/ partnerships between Aboriginal and non-Aboriginal people in knowledge-related activities and business development.

• The site will have a strong visual impact from both the ground and the air. People flying into and out of the Alice will see the circle motifs and the broader development area.

• The Precinct will be a national icon depicting the efforts of desert Australians to enhance their livelihoods by engaging with the world.

• The Precinct will build on the international context of Desert Knowledge Australia and the Desert Knowledge CRC through partnerships and collaboration with international agencies like the Desert Research Institute of Nevada and the University of Texas.

• Creating a Desert Knowledge Precinct to provide a physical centre for Desert Knowledge Australia, the Desert Knowledge Cooperative Research Centre, Desert Peoples Centre, Solar Demonstration Facility and other flagship programs.

Core development area from the air.

Sharing the knowledge of desert people.

- Supporting desertSMART, a community, business and government partnership that provides a holistic approach to energy use, building design, water and waste issues.
- Preserving water supplies by linking government and community together, supporting water conservation education through initiatives such as desertSMART and Desert Knowledge Australia COOLmob and investing in water planning and conservation measures.
- Continuing to support recognition of Alice Springs as Australia's solar centre, a program to demonstrate how solar power, energy efficiency and new approaches can combine to provide a sustainable energy future.
- Extreme care will be taken to preserve the natural character of the Precinct and especially in minimising impact on the large corkwood trees and other vegetation. Ecologically sustainable development is a central feature of the construction program with buildings designed to minimise energy and water requirements.

Key Organisations

The Desert Peoples Centre, is an exciting cooperative initiative of Batchelor Institute for Indigenous Tertiary Education and the Centre for Appropriate Technology for the delivery of post-secondary education and training for Aboriginal students. A major initiative of Indigenous people, it will work to further education and economic aspirations of Aboriginal people throughout desert Australia. The centre will include campus facilities at the Precinct with a network of remote study centres located across desert communities.

Desert Knowledge Australia is a networking organisation that is building opportunities to diversify the economy of desert Australia though gathering, sharing, developing and marketing the knowledge of desert people. The Desert Knowledge CRC is a collaboration of the Northern Territory Government, 28 other partners from across Australia and the Commonwealth Government to research towards desert solutions to key issues such as natural resource management, community viability, governance and integrated regional business systems for regional development.

The Desert Knowledge Business and Innovation Centre will provide a meeting place within the Precinct as well as headquarters for Desert Knowledge Australia and the Desert Knowledge CRC. It will be the centre for a developing network of business and research activities across inland Australia with some initial steps also being made at an international level.

Creation of a Living Desert Centre will also be considered for Stage Two development at the Precinct. It would showcase people of desert Australia, their lives, livelihoods, culture and interactions with the natural environment, celebrating the contemporary interface between Aboriginal and non- Aboriginal cultures, providing an opportunity for visitors and tourists to experience the vibrant artistic and knowledge capacities of the central Australian region.

Masterplan review

Kiah-Infranet was awarded the landscape design documentation for stages 1 and 2 of this development in April 2007. To ensure that this first stage of landscape design documentation does not conflict with possible future developments, it was necessary for us to review the original landscape masterplan prepared by Clouston Associates, as the detailed resolution of this masterplan had undergone significant changes, especially with road and building layouts. As a result we updated the masterplan, including infrastructure components and waste management strategies, with the aim to ensure that a cohesive overall plan was achieved. Key to the review was the overall assessment of topography and drainage- with the following Principles:

• Wherever possible locate roads along ridgelines to maximise the positive distribution of rainwater- it is easier to distribute and collect rainfall running from ridgelines down the slope, than to interrupt flows across a ridgeline.

• Strengthen planting along ridgelines where possible to give visual definition to the landscape.

• Utilise the minor drainage lines for rainfall discharge throughout the development- i.e. concentrate water where it naturally flows, and enhance the water corridor.

• There are three different types of water provided for the complex: Recycled water (bore water), Recycled water (grey water), and Potable water (for drinking).

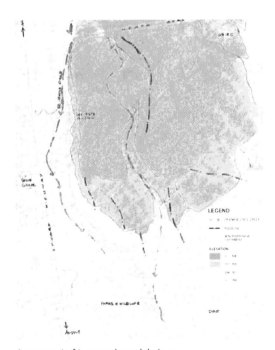

Assessment of topography and drainage.

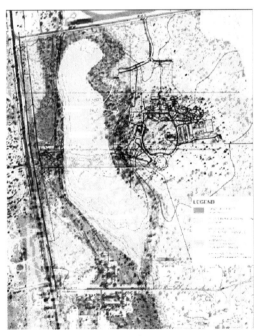

Assessment and Design Approach.

Design Approach

- *Reinforce the powerful relationship of the site to the MacDonnell Ranges.*
- *Reinforce the sense of place of the physical site.*
- *Strengthen the natural attributes of the site and links to adjoining land uses and land-marks.*
- Consider the *potential expansion* of the surrounding areas and the flexibility of the site usage.
- Design an adaptive scheme. Create a design that provides for multi-functional usages; spaces that can operate equally as meeting places, outdoor teaching areas, passive recreation areas and possibly ceremonial areas.
- Create an *interactive process with community* to add value and encourage indigenous involvement. e.g. for community art/sculpture projects; natural heritage interpretation: education regarding indigenous species/desert plants from the area/region and naming plant species for bush food, medicinal purposes, economic market opportunities and educational value; cultural heritage interpretation- story telling about the land, the history, the interpretation of the landscape; and investigate opportunities for forging links through this project, between the CSIRO, Yiarra College and the NT Government Departments in the Arid
  Zone Research Institute;
- *Relate to the Living Desert Centre Vision and Goals and Objectives.* Incorporate the primary values of harmony, sustainability and wealth creation in the landscape design. Integrate the gardens with research programs to learn more from desert plants.

Design approach: The site and its cultural background

Aboriginal relationships to water

Most civilisations have manipulated water sources/assets by re-routing, and manipulating water through channels and creating dams. In Western civilisation,

Masterplan left, and excerpt of Central courtyard (in progress) to the right, with the symbolic soakage area at entrance of the development

for example, with the impact of industrialisation on our landscape, water management to prevent flooding was important.

Both Da Yu, in Chinese culture and Da Vinci in Europe, for example, both taught people how to manage water better in urban areas to avoid flooding. Da Vinci described water as "the vehicle of nature", believing water to be to the world what blood is to our bodies. Today in western society, there is a need to increase the awareness and comprehension of people with respect to the basics of the water cycle; there is a need to increase the understanding of water's therapeutic qualities, there is a movement called "Water sensitive urban design"- there is a need for the development of a new consciousness for water.

Comparitively, the Aboriginal culture is one of the few remaining cultures that have always treated water as a sacred resource. As a result, the aboriginal culture has a minimal impact on the environment including waterways allowing the natural environment to manage itself.

Aboriginal People, and Groundwater

Traditional Aboriginals largely relied on lagoons, springs, rockholes, and shallow unlined wells for their water supplies. Due to the importance of water for their survival, especially in the inland regions of the NT, many watering points have been incorporated into their stories of the Dreaming. Many people still lead a partially traditional lifestyle so these sites and stories are an important part of their culture. Dreamtime stories tell of the creation and events about that particular waterhole. At some rock holes, which contain clean water, custom requires that people sip the water without using their hands, for hygienic purposes.

Permanent settlements have now replaced the former nomadic lifestyle with many communities ranging up to over a thousand people, most of these settlements rely on groundwater tapped with bores (www.nt.gov.au/nreta/water/ground/people/aboriginal.html). The problem today is contamination of water holes in the desert by camels. This severely restricts water being available for human consumption.

A permanent rock hole in Central Australia (Papunya).

Old Henry Tjugadi Tjungurrayi, Water man, 1974 (J. Doyle, Papunya)

Exploring the connections between water, spirituality and consciousness with Indigenous civilisations

From early civilisations, water has played a key role in the spirituality of societies. Examples include for example, Christianity (Baptism, the great flood, Noahs Ark) and the South American Indians and Australian Aborigines. Schulz describes how the Indians developed dances and rituals to persuade the rain to come, and draws parallel to the Australian Aborigines who also developed rain dances and communication with water with the soul. This intimate relationship with the sacred element water that these cultures maintained, is in stark contrast to Western cultures – that with their scientific background mainly understand water in terms of temperature differentials, and other chemical and physical properties. Indigenous peoples, whom we see as childlike and naive when measured against the degree of technological advancement in our societies, make us aware of the need to protect nature and the element of water.

„Men performing their sacred ritual believed that they could exert vital influences upon the animals, the plants, and the natural phenomena that constituted their totems only through the common supernatural beings that linked them. To promote the increase of animals and plants, to summon winds or rain, it was hence necessary that the ritual first instituted by the appropriate totemic ancestors should be performed again without any deviations, and that the creative words first intoned by these personages be sung again in their unaltered original form." (Central Australian Religion,T.G.H Strehlow)

This religion was so connected to the land, to the animals, to the trees, the soil, the water- it demonstrated a connectiveness that we, have not been exposed to.

As Schulz (2005) says: The Aboriginals possess the ability to discover water in the desert even if the springs are not really noticeable on the surface. White people by comparison find it difficult to find water in the desert; it is the alienation of nature in western civilisation that has been accompanied by a loss of the relationship to water quality, a relationship that has always existed amongst native people.

Left: Water fountains, Pisac, Peru: past, present and future fountains for bathing, to cleanse the soul before entering the town. Middle: River in Arnhem Land (Aboriginal Dreaming 40,000 Years of Aboriginal History). Right: Aboriginal art (www.aboriginal art.com.au)

Water dreaming of the Aboriginals is reflected by their paintings and songs

"The Water Dreaming paintings were, a resolution of five elements, either expressed or implied: the waterhole, the running water, the cliff, the bush tucker growing after receiving water, and the Water Man or ceremonial singer, or his substitute." These meaning clusters in the Water Dreaming paintings were trans-figurative and life-giving, for water Dreaming paintings were about the singing and dancing for water, and its celebration as a life-giving force. Johnny Warrangkula Tjupurrula painted "Water Dreaming" (below). In this design there was a network of 5 water holes with running water often underground and the bush tucker nourishment of the landscape terrain.

In "Man's Water Dreaming" by Old Walter Tjampitjnpa (right below) the basic elements of the Water Dreaming are revealed in the "U" sign, the symbol for the

Johnny Warrangkula Tjupurrula -"Water Dreaming"- design for a network of 5 water holes with running water often underground and the bush tucker nourishment of the land-scape terrain (Papunya, p. 157; 163).

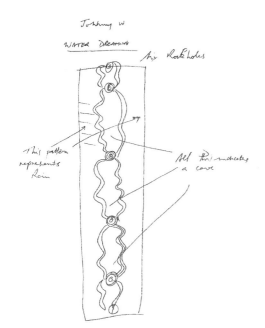

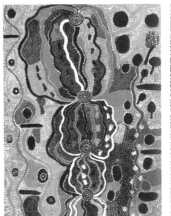
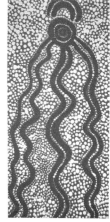

Old Mick Tjakamarra, "Children's Water Dreaming with Possum Story" (left) and "Man's Water Dreaming" by Old Walter Tjampitjnpa (right).

Water Man. Concentric circles represent the waterhole and the undulating lines indicate water running across the sand (Papunya-the Place Made After the Story, p.183). In the painting by Old Mick Tjakamarra, "Children's Water Dreaming with Possum Story" (see figure on previous page) - the water is passing like some eternal thought over the desert sandhills surface, held in by four rounded bull's eye waterholes. It includes separate creeks and a possum journey among the trees looking for bush tucker (Papunya-the Place Made After the Story, p.180).

Our overarching design objective/approach was to reflect the attitude of aboriginal people towards the environment as much as possible - to touch the earth lightly and to capture and infiltrate the water into the landscaped areas and into the ground water table. In further applying the principles adopted in the masterplan, I reflected on the relationship of aboriginal people to the land- to water- and the representation of water holes, water flowing in Aboriginal art. We should not copy these concepts as they belong to the artists themselves, however the images presented an inspiration / ideas behind the formulation of pattern language in the new landscape that was developed.

Unfortunately only one meeting with Aboriginals was held during the design process to discuss the "soakage pit" at the entrance - this was seen as symbolic entry statement, as in years past, this site was known for the access to water along the river banks. They used to dig with sticks for water, along the river banks.

Design approach: The site and its natural elements, parameters for sensitive water design

The natural elements of the site summarize as follows: a flat desert environment focussing on the symbolic MacDonnell Range; sandy red soils; less than 200mm rainfall per annum; St Mary's Creek; drainage channels; Corkwoods and buffel grass(weed); a depleted ecological system.

Parameters for sensitive water design were given by the nature of water. Naturally flowing streams always endeavour to follow a meandering course, the

The site: sandy soils, infiltration rate high, minimum falls (site grade of 1:150!); buildings on benches above plain.

path of least resistance. Schwenk's studies on the revolving currents in the bed of a stream indicated that the revolving circulation and the movement downstream create a spiralling motion which regulates the flow of the water, and controls temperature. This research, if applied to designing new water systems should ensure they are healthy, sustainable systems.

Schauberger's studies of natural flows of rivers indicated, similar to Schwenk's studies, that temperature gradient plays an important role both in the way water moves in rivers and also in the structure of the water masses within the river.

The more the engineer is ignorant of the nature of water, tries to channel water by the shortest and straightest route to the sea, the more the flow of water weighs into the bends, the longer its path and the more destructive and the worse the water will become (Bartholomew 2003).

Water sensitive design

Catch the water, infiltrate the water, create soakage areas, emphasis the drainage soakage areas and swales with wet planting species to reflect the bush

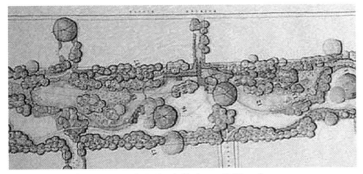

Applying principles to Scott Park Wetlands (Judy van Gelderen).

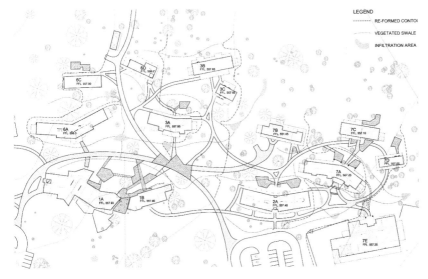

Initial Drainage Concept, showing swales infiltration areas, distribution lines.

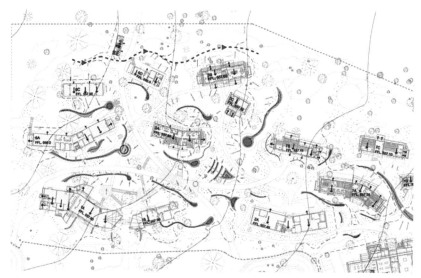

Sensitive Water Scheme, showing swales and infiltration areas (KIAH Infranet, 2008).

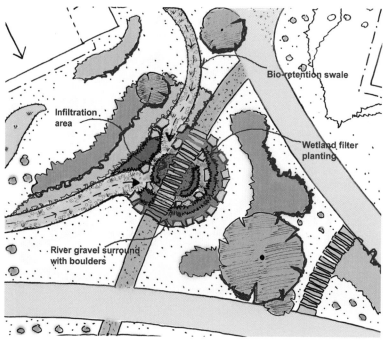

Sketch of drainage soak area (KIAH Infranet, 2008).

tucker/ green oasis that grows around the billabongs in the desert.

Roof and road water is directed into the series of distribution drains, bio-retention swales, infiltration swales; etc. Water is fed from the gutter "shutes" into the infiltration swales that then lead into the drainage soakage/detention areas.

Planting Design

To complement the site, and the need for low water demand, the planting design reinforces the ecological patterns that were there previously. There will be a transition from the more highly used areas/ courtyards surrounding the building to the perimeter areas of desert rehabilitation planting.

Re-vegetation themes for the site will reinforce the natural land unit/vegetation zones as illustrated in the masterplan. These are zones derived from the geology, topography and soil profiles; and the vegetation zoning is based on the natural vegetation associations that used to be there before they were interfered with by man or climate changes. The main vegetation zones within the stage one/two landscape site include the *Coolabah, Swayback Nardoo, Silky Browntop dominant* and *Fork-leaved Corkwood dominant*. To add visual interest to the scheme we have proposed using plants derived from the *River Red Gum (sandy river/creek beds) Eucalyptus camaldulensis var. obtusa dominant* mix as well within the wetter areas of the site where bio-retention swales and infiltration areas are proposed. In addition, the mixes within areas of high use contain "modified indigenous" species to create adequate shade and some variety through more "amenity" plantings. Key to the success of the planting scheme will be the removal of the Buffel grass.

Key elements of the planting design are to reflect the informal, woodland set-

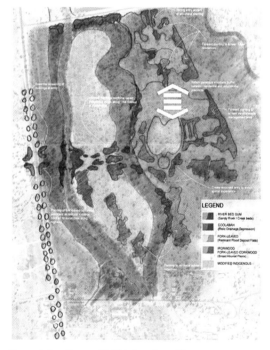

Revegetation themes (KIAH Infranet, 2008).

ting and nature of the building layout; reflect the horizontal/strong east-west orientation of the landscape, as viewed from the plane. This has been achieved by extending planted groups in an east – west fashion on the perimetre /outside, larger spaces adjacent the building; and to reflect the three colour schemes proposed for the different buildings of the site, as reflected in the colour strips as per figures below;create wildlife/birdlife refuges within the development; integrate concepts for "bush tucker" garden (yet to be defined), research gardens and any other initiatives; and to create a solution that minimises maintenance and maximises use of water harvesting.

Colour schemes proposed for the buildings.

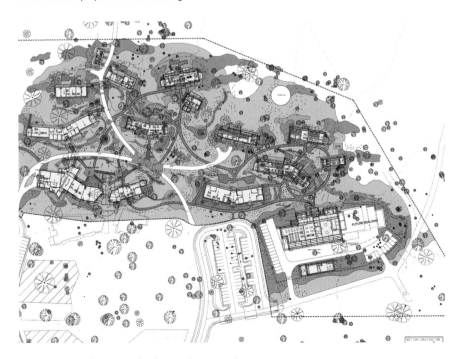

Landscape Design for Stages 1 & 2 (KIAH Infranet, 2008).

Sustainable design concepts for building a Scarce-Watercity

~ **Melanie Klein** ~ Professor, Kansas State University, USA

Introduction

On May 4, 2007, a two-mile-wide tornado ripped across Kiowa County, Kansas, USA, leaving catastrophic destruction in its wake. Ninety-five percent of the town of Greensburg was leveled while the rest of the town was severely damaged. Shortly after the tornado, a 12-week process involving multiple meetings and discussions by teams of local, state, and federal officials, business owners, civic groups, and hundreds of citizens resulted in "Long-Term Community Recovery Plan: Greensburg + Kiowa County, Kansas " (LTCRP), which expresses the Greensburg/Kiowa County community's vision for recovery (Federal Emergency Management Agency [FEMA], 2007). In October 2007, some professors and landscape architecture students of Kansas State University began addressing the landscape architectural needs of Greensburg by envisioning design concepts for projects specifically listed in the LTCRP. Realizing an adequate and sustainable water supply is critical to sustaining Greensburg. City Officials stated in October 2007 that designs will be weighed against the following goal: "Water: Treat each drop of water as a precious resource." (http://www.greensburgks.org/recovery-planning/5-additional-goals-added-to-long-termrecovery-plan). Students incorporated this goal into their design concepts, which were conceived as a partial response to the Long Term Community Recovery Plan and a catalyst for conversation as the town considers their reconstruction efforts.

With an average annual precipitation of 22.35 inches (568 millimeters), Greensburg's rainfall is scarce compared to many areas. Greensburg's aquifer, the Ogallala, is being drawn down at a rate much higher than natural recharge. Design strategies must mitigate water use.

Whole-city infrastructure choices can protect water quality. Incorporation of stormwater and sewerage systems into city-wide parks and open spaces is an opportunity landscape architects and planners can consider in worldwide projects that have a shortage of water. How this opportunity is being considered by Greensburg will be discussed in this paper.

While student design proposals focused on many environmentally sustainable design techniques, this paper will discuss the students' methods used specifically for "water as a precious resource." Sections of the paper discuss how individual site designs can contribute to mitigating water use and lessening the load on the city's stormwater and wastewater systems. Students envisioned the water-saving design principles or design strategies as being highly visible in the Greensburg built environment, to educate citizens and visitors about water as a precious resource as well as Greensburg's commitment to water stewardship. This paper focuses the students' chosen water-saving design proposals and how these proposals were communicated to Greensburg citizens. Incorporation of site-scale water-saving design principles and how to communicate the principles to stakeholders are issues that landscape architects and planners must consider for scarce-water regions throughout the world.

Water System and Design Principles at the City-Scale

While it is tempting for Greensburg to complete individual projects as funding and volunteers become available, it is important to follow a well-defined overall plan to insure new projects are not contributing to water-system problems. To protect water systems, a basic understanding of existing topography, water flow, floodplains and other geography is necessary before planning decisions can take place (see Image 1). Overlying geographic features such as waterways, potential restoration zones, and floodplains with major circulation and development patterns reveal the best locations for active and passive park spaces, restoration zones and proposed trails (Berkebile Nelson Immenschuh McDowell Architects [BNIM], 2008, pp.64-66). Image 2 shows an overlay of these geographic features which should be considered along with stormwater and sewerage systems. Incorporating storm sewer systems into city-wide parks and open spaces is an opportunity that can be helpful for the natural water system. "Soft" engineering practices could recreate the natural water treatment train throughout

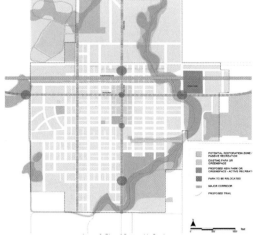

Image 1: Plan of Greensburg topography, 100 year flood-plains, intermittent creek, and existing park sites. Generated by BNIM Architects, Kansas City, Missouri, USA. Used with Permission. The area shown in blue is defined by FEMA as being affected by flooding during a one hundred year storm. This area could be improved with a system of more integrated flood control practices.

Image 2: Plan of Geographic Overlays. Generated by BNIM Architects, Kansas City, Missouri, USA. Used with Permission

Greensburg. Once studied and implemented, a truly integrated system has the potential to: "eliminate flooding by slowing and decreasing runoff volumes and increasing perviousness, dramatically improve water quality to ensure aquifers are recharged with pure water, [and] ultimately create a community with zero stormwater 3 runoff" (BNIM, 2008, p. 72). Individual site-scale designs can then be influenced by this system.

Individual Site-Scale Water-Saving Design Principles and Techniques

There are several ways that individual site-scale designs can focus on mitigating water use and lessening the load on the city's stormwater and wastewater systems. Students investigated, and later, communicated the following techniques to Greensburg residents: implementing natural filtration techniques to clean runoff; restoring and celebrating an existing intermittent creek running through a portion of the city; slowing and decreasing runoff volumes and increasing perviousness in "urbanized" areas; water capture, storage and reuse for non-potable uses; using native plantings that require minimal irrigation through storm water harvesting; and developing living machines for groups of buildings sited together. Investigations of these principles and techniques led to site-specific design concepts that communicated water-saving potentials for Greensburg to consider when rebuilding the city.

Implementing Natural Filtration Techniques to Clean Runoff

City-wide, Greensburg is relatively "flat," with less than two percent slope (west to east) for most sites within the city limits. Most Greensburg sites allow runoff to move in sheets across the site. Utilizing Geographic Information System (GIS) data obtained the United States Federal Emergency Management Agency (FEMA), students were able to determine there was one intermittent stream and 100 year flood plain in the eastern portion of the town (see Image 1), primarily in an area currently used for agriculture. When water is flowing in this shallow channel, it flows from south to north. In the LTCRP, the citizens determined the site with the intermittent stream should be the location of a future educational and recreational campus. The campus would would be designed to accommodate elementary, middle and high schools, a community center, park, and biking/walking paths. The campus design would serve as a southern Main Street anchor and help solidify the connections to downtown and residential areas (FEMA, 2007, pp.71-72).

The student design of the Educational and Recreational Campus (see Image 4, 5 & 6) embodies sustainability through a sensitive site design that allows for large areas of native plantings to slow overland flow of surface water before it reaches the shallow channel. Rather than allowing surface water to flow through agricultural plantings and related farming chemicals, slowing overland flow through organic, native plantings aids in water quality as well as controlling runoff damage. In the campus native planting areas, student designers added bike trails and walkways which celebrate this existing intermittent creek. As the native prairie vegetation becomes mature, these restored prairie areas become teaching laboratories for schoolchildren and the public (Image 5 & 6). In the restored prairie areas, the public can learn about regional natural systems, including the visible demonstration of overland flow through native prairie grasses and forbs aiding infiltration and purification of water by simulating water flow patterns found in native Kansas landscapes.

Slowing and Decreasing Runoff Volumes & Increasing Perviousness

Student designers recognized that the highly developed downtown area of Greensburg (see Image 3) must minimize imperviousness, maximize infiltration, and capture as much water as possible for reuse. Therefore, students proposed a variety of "soft" engineering techniques. While student designers wanted to minimize imperviousness as much as possible, it is important to note that Greensburg is a farming community and needs two-lane roads wide enough to accommodate farm implements. Even the downtown area must accommodate such widths, as locals enjoy gathering and watching the "parade" of farm-related equipment during harvest times. In addition to this road width requirement, the

Image 4: Educational & Recreational Campus Plan shows prairie grass area that utilizes natural filtration techniques to clean runoff before it meets the intermittent stream in the southern portion of the town

Image 5: Proposed Prairie Area near Elementary School: Natural Filtration techniques clean runoff before it meets the stream in the southern portion of the town

Image 6: Section of Bike and Walking Path within Proposed Natural Filtration/Prairie Area on the Educational & Recreational Campus

citizens felt strongly that diagonal parking on either side of the drive lanes would help accommodate the needs of the businesses. Therefore, students proposed that the street itself was paved differently in the unique zones: driving lanes are of a highly durable, impervious pavement that is crowned to allow runoff to flow into the parking zone pavement; parking zone pavement is pervious (Images 7 & 8). Water can infiltrate through the parking zones pervious pavers, into a sand sub-base and an area of crushed concrete below (Image 8). Water can then percolate into the soil, recharging the groundwater system.

Another downtown water-smart technique is capturing runoff from precipitation that falls on south-sloped roofs fitted with solar panels (Image 8). This runoff, which becomes non-potable or "grey" water, can be stored temporarily and used to irrigate the downtown native plantings. Roofs not sloped for solar panels can be planted with low-maintenance vegetation which absorbs precipitation, reducing runoff as well as the amount of energy needed to heat and cool the building's interior (Image 8). Finally, "rain gardens," or slight depressions in grading that allow precipitation from the walkway to flow into small areas planted with native vegetation, were utilized downtown (Image 9). Any irrigation needs not met through the rain garden method can be supplemented with grey water stored in the rain water collection system.

Using Native Plantings with Minimal Irrigation through Storm Water Harvesting

In addition to the rain gardens proposed for the downtown (Image 9), another student design project, the Memorial Park and Sustainability Center, also proposed native plantings and storm water harvesting. Student designers proposed

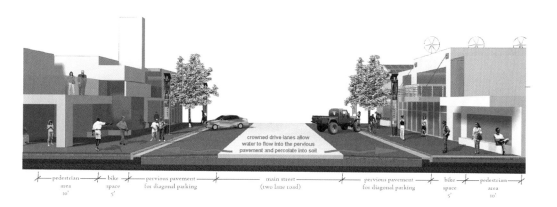

Image 7: Section of Proposed Main Street , Downtown Greensburg

that the LTCRP-designated site for Memorial Park (see Image 3) could also be used as the location of the Sustainability Center proposed in the LTCRP. Since this site is a rather large, highly visible area between the downtown and the education/recreation campus, it is ideal for "chance encounter" educational opportunities. Intended as a resource for the community as it rebuilds, the Park and Center would help educate the public on opportunities for future structures and landscapes to be built as energy efficient, environmentally sensitive and life-enhancing. The Center would include conference and classroom spaces, a green building reference library, and a public greenhouse. To fulfill its mission to educate the public on "green" building techniques and practices, the Center and surrounding landscape would also be a built example and visual resource of sustainable building strategies and systems.

Because these sustainable systems can be hard to understand or visualize, the student designers placed the systems in very visible areas. To expose the principle of using native plants irrigated through storm water harvesting, student designers took several steps. First, since the site slopes down gently from the southwest corner to the northeast corner (see Image 3), the northeast corner was utilized for the native plant storm water garden. The northeast corner is also the portion of the site most viewed by pedestrians and motorists due to its proximity to downtown. Since the designers propose that the Sustainability Center buildings be lustered at this corner, storm water runoff from building roofs and entry plaza pavement can be harvested to irrigate nearby gardens of native plants (Image 10 & 12). In addition to the native plant storm water garden, passive solar gain, rain collection from roofs, "living" green walls, Structural Insulating Panels (SIPs), geothermal heat pumps, photovoltaic panels, energy efficient HVAC systems, and a living machine are also utilized in the Center and Park design.

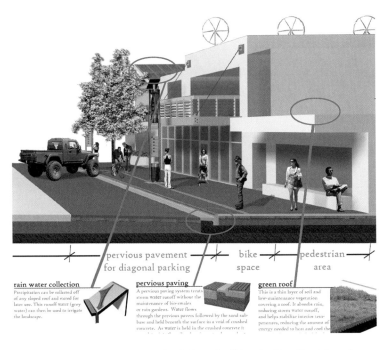

pervious pavement for diagonal parking — bike space — pedestrian area

rain water collection
Precipitation can be collected off of any sloped roof and stored for later use. This runoff water (grey water) can then be used to irrigate the landscape.

pervious paving
A pervious paving system treats storm water runoff without the maintenance of bio-swales or rain gardens. Water flows through the pervious pavers followed by the sand sub-base and held beneath the surface in a void of crushed concrete. As water is held in the crushed concrete it

green roof
This is a thin layer of soil and low-maintenance vegetation covering a roof. It absorbs rain, reducing storm water runoff, and helps stabilize interior temperatures, reducing the amount of energy needed to heat and cool the

Image 8: Rain Collection, Pervious Paving & Green Roof ideas for Main Street, Downtown

Developing Living Machines for Groups of Buildings Sited Together

A living machine uses screens, biofilters, large tanks, wetland plants, microorganisms, fans, re-circulation pumps and other mechanical devices to treat "black" water or water containing sewage. When properly designed and constructed for the needs of a building group, a living machine can treat this water without chemicals to the point that the water can be used for irrigation or toilets. In Greensburg's climate, a greenhouse would need to be used to keep water temperatures warm so that plants do not winterize. The system would need to be tailored to the volume and makeup of the sewage being treated. It could be a stand-alone greenhouse or built into larger buildings (Todd & Josephson, 1996, pp.109-136). Because a living machine and other sustainable systems can be difficult to understand, the student designers of the Memorial Park and Sustainability Center placed the systems in highly visible exterior areas, at times behind glass panels so the public may observe the systems operating (Image 11). Persons walking through the public site (Image 12) can begin to understand these demonstrations of sustainable practices, and come inside to learn more.

Conclusion

Though different in scope and scale, the landscape architecture students sought design proposals that addressed sustainable design features and community visions as stated in the Long Term Community Recovery Plan. The examples shared in this paper were created to help empower Greensburg in fulfilling their

rain garden

Slight depressions in grading allow precipitaion from the walkway to flow into planter boxes. Any irrigation needs not met through this method can be supplemented with grey water stored in the rain water collection system.

Image 9: Rain Garden Ideas for Main Street, Downtown

Image 3: Key Plan of Student Project Locations in Greensburg

mandate to "treat each drop of water as a precious resource." The water-saving design principles are intended to do the maximum good for the City's mandate, utilizing simple yet effective strategies to protect the city's precious water resource.

Students envisioned these design strategies as being highly visible in the Greensburg built environment, to educate citizens and visitors about water as a precious resource as well as Greensburg's commitment to water stewardship. If these sustainable design features are built in a way that allows them to be highly visible to the public, simple sustainable-practice educational opportunities will be provided for residents and visitors to Greensburg. Perhaps this will lead to other communities making commitments to water stewardship.

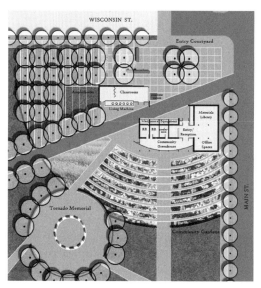

Image 10: Proposed Sustainability Center & Park with visible systems, including a Native Plant Garden irrigated through storm water harvesting and Living Machine which will treat wastewater.

Image 11: Proposed Sustainability Center with visible systems, including a Living Machine which will naturally treat wastewater to a level of purity suitable for irrigation.

Image 12: View through Sustainability Center and Native Stormwater Gardens

Water Purificative Landscapes

Constructed Ecologies and Contemporary Urbanism

~ **Antje Stokman** ~ Professor, Faculty of Architecture and Landscape

Sciences, Leibniz University Hannover, Germany

Introduction

Traditionally the landscapes that ensured human survival were closely related to "Living with water" in a way which tied urbanization patterns closely to the underlying hydrological conditions. But in contemporary times "Living with Water" basically is related to the dependency of human survival on the centrally organized and mostly invisible infrastructure systems that transport drinking, rain, and waste water for hundreds and thousands of miles. These systems have disconnected the land-use from the logics of the watershed as well as people's experience from the water-related processes of the landscape. The potentials of these water infrastructure systems for shaping urban form and meeting broader human, ecological and aesthetic objectives have almost been lost. However the simultaneous worldwide processes of extreme and unpredictable urban growth and decline are leading to huge challenges concerning the affordability and functioning of present water infrastructure conceptions and thus demand new solutions. Taking these challenges as a departure point, this paper will introduce a landscape approach for the design of water management, movement and purification systems as an integrated part of an open space framework.

Water Infrastructure and the Development of Urban Landscapes

Historically, the cultivation and urbanization patterns of cultural landscapes used to be tied very closely to the logics of their watershed, with the flow of water being one of the most important factors creating landscape relations (van Buuren and Kerkstra 1993, Picon 2005, Shannon 2007). Water infrastructure systems, meaning the methods of distribution, storage and recycling of water, were based on a deep understanding of a site's geography, topography, hydrology, climate and ecology. Grafted on the existing "hydrological landscape structure" (Buuren and Kerkstra 1993) in order to make the best use of natural water resources, a man-made system of canals, ditches, ponds, dams and reservoirs was introduced during the process of cultivation and urbanization. The appearance of these man-made water infrastructure systems, further accentuating the underlying natural physical landscape structure, became a major visual and spatial component of structuring and organizing cultural landscapes. The applied techniques of both linear and punctual water infrastructure are inextricably related to the resulting patterns of land-use and urbanization. The sensibility for a site, its natural characteristics and ecosystem performances, were the key skills of farmers and essential in order to achieve efficiency and survive. The relationships between natural and human processes, based on a deep understanding of complex and dynamic ecological processes, were actively applied into the physical construction of infrastructure landscapes and settlement patterns.

With the increasing concentration of human activities and settlements during the development of pre-industrial cities and urban landscapes, the water systems had to perform even more functions. Water infrastructure could create synergies with other important urban functions such as providing transportation routes for goods and building materials, serving as an open space network for social needs, supplying water for domestic and industrial uses as well as serving as a system for stormwater retention, irrigation and waste water disposal. In this context hydraulic engineering used to be a major component of territorial planning and water infrastructure systems were extremely prominent in most cities. Not just that most urban agglomerations were located on the banks of natural rivers – at the same time the urban tissue was criss-crossed by a dense system of man-made open canals and ditches. Picon (2005) points out that most European cities resembled Venice or Amsterdam before the canals were filled in during the 19th and 20th century for space, traffic and sanitary purposes. It is hard to believe that also Tokyo still in the 19th century used to be a very open, green and wet city. A system of segmented rice fields was planned as an integral part of the urban tissue, which did not only provide food to the citizens, but at the same time performed as a system of preventing floods and irrigation (Yokohari 2000). Overall it can be stated that in the first phase of urbanization and intensification of landuse, water was gaining even more importance as a structural and visual component of urban and regional form than in cultural landscapes dominated by agri-

Figure 1: Cultural landscape patterns resulting from the adaptation to the characteristics of the Watershed.

Figure 2: Settlement patterns resulting from the logics of the watershed being evident within the City.

cultural land use. Many of the few still existing examples of such kinds of cities have become popular tourist sites - clearly showing that the most profoundly moving urban water landscapes are nothing more than the irrigation, domestic water supply, transportation, sanitary sewer and flood control systems of the time. These landscapes allow the site-specific natural processes to still be revealed and utilized within the urban setting.

However the increasing pressure, intensity and speed of urbanisation lead, and is still leading to the disappearance of any visible form of water infrastructure in most cities. In almost all fast-growing urban agglomerations especially of the developing countries this process can be observed happening within a much shorter time than in the Western countries. Analyzing the effects of the urbanization processes on water systems by the example of Cantho in Vietnam, the typical development towards the disappearance of water from the originally water-based urban settlement patterns becomes comprehensible:

In the rural areas of Cantho each farmer's house is located next to come watercourse, either a stream or a man-made canal used for irrigation and drainage as well as transportation. The pond next to each of the houses on the one hand serves for the disposal of human faeces which are used for raising fish, on the other hand provides the soil for mounds which protect the buildings constructed on top of them from floods. The citizens are not dependent on any kind of municipal infrastructure but are self-responsible to make the best use of resources and take the advantages of nutrient recycling. But as the population rapidly expands due to the urbanization pressure these independent methods are not effective against the rising problems of water pollution – with the open water channels being used mainly for wastewater disposal resulting in very bad sanitation and health conditions. To solve these pressing problems as the urbanization increases even further the water channels are being covered up with the buildings and sealed surfaces connected to them by underground pipes – which eventually leads to very dense urban fabrics and the loss of all visible water and open space.

Such as in downtown Cantho, in most of today's urban agglomerations there are hardly any visible open water systems and the cities have become dry. A vast

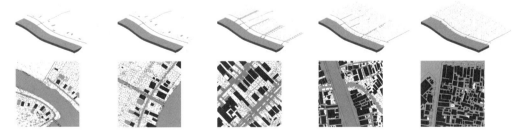

Figure 3: The loss of visible water systems within the urban landscape of Cantho, Vietnam (Nemcova and Wust 2008)

network of underground water pipes and sewer systems is replacing the smelly and dangerous open water courses, being considered a major progress in the field of engineering and urban planning. At the same time the urban structures of cities are increasingly dissociated from the organisation of the hydraulic system, erasing the visual and spatial logic of the urban watershed. The water problems are solved by engineers in a technical and preferably invisible way, so the urban and landscape designers gain the freedom of being able to focus on aesthetic and spatial design issues of the urban layout – with the effect of their designs becoming arbitrary, exchangeable and one city looking much like another, regardless of where it is being built.

Today´s autonomous technical water infrastructure systems designed by engineering specialists are widely considered the only way to solve the huge problems of water pollution and flood control related to urbanization. But can we afford this kind of merely technical approaches to problem-solving in the future, looking at actual tendencies of urban development and their effects on conventional water infrastructure systems? And how could landscape architects contribute to the discussion about affordable and effective water management strategies?

Problems of Centralized Water Infrastructure Systems and Prospects for Intervention

The construction and maintenance of a conventional waste water system's vast underground sewer network covering the whole urban built-up area is very costly. Thus the necessary investment for these centralized systems needs to be distributed over a long amortization period of at least 50-100 years. This also means that decisions have to be made on the spatial layout, dimensioning and technical standards based on predictions concerning population and urban development processes for the following 50-100 years. However the actual simultaneous and unpredictable development processes of extreme urban growth as well as urban decline taking place within only a few decades cannot be comprised by centralized large-scale systems.

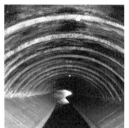

Figure 4: Networks of invisible water infrastructure replacing open water systems

Infrastructural challenges of shrinking cities and urban population decline

While global urbanization is progressing quickly with already more than 50% of the global population living in cities, the urban growth is becoming increasingly unevenly distributed: In the 1990s more than a quarter of the world's largest cities shrank with their number continually increasing (Oswalt and Rieniets 2006). This means that many cities, such as Detroit in the U.S. or Halle in Germany, were built for populations two or three times their current size. However planning concepts and engineering techniques traditionally always only had to deal with problems relating to urban growth and densification, not with shrinking cities and sparser urban population. Many cities in Germany are already affected directly by the problems and consequences resulting from keeping up the existing water infrastructure paradigms under changing urban conditions:

After the German reunification huge sums of money were invested into upgrading and extending the water infrastructure of Eastern Germany's cities, expecting their prosperous development for the future. However, due to high levels of outward migration, in many areas within only ten years the amount of wastewater dropped down to less than one quarter of the expected intake that the systems had been dimensioned for (Koziol 2005). Even in cities that so far did not lose any population, like for example Hannover in Western Germany, people and companies tend to move out of the city centres into suburban areas. This means that even in the non-shrinking cities the amount of wastewater flowing through the pipe systems is much reduced due to decreasing urban density with sparser populations distributed over larger areas. As a result in many German cities the underloaded sewers need to be flushed constantly to avoid smell and the accumulation of pathogens.

The maintenance of the over-dimensioned water infrastructure demands enormous expenses. At the same time there are rising costs for the design and maintenance of the increasing area of open space within cities, due to reducing population densities and building vacancies which partly lead to the demolition of

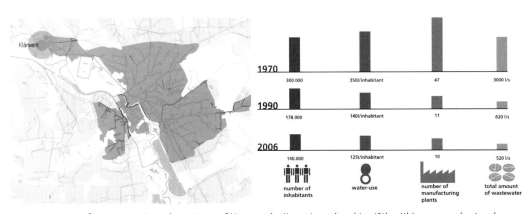

Figure 5: Amount of wastewater in catchment area of Hannover´s city centre reduced to 1/6th within 30 years due to urban development trends

built-up areas. It becomes more and more obvious that under these circumstances the existing kind of urban landscape and infrastructure cannot be maintained to keep functioning in the future. There is an increasing need for concepts addressing transformation and deconstruction issues while safeguarding function, compatibility and appearance.

Infrastructural challenges of growing cities and uncontrolled population growth

While the processes of shrinking and declining cities are most evident in the industrialised countries, the rate of urban growth rapidly increases in the developing countries in a high-speed process of catch-up urbanization. In less than 30 years some cities like Bombay, Beijing or Lagos developed to become large metropolises – whereas in the industrialised countries it took a metropolis such as London, New York, or Tokyo more than a century to grow to a megacity. Urbanisation processes in these new megacities are taking place with a speed and intensity that puts the strategic and innovative capabilities of planners and politicians to a difficult test. Due to the ongoing high influx of urban migrants and high rates of natural population growth the cities are increasingly subject to a loss of governability and control – with the consequence that more and more processes are unregulated and take place informally or illegally. There are all kinds of living and urbanisation stages and conditions next to each other – merging of villages and urban expansion, slum districts alternating with upper-class residential districts, chaotic and random patterns of land use with a large spectrum of varieties, formal and informal patterns of "patchwork urbanization".

The speed and intensity of densification processes seriously outpace any kind of planned water infrastructure provision and the expensive construction of pipe and technical treatment systems cannot be adjusted to the rapid and unplanned processes of construction developments. Supported by international organizations like the World Bank a lot of money is invested into building up hightech wastewater treatment plants. However they often can not be operated properly due to the incomplete or deficient sewer networks. As a consequence most megacities suffer under extreme water pollution and hygienic problems due to

Figure 6: Water pollution and water infrastructure problems in developing countries.

unsolved water management. In many cases the provision of drinkable water and sewerage services especially to the residents of informal settlements has been abandoned. At the same time the sealing of huge areas leads towards big problems of groundwater subsidence and increasing floods.

However contemporary landscape and urban design still usually do not address these issues, looking at urban landscapes with mainly aesthetic considerations constrained by an attachment to the picturesque. To become more attractive most cities are developing programmes to open up their inner-city waterfront locations on canals and rivers and attract new residents with concepts like "lake paradise" or "blue lake county". Landscape architects so far mostly have not questioned the technical nature of infrastructure, either applying the "camouflage approach" of hiding and cosmetically beautifying infrastructure or the "mitigation approach" by implementing laws and compensation measures to limit its negative effects. While the expensive ornamental landscape beautification of cities is increasing very fast, the infrastructural and ecological conditions within the urban environment are deteriorating even further.

Appropriating Water Infrastructure as Urban Landscape

The need to rethink concepts of water infrastructure can be considered a strategic chance to strengthen the profession of landscape architecture. As Elisabeth Mossop and Kongjian Yu suggest in their claims for "affordable landscapes" (Mossop 2005) and "Recovering landscape architecture as the art of survival" (Yu 2006), the profession of landscape architecture should shift away from its current focus on privileged and expensive landscapes towards landscape-based solutions to current issues of landscape problems related to urbanisation. One of the key problems of the current urbanization trends described in this paper is related to conventional concepts of urban drainage and purification systems – and a lot of money needs to be invested into exploring new solutions in the future. Rather than leaving this field to engineers the profession of landscape architecture should use this window of opportunity to take a leading part in the reconstruction and development of urban infrastructure systems – taking the landscape as a starting point.

Why could the profession of landscape architecture take a major role? The strength of landscape architecture lies in its ability to extend our current understandings of infrastructure, linking the performance of natural processes with engineering and urban design strategies. By reuniting the built and the natural we may find new logics towards a more resilient development of infrastructural landscapes as a base of sustainable urban and regional form. One of the precursors of our profession, Frederick Law Olmsted, is often mentioned as the first landscape architect actively applying this approach as early as the 1880's in his proposal for Boston's "Emerald Necklace" – integrating ideas of transport infrastructure, flood and drainage engineering, purification functions of wetlands and ecological restoration into the creation of an aesthetic scenic and recreational park landscape for citizens (Zaitzevsky 1992).

Considering the described challenges related to water infrastructure provision within shrinking and growing cities it is all the more necessary to develop systems involving both human and natural processes. Rather than trying to eliminate ecological processes and invest huge sums of money to replace them within controlled technical systems, we need an "intellectual leap by comprehensively applying the understanding of ecological processes and natural systems to human settlements and planning" (Mossop 2006). Some areas within German cities may resemble scenes of Alan Weisman´s book "The World without Us" describing what happens to our cities´ seemingly solid infrastructures and buildings if nobody cares about them any more. There are buildings without residents, roads without buildings, green spaces without parks, sewer systems without any waste water. One of the main reasons of the past to invest into expensive underground water infrastructure does not exist anymore: the limitation of urban space and high concentration of citizens. On the contrary, in shrinking cities it is hardly possible to maintain urban coherence and functions which speeds up the process of the citizens leaving and these areas deteriorating even further.

Case study "Mueßer Holz", Schwerin - towards an infrastructural landscape approach within shrinking cities.

One example of these shrinking urban areas is a district of the German city Schwerin, named "Mueßer Holz". It is located in the south of Schwerin and is one of the younger districts of the city built from 1978 to 1989. All the buildings are constructed of large prefabcricated concrete slabs with an average height of 5-6 stories – they are the typical style the former German Democratic Republic´s large housing development schemes which were the most favourable places to live before the German reunification in 1990. The city of Schwerin is located within a landscape of lakes and forest. Originally laid out for 29.000 inhabitants, in 2004 there were only 13.000 inhabitants still living in "Mueßer Holz" and additionally one fifth of the apartments were unoccupied. Thus the municipality decided to tear down some houses in order to relieve the housing market but can only invest very limited financial resources into upgrading the remaining open space and infrastructure systems to improve living conditions.

Figure 7: Shrinking urban areas in Germany: the example "Mueßer Holz", Schwerin.

Within her diploma thesis Berit Miehlke developed a concept taking the water infrastructure challenge as a starting point for the generation of a new urban landscape to meet the challenges of the future development of this district. Every time a building is pulled down, its remaining concrete basement will serve as a basin for a plantation of willows within a gravel filter for wastewater purification. Hence the remaining domestic sewage water can be treated within the district and the area can be disconnected from the sewage network. The sewage water serves as fertilizer for the short-rotation willow plantations which can be harvested every 3-4 years to provide biomass for energy production and heating of the district's remaining buildings. The money saved, which would otherwise have to be invested into the maintenance of the under-worked wastewater pipe systems, can now be used for the construction of the proposed new and affordable landscape infrastructure. This landscape infrastructure at the same time gives a spatial and aesthetic framework indicating the positions of the lost buildings, with their volume substituted by growing blocks of trees and their appearance continuously changing. At the same time this concept provides the flexibility for different future options of development: to organize the building demolition and infrastructure construction process step by step, to develop the green infrastructure as a framework for developing new urban functions here or eventually to give up the whole district and leave the willow plantations to develop into forest.

Case study "HuaXin", Shanghai - towards an infrastructural landscape approach within a growing megacity

Within the fast growing areas of megacities the conventional planners' tools trying to control landuse and organize infrastructure services are put to a difficult test. As the cities are becoming more and more densely populated and industrialized it is indispensable to improve the sanitary and ecological conditions and at the same time introduce a system of urban green spaces for recreation reasons. However those parts of the city with the worst environmental and living conditions usually are the poorest parts that can neither afford any privileged

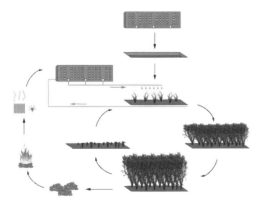 

Figure 8: Construction of new landscape infrastructure as a landscape framework for "Mueßer Holz" in Schwerin, Germany (Miehlke 2007)

landscapes of parks and gardens nor expensive technical infrastructure systems. In this case the basic necessity of infrastructure provision can be used by landscape architects as the most important and maybe only possible generator of public green space which is otherwise getting lost for other construction development.

This approach can be demonstrated by a project in HuaXin, Shanghai designed by the ecological engineering specialists Janisch & Schulz mbH. This district on the outskirts of Shanghai is still criss-crossed by a dense system of canals which have to take up more and more sewage water as the fast developing area is not connected to any water drainage and purification systems. The municipality was already planning to construct a wastewater treatment plant within a nearby park and to cover up all the small canals next to the roads, converting them to an underground drainage system leading the water to the plant. Janisch & Schulz suggested another plan: to reuse the existing infrastructure of water canals by converting them into linear purification landscapes that can substitute a central water treatment plant. The municipality accepted their suggestion and within four months the first construction phase of this urban constructed wetland was completed. This way the territory of infrastructure was reclaimed as significant to the city's open space design. At the same time the interrelations of the system were kept visible by highlighting the purified water outflow through the installation of a fountain with clean water – for the citizens to understand the processes within this not only attractive but also meaningful landscape element as part of their living environment.

Conclusion

Globally we are facing complex urban development processes leading to completely new challenges concerning the management and design of urban infrastructure systems and landscapes. Looking to the past it becomes clear that some of the most impressive and moving cultural and urban water landscapes are nothing more than solutions to the irrigation, domestic water supply, transportation, sanitary sewer and flood control problems of the time. And again today

Figure 9: Constructed wetlands to create green and meaningful residential open space in HuaXin, Shanghai (Ingenieurgesellschaft Janisch & Schulz mbH).

infrastructure networks, flows and their relationship to urban form and development are emerging as an increasing topic among contemporary urbanists (Graham and Marvin 2002, Angelil and Klingmann 1999, Allen 1999) as well as in the "Landscape Urbanism" discourse (Corner 1999, Shannon 2004, Waldheim 2006) and the "Green Infrastructure" discourse (Hough 1984, Tjallingii 1993, Sijmons 2004, Ahern 2007, Yu 2006). However the practice of landscape architecture still usually follows the landscape mitigation and camouflage approach, hiding and masking the urban water infrastructure rather than revealing its complex ecologies of intermingling connections between natural, social and technical processes. It is time to consider landscape design to be more than just the beautiful decoration of open space – designed landscapes should rather be inevitable, affordable, usable and ecologically performing components of our urban environments. For the landscape to become infrastructural landscape architects need a more profound and practical knowledge about ecological and infrastructure systems and dare to cooperate with the engineering and urban design disciplines.

The cases from a shrinking city in Germany and a growing city in China show approaches how a drainage and water purification system as a hybrid of built infrastructure, ecological functions and people's green space can serve as a fundamental component of changing urban and regional form. Making use of dynamic and self-correcting natural processes, the designed urban landscapes are working like "artificial ecologies". They contain a higher degree of ecological resilience, require less intervention and technical control than conventional systems and at the same time offer attractive landscape experiences. This way of thinking can shift the paradigm to a different understanding of landscape architecture: it is not something anymore that the society can bear the cost of, but that offers viable solutions for the sustainable design of urban systems.

Water in Malaysian Landscape Architecture

~ **Rotina Mohd Daik** ~ Landscape Architect, National Landscape Department, Malaysia ~ **Mustafa Kamal Bin Mohd Shariff** ~ Professor and Dean, Faculty of Design and Architecture, Universiti Putra Malaysia, Malaysia

Malaysia is strategically located in the center of Southeast Asia. It consists of the Peninsular and two states on the Island of Borneo. The landmass is largely surrounded by water - the Straits of Malacca in the West and the South China sea to the East and South. The country has 4675 km of coastlines. Its early civilizations were maritime-based and important cities had their beginnings along the coast or close to rivers. Being a nation blessed by an abundance of water, Malaysia hopes to optimize the use of its water resources in creative ways. This paper describe four examples of how water is used to good advantage in overcoming the dreaded monsoon season, creating enhanced living conditions out of an oil palm plantation as well as rehabilitating a once neglected and polluted river estuary and turning it into a major attraction for tourists and local residents.

Introduction

Malaysia is a federation consisting of 12 states and 3 federal territories. Twelve of the states and federal territories are located on Peninsular Malaysia while the other 2 states and a federal territory are located on the Island of Borneo. Peninsular Malaysia and the Island of Borneo are separated by the South China Sea. Thus, Malaysia is surrounded by the sea and possesses 4675 km of coastlines. The country also has an extensive network of river systems. There are about 150 major river basins and the longest river is the Rajang River in the State of Sarawak, which meanders along for 563 km connecting the Borneo Highlands to the South China Sea.

Malaysia enjoys a year-round warm and humid equatorial climate, with a temperature range of 20°C - 35°C. Most of its land is covered with lush and diversified tropical rainforest making it one of the mega biodiversity regions in the world. Rainfall is copious and evenly distributed throughout the year. However, in November and February the amount of rainfall will increase up to 2500mm due to the prevalence of the north- east monsoon winds which brought heavy rain to the east coast of the Peninsular, Sabah and Sarawak. During this period, annual flooding has become a norm in the affected states.

In Malaysia, cities grew out of humble settlements along its long coastlines and major rivers. This makes the people of Malaysia and their cultures adapt well to water. Nevertheless, with rapid development towards a developed nation, Malaysia needs to find better ways of managing its water resources. This paper will highlight some of the development and management initiatives that Malaysia has developed in creating a harmonious living with water.

Role of the National Landscape Department.

The National Landscape Department was established in 1996 and is entrusted to be a body responsible for the development of the country's landscapes including the development of water bodies. Since its establishment, it has organized numerous programs in order to encourage the growth and development of the nation's landscapes and the landscape industry in the country. Among the functions of the department is to outline the landscape development policy, enhance the implementation of the policies, programs and landscape related activities and ensuring the preservation of the natural landscapes. The department has drafted a National Landscape Development Policy (NLDP), which when adopted, will provide the framework for effective planning, management and utilization of all landscape resources in the country. The Country's landscape vision of transforming Malaysia into The Most Beautiful Garden Nation has encouraged the National Landscape Department to embark vigorously on numerous landscape activities and promotional programs to stimulate interest and commitment of policy-makers and the public on the importance of high quality and sustainable landscape development.

The Importance of Water Resources in the Draft National Landscape Development Policy

Malaysia is a country with an abundance of coastal areas, water catchments and wetlands. The draft National Landscape Development Policy (NLDP) pays special attention on issues regarding water. In developing the national landscape towards The Most Beautiful Garden Nation vision, many projects have been planned to enhance these water bodies to provide amenities to the public and at the same time contribute towards the economic well-being of local population. Thus, it is important that development involving water bodies be planned wisely without jeopardizing their ecosystems and water quality.

The landscape development in Malaysia is currently guided by Landscape Master Plans. The plans encompass comprehensive long-term action plans for the development of landscapes and public parks of all major districts in the country. It is formulated as a framework and a guide for landscape development at the state, district, and town levels. These include the identification, utilization and management of water bodies in these districts. With the availability of the landscape master plans, local authorities will be able to control, streamline, enforce and prepare projections for future landscape implementation programs including waterfront development in their jurisdictions. In line with the draft NLDP, the

National Landscape Department has also been encouraging the wise use of water in landscape development. To date there has been an increasing use of water elements in urban landscape development. Water is used in the development of townships through the development of waterfronts, lakes and ponds, weirs, retention ponds, and river beautification. All water resources available in cities will be used not only for beautification works but to cater also for other functions including flood mitigation, climate amelioration, and potable water supply.

Case Studies of Creative Uses of Water in the Malaysian Landscapes.

The following four case studies of projects implemented in Malaysia demonstrate how water has been used creatively to add aesthetic, functional and economic values that benefit the country.

Incorporation of Water in the Development of Putrajaya

The Federal Government Administrative Center in Putrajaya is a city planned and built to provide a living environment which is conducive for administrative, leisure, recreation as well as economic activities. The city is laid on an undulating terrain carved out from a former rubber and oil palm plantations. The undulating nature of the 4581 hectares site provides an opportunity for the creation of a garden city surrounded by green spaces, urban parks and a 600 hectares man-made lake. This central lake visually connects important institutional buildings, residential areas and the scenic landscaped areas. A series of man-made wetlands were constructed to naturally maintain a high standard of water quality for the lake. The system of wetlands in Putrajaya is the first man-made wetland to be constructed in Malaysia and it is also one of the largest fully constructed freshwater wetlands in the tropics. The construction of the wetland was completed in August 1998 and is currently functioning well and contributing to provide cleaner water for the city lake ecosystem as shown in Figure 1.

Among initial functions of the Putrajaya wetland are to treat urban surface runoff and act as a filtering mechanism of the catchments, intercepting water flow, trapping sediments and pollutants, removing toxic substances as well as

Figure 1: Activities centered on lake area, government administrative buildings....

assimilating nutrients collected from the catchments area. The created ecosystem eventually provides a breeding environment to numerous aquatic plants, invertebrates, reptiles, birds and fishes. The wetland also contributes to control flooding by providing temporary storage of storm water over wide coverage of lake area.

The 600 hectares central lake was created by inundating the valleys of two main rivers (Sungai Chua and Sungai Bisa) that pass through the township. The lake has been primarily designed to enhance the aesthetic appeal of Putrajaya. It is a man-made system that involves altering the existing terrain to simulate wetland conditions. They primarily attempt to replicate the treatment that has been observed to occur when polluted water enters the natural wetland. These wetlands help to clean water by removing pollutants. Besides being a water cleansing and filtration systems, the wetland area is also being used for a host of sports and recreational activities, flood mitigation, research and education related to environment as well as a tourist attraction. The Putrajaya wetland system comprises of six arms with 23 cells (Figure 2.). All the arms eventually discharge to the Central Wetland, which actually makes 24 cells in all, before the water flows into the central Putrajaya Lake. They straddle the water courses of Sungai Chua, Sungai Bisa and three tributaries. A series of rock-filled weirs divide the 23 cells. Although all the six arms are connected, they differ in size, depths, plant com-

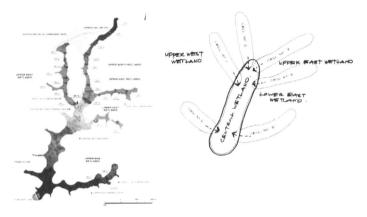

Figure 2: Wetland system which comprises of six arms and 23 cells flow to the Central Wetland

... residential area, recreation and breeding ground for migratary birds

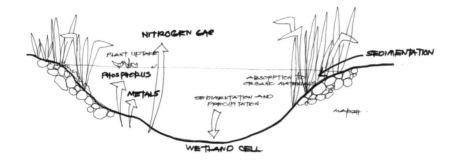

Figure 3: Various reactions happening in the wetland cells

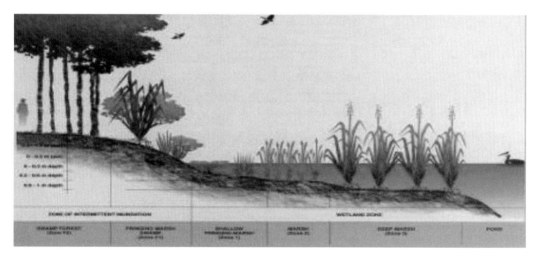

Figure 4: Section of a typical wetland cell showing the zone of intermittent inundation,
wetland zone (Zone 1, 2 and 3) and the open pond

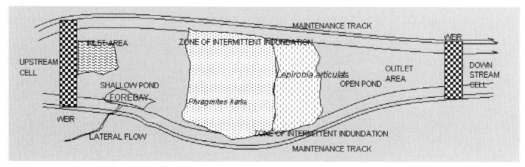

Figure 5 : Typical lay out of a wetland cell

munities and pollutant loads that they are designed to handle. The wetland is also complemented by riparian parks and gross pollutant traps.

The main contribution of the constructed wetlands is to ensure that the water entering the central lake meets the standard set by governing authority. To achieve this filtration function, the wetland was planted with a variety of indigenous aquatic plants that remove excess nutrients and pollutants from the catchments water. The basic processes occurring in the cell zones are as illustrated in Figure 3. Typical longitudinal cross-section and typical layout of a wetland cell are shown in Figure 4 and Figure 5 respectively. The design features a multi-cell multi-stage system with flood retention capability to maximize the space available for colonization by water plants. The roles of the plants are to intercept pollutants and to provide a root zone where bacteria and microorganisms that assist in filtering and removing water pollutants can flourish.

Maintaining the wetland in working order present another challenge to managers of the man-made wetland. A number of guidelines and operating manuals were formulated to ensure the sustainability of the wetland and its surrounding environment. The monitoring programs are part of the management activities that are undertaken to ensure a fair assessment of the wetland functions in relation to its ecological and management requirements. They are also formulated to ensure the sustainability of water quality in the lake. The Putrajaya Lake and Wetland Management Operational System (PLWMOS) is intended to serve as the main environmental database and spatial analytical tool for the current state of hydrology, physico-chemical, and biotics parameters of Putrajaya's lake and wetlands. The monitoring programme includes the studies of water quality, phytoplankton, zooplankton, waterborne pathogens, plants and wildlife and the movement of contaminants in the biotic system. PLWMOS was designed as a knowledge-based decision support system particularly to serve as an early warning system to alert for potential environmental problems. The success story of Putrajaya in promoting the use of water in creating a new urban landscape has attracted other developers to emulate its approach. A number of other township and residential developments have also incorporated water into their projects using a variety of approaches and technologies. Besides satisfying the requirement by local authorities, developers are beginning to realize the potential of using water elements in their projects to enhance urban landscapes and add to their economic values.

The Monsoon Cup of Terengganu

The state of Terengganu is part of the federation of Malaysia. Located in the eastern coast of the Peninsular, it is one of the very few states that still retain the traditional cultural values of the indigenous Malay race. The eastern coast of Malaysia has distinct dry and wet seasons. During the wet seasons, the coastal states normally receive heavy rain and strong winds from the Northeast Monsoon. This monsoon winds normally blows during November to February each year. This is followed by the annual flooding in the east coast states. However, the states of Kelantan and Terengganu normally received the brunt of the seasonal flooding. Thus, in these affected states the weather plays an important role in the development and daily activities of the local population. The dry season allows locals to indulge in land-based and sea activities. These include rice cultivation and farming, fishing, and also leisure pursuits such as the world famous kite flying competition. However, the onset of monsoon starts accompanied by frequent thunderstorms, strong winds and rough seas forces dry season activities to a halt. The local population stays indoors and economic activities are confined to doing traditional handicrafts such as batik painting, wood carving and backyard food industries. During this season even tourism and recreational activities significantly decline leaving hotel rooms vacant and affecting the local economy. However, the state government of Terengganu recently organized the Monsoon Cup during the peak of the monsoon season. The 500km long coastlines facing the South China Sea and the availability of high winds during this season are ideal for yachting. The Monsoon Cup, which was first organized in Malaysia in 2005, was dubbed the Formula One of sailing competitions. This professional sailing series was formed in 2000 to unite the world's best match-race regattas under one banner. Thus, the organization of the international Monsoon Cup yachting competition in Kuala Terengganu demonstrated how water at its worst (with high winds and rough seas) could be utilized to bring in tourists and provide a boost to the local economy and improve people's livelihood.

Malaysian Flood Mitigation System for Urban Residential Areas

Malaysia, is blessed with frequent heavy rains that provide an abundance of water can lead to calamities such as flash floods and landslides causing severe damages to properties and loss of lives. As Malaysia continues with its development, more built up areas appeared and this has increased tremendously surface water run-offs resulting in flooding and soil erosion during severe thunder-

Figure 6: Traditional activities by the sea which come to a standstill during monsoon.

Figure 7: Transformation of the estuary that are usable throughout the year.

storms. Retention ponds in housing areas are known for its benefits in providing storm water abatement as well as removal of pollutants. These man-made ponds are frequently used to help substitute for the natural absorption of forests or other natural processes that are often destroyed during development. Loss of natural "sponge" in urban areas leads to massive flow of surface run-offs during heavy rain. The construction of retention ponds close to heavily built-up areas will aid in storm water management by temporarily storing storm-water. Furthermore, retention ponds can also be landscaped to enhance the aesthetic appeal and fulfill amenity needs of residents. This effective use of retention ponds for storm-water management and amenity development is demonstrated in the neighborhood of Bukit Jelutong and Setia Ecopark housing estates. Both of these middle-class development used storm-water retention basins to create interesting water features that enhance their surroundings. The Bukit Jelutong housing estate was developed by Guthrie Properties Development Holdings Berhad on a 893 hectares of prime land close to the Selangor state capital of Shah Alam. it is a low density housing development that promotes back to nature lifestyle for its residents. The developer planned and developed 12.14 hectares of retention ponds with an excess capacity of 50%. This has helped Bukit Jelutong overcome its excess storm-water and avoid serious flooding in low lying areas. Due to its sensitivity to flood mitigation and the provision of well-landscaped water features, the Bukit Jelutong housing estates has received a number of awards including the prestigious Best Town Planning Scheme Award from the Malaysian Institute of Town Planners in 1997. The success of Bukit Jelutong in controlling its flood problems has encouraged another property developer, SP Setia Sdn Bhd., to incorporate fully landscaped water retention features in its development. The Setia Eco Park is a sprawling residential development covering over 320 hectares

Master lay out plan.

of prime land also close to the Selangor state capital of Shah Alam. The developer also wanted to offer buyers with an opportunity to live in a garden-like natural surrounding of a tropical paradise. Thus, the estate incorporate 25% of the development to landscaped parks, walkways, streams and lakes and a forest park. Setia Eco Park consists of 74 hectares of green areas, 68 hectares for infrastructure development and 178 hectares of built-up land area. The development replaced what was previously an oil palm plantation with undulating landform of isolated hills and small valleys. Owing to the land's rolling terrain and its location neighboring the Seri Cahaya Alam Agricultural Park with a rich diversity of flora and fauna, the landscape architects proposed to create an "eco-sanctuary" that blends with its natural surroundings rather than the usual storm water retention ponds. The central body of water is a 12 hectare lake. To encourage wildlife, 3 islands were created in the middle of the lake to encourage the growth of vegetation that attracts wildlife. The artificial ponds were incorporated early in the master plan of the residential development. The project considers the existing natural systems and avoid unnecessary disturbance to existing neighboring natural vegetation. The layout of Setia Eco Park was designed to preserve the natural stream and undulating characteristic of the land. The main drainage and retention pond were then enhanced with visually attractive landscaped elements with habitats for flora and fauna. The whole 12 hectares recreational lake, 20 hectares of forest park and another 37 hectares of land were dedicated to create 26km of waterways, lakes and creeks running all around the Setia Eco Park enclave. Islands within the lakes serve as nesting grounds for beautiful birds and swans. Efforts have been taken to retain the natural water courses or valleys and most are retained as linear parks incorporating streams and ponds. The ridges and hills between the valleys have also been retained but have been reduced in level to facilitate accessibility and construction of homes. The layout of water bodies and parks were planned to flow from the northern part of the development to throughout the parcels of the southern part. This layout minimizes stagnant water which affects the aquatic life within the water bodies. The inter-connected green parks around the parcels soften the hard structures of the surrounding area and also act as a green lung to the development. To preserve native habitats and the existing flora and fauna in the area, the services of spe-

Figure 8: Images of residential landscape that has been emulated in most of the urban are.

cialists were engaged to conduct extensive research and advice on how to promote the type of plants and create a habitat conducive to birds, butterflies and fishes. Among the steps taken to implement this included the setting-up of a nursery to cultivate the food plants of butterflies. Other vegetation were planted to attract the migration of local butterflies, birds and other species to the park.

The Lumut Waterfront

Lumut is a small town in the state of Perak. It is located close to the estuary of the Dinding River, which flows into the Straits of Malacca. The town is the gateway to Pulau Pangkor, a popular island resort in the Straits of Malacca. The town itself has always been historically associated with fishing and maritime activities. The development of a waterfront and park enhance the image and added value to this sleepy seaside town. Due to its past maritime association, it is only appropriate that the theme of the park reflects its maritime roots. The master-plan of the waterfront and park is based on the outline of a ship complete with anchor and sails. The park consists of two main plazas connected by a central axis. The walkways curves out to the sides of the main axis and made to resemble the horns of the ship's anchor. The decorative patterns of the plazas' pavement resemble the compass of a ship and the roofs of its two main pavilions were designed to mimic the sail of a boat. Other parts of a ship such as the mast, yard, stay rudder and boom appear in the design of benches, gazebos, playground, flag and light poles, bollards and various sculptures. Sculptures representing fishes, turtles and other sea creatures were also designed into the park. The Lumut Waterfront and park provide visitors with many facilities including restaurants and outdoor eating places. Wide open plazas planted with palms frame scenic vistas of the river landscapes and the sea. A river walk that connects the park to the town centre brings visitors close to the water's edge and provides them with a close-up experience of the Dinding River. The park is also provided with a jetty, a marina and fishing decks. The development of the Lumut Waterfront and park has turned a once heavily polluted Dinding River and the seafront into a clean and useful place for the public to use and attracts tourists, whom in the past merely used the town as a gateway to get to other tourists destinations. This again demonstrates how the creative use of water can add value to existing space and place.

Conclusion

Water is an important resource in the world. Water is essential to support human consumption and other activities as well as ensuring that the natural system continues to function well. As water becomes scarce due to its increasing demand and human carelessness, we need to protect it by using it in more creative and sustainable ways. This paper shares case studies in Malaysia where water has been creatively used either directly or indirectly to enhance the lives of its citizen, add economic values to the country and maintain the stability of local natural systems through the contribution of landscape architecture.

The Water Adaptive Landscapes in Ancient Chinese Cities

~ **Kongjian Yu, Dihua Li** and **Zhang Lei** ~ The Graduate School of

Landscape Architecture, Peking University, China

Global warming and Climate change may increase flood hazards in some regions, and draught in others. The past experience of adaptive strategies evolved in the long history of survival under hazardous conditions is inspiring for us to face future uncertainty. Based on the study of several ancient cities in the Yellow River floodplain, this paper discusses the disastrous experience of floods and waterlogs and found three major adaptive landscape strategies: sitting on highlands, constructing walls and protective dikes, and reserving or digging ponds within cities. These adaptive strategies result in three types of water city: Water-within-city, city-in-water, and Ying-yang-city. It is argued that all these traditional experiences and landscape heritages help us to understand the vernacular cultural landscape of cities in the Yellow River floodplain, and that have important values to landscape architecture and urban planning as universally applicable strategies in facing global warming and regional climate change as well as practical landscape strategies for better urban design for cities in this region. It is further argued that the water-adaptive landscapes are valuable cultural heritages, and should be integrated into landscape and urban planning for urban development today.

Introduction

Global warming and Climate change may increase flood hazards in some regions, and draught in others. While reducing the green-house gas emission is a priority, it is of no less significance to develop adaptive strategies to mediate the potential hazards caused by climate changes. The past experience of adaptive strategies evolved in the long history of survival under hazardous conditions is inspiring for us to face future uncertainty.

The Yellow River, famed for its high sediment yield, is probably the most difficult river to be regulated in the world. The downstream region of the Yellow River has been rather inundated in history, especially when encountering a big flood, levee failure, or river diversion. Therefore, the flooding frequency of the Yellow River is relatively high compared with other rivers around the world. However, during the long struggling history against flood and silting disasters, these ancient cities acquired lots of valuable experience about how to control and mediate floods, which can be identified from the unique local landscapes. These kinds of landscapes have already been mentioned before (Liu,1936; Li,1895), and are further explained in the modern time (Zheng, 1985; Wu, 1995; Zhang, 2000). Furthermore, there are also related studies on specific cities in the fields of archeology, history and geography etc.(Ding,2004; Li,1988; Chen,2002; Zhao,2000). Nevertheless, when considering the ancient cities in the Yellow River alluvial plain as a whole, there is a lack of research and the systematic study on the origin and evolution of this adaptive landscape is also deficient.

Recently, the unique landscape of these cities has been highly valued, and also been used in slogans such as "Water city in the north of the Yangtse River", "Water city in the north country" in the urban comprehensive plans to enhance city images so as to boost the development of tourism and attract investment. However, the origin of the water-featured landscape in the cities is always misinterpreted as using geomancy or Feng-shui (Chen,2002), while the unique value of the landscaping as an "Art of Survival", is not well recognized yet (Yu, and Padua,2006).

Facing today's ecological and environmental degradation around China, "The art of survival" which is a unique cultural heritage of the ancient Chinese people could still be beneficial to refer to, especially in present urban water system management, flood and waterlog control planning and land use planning. Therefore there is potential theoretical and practical value in studying the flood-adaptive landscape of the ancient cities. The priority of this paper is to give a general introduction of the background and an in-depth analysis about the origin and evolution of the adaptive landscape in the Yellow River Alluvial Plain.

A history of suffering from, and experience with flood and waterlog

The Yellow River alluvial plain is between the Hai and Huai rivers on the north and south sides, while the west-east extent is limited by the Funiu and Taiyin mountains. The area includes the administrative boundaries of Kaifeng, Puyang and Zhoukou cities and the eastern part of Xinxiang city in Henan Province; Heze

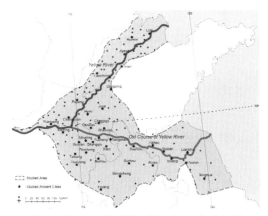

Fig. 1 The studied area: the Yellow River flood alluvial plain.

and Liaocheng cities in Shandong Province, and also the northern part of Jiangsu and Anhui Provinces.

As mentioned above, the people living in the Yellow River alluvial plain suffered a lot from floods in history. According to the statistics, between 1000 B.C. and 1949 A.D. the Yellow River had 1500 floods including overflow, bank burst, river diversion etc. and the flooded area was about 250 thousand square kilometers. During this time, the Yellow River had 26 considerably disastrous river diversions which happened once in very 4-5 years on average.

Kaifeng city experienced bank burst 70 times while between 1180 and 1944 the whole city was flooded 6 times and trapped in water 15 times (Li,1995). Similarly, in the 3000 years before 1949 A.D., the city of Heze was flooded 12 times by river diversion and 164 times by bank burst. It also suffered disastrous waterlog 224 times within the 614 years before the year 1949. Also the city has been trapped in floodwater many times. It is almost the same situation in Caoxian and Chengwu counties which have been reconstructed many times after being devastated by floods (WCRHCC,1994).

Disastrous silting always happens with flooding. After a flood, a large amount of silt is always deposited on the land, and this can bury the cities and ruin the farmland (Zou, 1993). In some cities with the shield of circumvallation and circumvallating levees, the silt carried by floods can be accumulated outside the levee or circumvallation, which elevates the altitude of the land outside the city or levee. This process has caused the phenomena that the city is beneath the outskirts of the city, while the outskirts of the city are below the outskirts of the levee (Li,1895), which looks like a well(Liu 1936) (Fig.2a,b, Fig.3). Therefore the elevation of the sites of the ancient cities would gradually lower as the sediment process continued, with accumulating waterlog and increased difficulty in flood

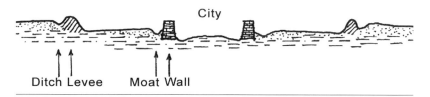

Fig. 2a A typical section of ancient cities in the Yellow River alluvial plain.

Fig.2b Typical elevation model of cities in the Yellow River alluvial plain (Heze City, GIS visualization of terrain).

Fig.3 City as a well: city is beneath the outskirts of the city (Photo: Kongjian yu).

control. Once the levee got damaged or even when the circumvallation failed, it would be a tragedy for the whole city, and the loss and casualty was unacceptable. The large amount of silt itself also has had the power to crush a city. Sometimes the sediment carried by the flood elevated the land several meters higher, and the cities were buried. The common phenomenon that more modern cities have been built above former ones is just an illustration of this power.

Flood and Waterlog Adaptive Landscapes

During the long-time struggle against the flood disasters, people have attained much experience about flood-control and the way to adapt in this difficult environment, which has allowed cities to survive and develop. The adaptive landscapes of the ancient cities in the Yellow River alluvial plain have exactly generated this experiences with survival, showing three main strategies, which are; (1) Inhabiting high land, (2) Building circumvallation and circumvallating levees, (3) Conserving and excavating retention ponds.

Inhabiting High Land

In the remote past when the Yellow River was overflowing on the large plain area, the soil was enriched by floods. The ancient people then gradually migrated from the highland terraces to the alluvial plain to cultivate the fertile soil for agriculture since the late neolith Longshan Period (4350-3950 B.C.) (Wang,1998). To avoid the floods, the ancient settlers chose high land in the plain to settle down in, for this was one simple strategy to stay away from the floodwater. In eastern Henan and southwestern Shandong provinces, there are distributed many relics of this type of ancient settlement between the time of the Longshan period, Shang (1700 B.C -1100 B.C) and Zhou Dynasties 1100B.C.-256 B.C).

After experiencing numerous floods, some of the relics have been crushed or buried by sediment, while some are still visible above the ground. These relics are called "Gudui" (Ancient Mound) in the local areas, which vary in size, shape

Fig.4 "Gudui" (Ancient Mound), the building base is raised above the ground and becomes a unique vernacular landscape element (Photo: Kongjian Yu).

and with a height of 2-5 meters in general. These relics reflect that the strategy of "inhabiting on high land" started from the Neolithic period and can be regarded as a unique local cultural landscape (Li,1988) (Fig.4).

In the Spring-Autumn (770B.C-476 B.C) and Warring-States Periods (476 B.C-221 B.C), more people migrated to the plain area from highlands for agriculture (YRCHSCC,2003; Ban,2005), and the population grew sharply. Many dikes were built beside the settlements along the Yellow River. Therefore in some settlements with convenient traffic, cities mushroomed. To these cities, inhabiting on high land was still an important strategy to control floods and mitigate waterlog. The forms and strategies were various and include the following:

Choosing natural high land

Many ancient cities were built on relatively higher places. The relics of the ancient cities Huaiyang and Pingliangtai are both located on high land (Wu,1995). One specific example is the ancient city of Suizhou in Suixian County. It is recorded that this ancient city was built on the Jinsuo mountain range, while in the Jiajing period(1522-1566 A.D.) of the Ming dynasty a new city was built on Phenix mountain after the the former city was destroyed by a flood (Wang,1968).

Some cities used the high land formed by the sedimentation of the floods. When the former city was too low-lying for living or overtaken by floods, people always moved to the high land to build a new city. Examples can be found in today's Shan, Shangqiu, Zhecheng and Xiayi counties etc.

Not only the cities were sited on the high land, but also the important architecture such as administration centers, temples, and colleges which were always built on high land to avoid floods. One example is the Kaifeng Temple Tower which was built on the top of Yi Mountain. Although it experienced floods many times, it still remained above water level (Li,1958). Another example is the governmental office of Suizhou, which was built in front of the Jinling mountain (Wang,1968). Besides that, it was also very common to build temples, colleges, and graves on the "Gudui" (Ancient Mound) relics in those ancient cities to avoid floods. This also generated a visual effect of grandness to the architecture.

Elevating ground for roads, blocks, and buildings

It was a common phenomenon that the ground level of the ancient cities became lower-lying relatively, because of the silt deposited outside the city when flooded. Therefore utilizing the deposited silt to elevate the ground of the city was an important approach to reverse the situation. This was referred to by Yang Tianjing: "The local officials had designated some land to allow the government and citizens to take earth for elevating the ground of the city or houses" (Li,1895).

As a consequence, retention ponds were also formed, which means that when the ground of the city was elevated, water from the waterlogged area could also be drained to the ponds. This was a strategy killing two birds with one stone. Wang Shangxian has recorded this about Yucheng city (Li,1895), and similar records can be found in Ningling county (Xiao,1911).

Building artificial high land for important architecture and as a refuge during floods

Building a high base for important architecture to avoid floods was a more common adaptive landscape strategy, and this can be dated back to the Spring-Autumn (770B.C-476 B.C) and Warring-States Periods (476 B.C ?221 B.C), Qin dynasty (221 B.C - 206 B.C) and Han dynasty(202 B.C -220A.D). Although afterwards, the frequency of using volumes of consolidated soil for architectural base decreased, building important architecture on a high base compared with the normal buildings was still a general principle. Many ancient cities have similar records that show after the city was flooded, most buildings were damaged, while the important architecture including government offices, colleges and Town God Temples could survive the floods because of their higher level (Yuan, 2004; Chen,2004).

The former Town God Temple of Caoxian County was always waterlogged during the rainy season. In the Jiajing Period of the Ming dynasty (1522 A.D - 1566A.D), when the temple was rebuilt, the first step was to elevate the base several *chi* (one chi=0.33meters) higher using the earth transported from the outside of the city. Then an extra base was built that was several times higher than the former base. The new project was tested by a flood in the year it was finished, and after the flood ,the temple was still there with almost no impact (Chen,2004).

Besides that, there are also instances where terraces or high land was built around the ancient cities as refuge for the citizens when a flood was coming. The ancient city of Suizhou is an example. Wu Gong, an officer in the Ming dynasty (1368A.D-1683 A.D), advocated to build the high land referred above for the citizens' escape from floods. He held that when the flood came, it always influenced hundreds of kilometers, and the depth of the water could be several meters. So the flat areas were always flooded, but the high land could escape that, and could be used as a refuge for the citizens. On the other hand, when raising the ground for buildings and escape mounds, volumes of earth were needed which came from the making of ponds that could store and reduce storm water runoff and mediate the waterlog problem. (Wang,1968)

Circumvallation

Although circumvallation normally is used as a military defense facility, it also has a flood control function in the Yellow River alluvial plain (Liu, 1932). The use of circumvallation as a flood control function has even been found in the ancient Chinese cities originated along the Yellow River, like the Pingliangtai city relic of Huaiyang city in Henan Province which was established 4000 years ago. Also there is the Xihao relic of Yanshi city in Henan Province which was established up to 3000 years ago in the Shang dynasty, and a similar historical site was also found from the Shang dynasty (1700 B.C -1100 B.C) around Zhengzhou city (Wu, 1995).

The earliest circumvallations were mainly made of consolidated soil. This material was vulnerable to the erosion of rain water or in the waterlog, so most of the ancient cities used bricks on the outside of the consolidated soil to prevent erosion. Sometimes even the whole circumvallation was build with bricks (Wang,1968), which could greatly increase the effectiveness of the circumvallation to prevent flooding. City entrances (passes) were generally the weak points of the circumvallation in terms of military defense. To increase the function of the entrances in defense, most ancient cities had smaller defensive structures enclosing the entrances outside the city, called "Wengcheng" (barbican entrances to the city). The ancient city of Shangqiu had four entrances, each of them enforced by the "Wengcheng" that had two gates. Through this arrangement, floods could be effectively prevented from entering into the city (SCRCC, 1991). Furthermore, setting city gates at the back side of the city away from the potential flooding was an important principle. The ancient city of Suizhou used to have a small gate in the northwest side of the city for day-to-day entrance in the Ming dynasty (1368A.D-1683 A.D), which was called the right-wing gate. Because it was found that floods always entered the city through this small gate, it was finally closed in the Qing dynasty (1636A.D-1912A.D) (Wang et al, 1968).

Circumvallating Levees

   Another common flood adaptive landscape was the circumvallating levee outside the circumvallation, which was generally a ring shape levee surrounding the city as a double reinforced protection. Due to budget deficit, many cities only had circumvallation built at the time when they were initially established. Then the outer levees were gradually built. Some cities had levees built only at the side facing the river, but this strategy reduced the effectiveness of flood prevention. So if finance allowed, many cities would make segments of levees connected gradually into an integrated one, such as in the ancient cities of Suizhou, Zhecheng (Li, 1896), and Chengwu (Yuan, 2004). To further increase their flood prevention capacity, some ancient cities also had multiple levees built along the river bank section vulnerable to flood. A good example is Kaifeng city in the Yuan dynasty (1206-1368 A.D)that had multiple levees built along the Yellow River (Wu,1995). Another example is in the Dangshan county, where many levees along the Yellow River were built (Liu, 1998). Also the city of Taikang county had nine levees built along the river (An, 1990).
   Compared to circumvallation, the circumvallating levee was mostly built of consolidated earth which was not waterproof. So the protection of the levee itself was very important, and it always needed trees such as willow, mulberry and elm to be planted to protect it. In 1513 when the levee of Caoxian county was rebuilt, woody stakes were planted to decrease the impact from the waves and prevent erosion. As well, poplar and willow trees were planted to consolidate the earth (Chen, 2004). Other cities like Heze (Ling,2004), Suizhou (Wang, 1968), Luyi (Lv, 2002), Xiayi (Han, 1920), etc. all have records of planting trees along the levee throughout their history. As well, Caoxian county set up protective fences outside their levee to keep it from being destroyed (Chen, 2004), while in Ningling city, building paths on the levee and grazing on its perimeters were forbidden (Xiao, 1911).

Circumvallation and circumvallating levees work!

In history, the function of circumvallation and circumvallating levees in flood prevention is indubitable. In 1855 when the Yellow River had a big natural diversion (Tong Waxiang bank burst), the whole Heze area was submerged under the water, while only the cities were above the water surface as isolated rescue islands. People who lived in adjacent villages all went into the cities to escape the flood. Just because of the protection of circumvallation, Heze city survived this disaster (HZZHRCC, 1993). Yuncheng city would have almost been totally wiped out from the earth, had the citizens not repaired their circumvallation and levee in time under the organization of the government during the flood. However, the villages around the city were all submerged in the water (YRRCOHRRB, 1989). Similar situations were recorded in almost every ancient city in the Yellow River alluvial plain, and all these proved the powerful function of circumvallation and circumvallating levees. Circumvallation was mainly used for military defense, while the circumvallating levee was mainly established to block floods. The levee was always the first defense line in flood prevention. Therefore the ancient cities all regarded repairing the levee before or during the flood season as the top task, and the records of cooperation between government and citizens to amend levees are numerous.

Generally floods could be kept outside of the levee, while the silt also deposited outside the levee would gradually elevate the land surface there.. This demonstrated the function of the circumvallating levee in controlling floods, while at the same time, the risk would increase as the silt accumulated outside of the levee. Therefore, even more attention had to paid to this by the government officials and residents. Officers of Suizhou city in the Ming dynasty (1368A.D-1683 A.D) pointed out that: the land elevation outside their levee was several meters higher than the city, and if the levee burst, the city would suffer a huge tragedy. Not only the houses would be submerged, but the residents would all die (Wang, 1968). This understanding among the government officials made the circumvallating levee a life-line. Since silt carried by the Yellow River deposited outside the levee, a precious buffer zone between the city wall and the levee was formed. This buffer zone could become the sink for the rainwater drained from the inner city which would prevent it being submerged in waterlog. For example, Caoxian county in the Hongzhi period (1488-1505 A.D.) of the Ming dynasty failed to maintain their levee for a long time, which lead to a silt deposit outside the city wall (circumvallation). Over a period of ten years, the ground outside the city wall rose gradually, and was almost as high as the city wall. When people were passing in and out, they could directly enter the city over the circumvallation, and the semi-buried gates were too narrow to allow a carriage to pass by. The inner city was always waterlogged which was not suitable for living, so many people emigrated. In the early Zhengde period (1506 -1521 A.D.) of the Ming dynasty, the local official suggested to rebuild a new city, but because of the unaffordable cost they rejected this and decided to rebuild a new circumvallating levee and elevate the circumvallation instead. The new levee functioned well in keeping away many floods, and the silt sediment piled outside the city beyond the levee, so that the city was able to be sustained (Chen, 2004).

However, once a flood destroyed the levee and circumvallation, a city would be submerged, and when such a tragedy occurred, the circumvallation and levee could also be used as refuges for residents to escape from the flood. Records about these kind of situations can be found in Kaifeng city (Jiang, 1987), Kaocheng city (Li, 1986), Dongming city (YRRCOHRRB, 1989), Yuncheng city (Wu, 1995), etc. One of the latest records was the 'once in a hundred years' flood of Suixian county which occurred in 1957, where both the circumvallation and the levee were crushed and the flood poured into the city. Thousands of residents and peasants ran up to the broken levee and circumvallation to escape the flood temporarily and wait for rescue (SCRCC, 1989).

Retention ponds

Another common feature of the ancient cities in the Yellow River alluvial plain was the large water surface inside or surrounding the city.. Therefore most of the ancient cities could be called "water cities", but this kind of "water city" was different from the water cities in South china which were formed with networks of streams and canals. The "water city" of the Yellow River alluvial plain featured a large body of water or lakes.

Types and Origins of Retention Ponds

Ponds and water surfaces in and around the cities can be classified into four types: moats, ponds inside the city?circum-city lakes, and former city lakes. The origin of the water surface was multifaceted, below some possible origins are discussed.

Ponds formed when constructing the circumvallation and circumvallating levee

It was a common practice among the ancient cities to build the circumvallation by digging the moat, a practice which killed two birds with one stone. This has

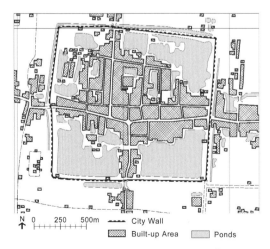

Fig. 5 Lake formed by silting: Caoxian county Plan (based on 1/50000 topographic maps of Caoxian county).

been recorded in Xiayi (Han, 1920), Liaocheng (He, 1999), etc. In some cases, the building of the circumvallating levee was also associated with the digging of channels encircling the levee, which could be used to drain the flood. Records can be found in Shangqiu (Liu, 1932), Heze, etc. But the moats and channels were always silted up with the sediment from the Yellow River, therefore periodical dredging was required, which was always combined with the reconstruction and expansion of the circumvallation or circumvallating levee. By this means, the capacity of flood prevention could be increased from time to time.

Ponds formed during urban construction

One of the major origins of the ponds inside the city was that they were dug out to provide earth for the construction of city walls and residences and public buildings. In Caoxian county it was noted that when building the college of Chaoxian county, people got earth from the nearby land and a pond was simultaneously created (Chen, 2004). A similar record was found in Heze city where the undeveloped land beside the governmental office was dug up for earth and gradually a pond was created (Ling, 2004).

Ponds formed by silting

Silting was the most common reason for the ancient cities to have large water features. Sand from the Yellow River carried by annual floods silted up outside the levee and circumvallation, and the city gradually became a low-lying basin, which resulted in waterlog inside the city and water catch in lower sites within the city to become ponds. One example was in the Caoxian county which was build in the Zheng Tong period (1436-1449 A.D.) in the Ming dynasty. But in the Kangxi period (1662-1722 A.D.) of the Qing dynasty, the land outside the city was silted up, and the urban drainage was blocked and four large lakes at four corners were thus formed (Chen,2004), which still exist today (Fig. 5). Another example was in Xiayi county, which recorded that the water features in it were formed by a flood which occurred in the early Kangxi period (1654-1722A.D) (Han, 1920). Similar records were found in the cities of Ningling, Heze, etc.

Ponds formed for drainage

Making ponds to retain rain water and mitigate waterlog in the city was very common practice in ancient cities. In Suizhou (Wang et al., 1968), Yucheng (Li, 1895), Ningling (Xiao, 1911) etc. all had records about digging ponds to drain water, and the earth was always used to build the circumvallation or bases of residential buildings, or to build the artificial highland as a refuge.

The measures referred as above were always practiced collectively, which brought the different water features or ponds. The water system in the cities experienced a dynamic process in their long history. The city moat was always the main water feature when the city was initially established, and the moat was dug when the circumvallation was built. Both the moat and the circumvallation acted together as a holistic flood defense system. The lake surrounding the city usually evolved from the moat. Whenever needed, the city moat was extended and many ponds between the circumvallation and levee were dug to drain rain water or mitigate waterlog. The moat would be extended for earth required to build and repair the city wall or building the houses, and finally became a large lake between the circumvallation and the levee.

It is recorded in Xiayi city that the moat was originally 25 meters wide bounded by farmland (Zheng, 1963), while years later in the Kangxi period (1654-1722A.D) of the Qing dynasty, the moat had been extended to 90-120 meters wide, which had became a huge lake outside the levee. The lakes were also used for production, including cultivating crops and fishing (Han, 1920). This kind of productive landscape was very common in the Yellow river alluvial plain, and other typical examples are found in the ancient cities of Liaocheng, Shangqiu, Huaiyang, Chengwu, Yucheng etc. (Fig.6, Fig.7, Fig.8).

Ponds inside the city usually did not exist when the city was first established, and they were formed when earth was needed for building the circumvallation and houses. When the inner city ground was getting lower and lower every year the ponds were gradually formed and enlarged as an adaptive solution to the flood and waterlog problem.

The water surface area of some cities finally could reach one third of the whole city, and the water surface area of Xiayi city covered even two thirds of its total area. In 1949 Xiayi city had to develop a new city outside the former one due to the limited dry land for further development (Tab.1).

	Heze city	Cao county	Chengwu	Xiayi	Changyuan	Feng county	Nanle
Percentage (%)	28.9	34.9	23.3	69.1	23.7	19.2	13.3

Tab.1 The percentage of water surface in some of the flood adaptive cities (data source: gross calculation by the authors based on the 1/50000 topographic maps of the cities from 1950s-1970s)

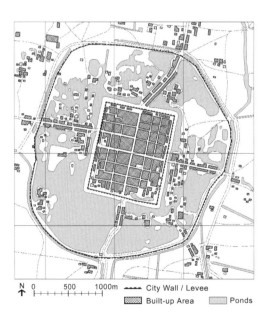

N 0   500   1000m ▬▬ City Wall / Levee
↑   ▨ Built-up Area   ▨ Ponds

Fig.6 Circum-city Lake: Shangqiu county Plan (based on 1/50000 Topographic maps of Shangqiu county).

N 0   200   400m ▬▬ City Wall / Levee
↑   ▨ Built-up Area   ▨ Ponds

Fig.7 Circum-city Lake: Yucheng Plan (based on 1/50000 Topographic maps of Yucheng county).

Lake Formed from a Submerged City

In extreme cases, the whole city could eventually be submerged to form a huge lake due to the continual silting process outside the circumvallating levee. This occurred when the city was getting lower and lower, and the water surface area in the city was increasing. Before this happened, the cities usually experienced a long struggling defense process, before finally being submerged by a catastrophic large flood. The new city would usually be rebuilt at a higher place next to the "dead city lake". This situation created a unique landscape called Ying-and-yang (The dead and living) cities. Examples can be found in Zhecheng, Sui county, Chengwu, etc. The strategy of abandoning the old city to become a lake and building a new city nearby can be considered as a last solution to adapt floods and waterlog, it is not, however, a mere passive strategy, but also an active strategy of metabolism between land, city and water, which can only be seen in such an hazardous environment.

One of the more dramatic examples is Suixian county, which was relocated and rebuilt three times through its history. This has left a spectacular landscape recording three different evolution phases of flood adaptation: (1) the oldest city was submerged to form a lake, which was gradually cultivated, and now is farmland; (2) the next city was submerged in the late 1500s, and is now a large lake to the north of the new city; (3) the new city built in the Jiajing period (1522-1566) of the Ming dynasty, now still has a large water surface and ponds inside the city, which make up 36.2% of the total urban area (1959) (Fig.9)

Fig.8 Circum-city Lake: Liaocheng Plan (based on 1/50000 Topographic maps of Liaocheng county).

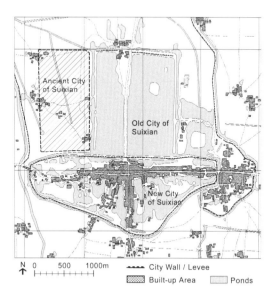

Fig. 9 Former city lake: Suixian county Plan (based on 1/50000 topographic maps of Suixian county).

Functions of Ponds

From the origin of the ponds, it can be concluded that the ponds' most important function to the ancient cities was flood retention and waterlog drainage. The pond system was the major water drainage and storage system, and when combined with the circumvallation and circumvallating levee, they formed the whole flood adaptive defense system. In the history of city management in the Yellow River flood plain, people not only recognized the importance of the pond and water body, but also the importance of managing them to function better. Wang Shijun refers to this in his book (Wu, 1995). Even today, the water drainage and storing system still functions well in some old cities. Many of the ponds in these cities are also famous local scenic spots, which were used by the scholars and elites to build their gardens or for recreation. Besides this, these ponds have other multiple functions such as aquiculture, irrigation, fire fighting, recreation, military defense, etc. (Fig.10) From the perspective of the modern sciences of ecology and urban planning, ponds in the cities are important wetlands, which help to keep regional water balance, act as significant habitats of native species and wildlife and provide other diverse ecological services.

Typology of Flood Adaptive City Forms in the Yellow River Alluvial Plain

Through the strategies of adaptation in the Yellow Alluvial, the water adaptive cities in this region have developed very unique city forms, which are quite different from the water cities seen in other parts of China and around the world, such as Suzhou in South China and Venice in Italy. Some of these unique features

Fig.10 A Productive lotus pond: the multiple functions of pond in the city (Photo: Kongjian Yu).

including: water bodies are seen in lakes and ponds, not as connected network as is seen in Suzhou; Cities are double surrounded with squared city walls at the inside and circular circumvallating levees at the outside. While the inner city wall has double functions of military defense and flood prevention, the outer levee basically functions as flood block. Various combinations of water bodies and city walls and levees make up different overall city forms, including (Fig.11):

• Water-within-city: water bodies of various sizes are largely contained within the inner squared city wall. This form of city can be used to describe cities of Kaifeng, Heze, Chaoxian, Fenxian, Juye, etc.
• City-in-water: Water bodies of various sizes are trapped in between the inner city walls and the outer circumvallating levee, examples include cities of Liaocheng, Shangqiu, Yucheng, Shanxian and Tangshan.
• Ying-yang-city (The dead and living cities): The city was adjacent with a huge lake. This unique type of water adaptive city is composed of the former submerged city which was strategically abandoned and became a huge water body and the new city built beside the dead city. It is a form landscape metabolism among land-flood-city. This type of city can be seen in Suixian, Zhecheng, etc.

In addition to these basic types, many cities are hybrids that are combinations of two or three above mentioned city forms.

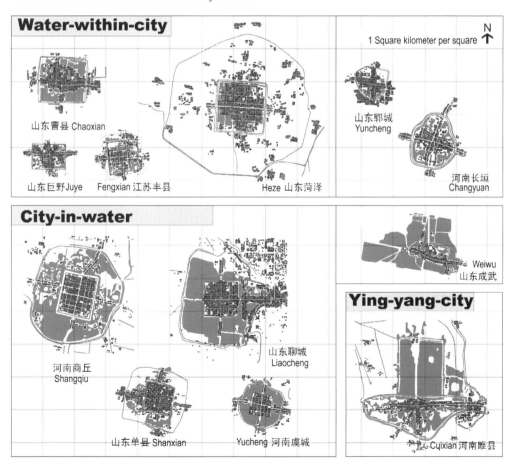

Fig.11 Typology of flood adaptive city forms in the Yellow River alluvial plain.

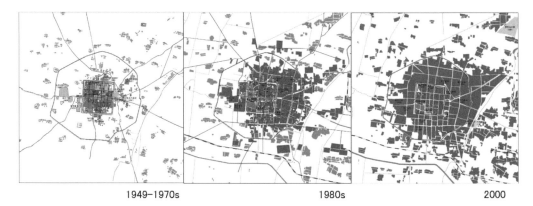

| 1949–1970s | 1980s | 2000 |

Fig.12 Heze city decreasing pond system.

Fig.13 Waterlog in the city of Heze due to the filling up of former flood adaptive pond system.

Conclusion and Discussion

The adaptive landscape strategies of inhabiting on high land, building circum-vallation and retention ponds system have played an important role in sustaining the cities in the Yellow river plain under the harsh environment, and have helped people survive numerous floods. The actual values of this "art of survival" are now mostly forgotten. Such ignorance about this adaptive art of survival has led to the loss of the valuable local landscapes and the functional traditional urban forms during the speedy urban development of the past few decades in China.

In history there were 72 ponds in Heze city which made up 30% of its total urban area, and the pond system functioned extremely well in flood control and waterlog mitigation, ground water recharge, creating urban micro-climate, etc. But due to years of urban development recently, the area of urban water surface has dwindled annually. By 2000, the urban water surface only accounts for 16.2% of the total area, which has decreased by nearly 50%. (Fig.12,13)

Due to the loss of ponds and lakes in and around the cities, the rainwater during the monsoon season – a large amount of water resource which could be used to recharge the groundwater – is lost. In the past years, the decreased water body has been proven to be responsible for various water related natural disasters, including waterlog, flood, drop of underground table, drought in the spring and summer, degradation of wildlife habitat, decrease of biodiversity, and the loss of recreational resources and local identity. Recently many cities in the Yellow river alluvial plain have shown interest in protecting or reconstructing the "water city". But unfortunately, more often than not, "water city" has been misinterpreted and simply become a slogan for a beautiful city. This study shall be useful to help people understand the essential meanings behind the morphology of the "water city", and for people to understand and take care of the flood adaptive landscape as the "art of survival."

Acknowledgements This research was co-funded by The Natural Science Fund of China (NSFC, #39870147 and NSFC, #59778010), and by the project of Urban Water and Green System Planning of Heze City, Heze Planning Bureau. In addition to the authors, many colleagues and students from the Graduate School of Landscape Architecture participanted in this research and planning, including Dihua Li, Lailei Yu, Wanli Fang, Jing Zhou, Chunbo Li, Sisi Wang, Hui Han, Yitian Wang, Weiwei Zhang, and officials from the Municipal Government of Heze including Liyan Wang, Wenlin Liu, Maolin Ying, Shanyi Xiao, Chunming Wang, Guoyun Chao, Jing Dong, Chengxiang Zhu, Dongsheng Zhou. The Authors thanks all of these participants in this research. The Authors would also like to thank Mingdan Zhang for his help in English editing of this paper.

Water and Space in the Netherlands

Living with Water in the 21st Century

~ **Renske Peters** ~ Director Water, Ministry of Transport, Public Works and Water Management, Directorate General Water ~ **Michelle J.A. Hendriks** ~ Ministry of Transport, Public Works and Water Management, Directorate General Water, Netherlands

Summary

The Netherlands has been living with water for ages. This is visible throughout the landscape. Major parts of the landscape are naturally shaped by and adapted to the water system that was present. Still water has major influence on the landscape. Recent shifts in water policy assign even a bigger role to water in space and spatial policy.

This paper will provide insight in how Dutch water policies are changing to a more integrated and adaptive approach to water and space.

By the end of the 20th century government and general public realised that the rather technocratic approach of reinforcing dikes and draining the land could not persist especially with regard to future climate change. More room for water became the leading principle. In regional water management as well as in national river flood safety, this asks for interventions that create more space for water. It is recognised that combination with other area specific functions, and attention for spatial quality are important prerequisites to find feasible and accepted solutions. Also other components of the flood safety policy are shifting to a more spatial approach. Consequences of possible floods are to be taken into account in spatial planning and design, and in the coastal areas it is tried to make more use of natural processes and to improve spatial quality as well. All these features are in line with the general policy on adaptation to climate change. Also water quality policy has got an increasing spatial element. Major parts of the measures taken are spatial and since the EU Water Framework Directive cooperation between parties within one river basin is strengthened.

This increased awareness of the link between water and space also announced a shift to a broader group of actors that is involved in water management. Water is no longer solely the concern of water boards and the Ministry of Transport, Public Works and Water management (V&W). Spatial actors are closely involved and take water into account in their daily decisions. The skills of spatial planners and designers are increasingly appreciated in processes of finding integral solutions to live with water. It illustrates the mutual relationship between water and spatial quality. Water can improve our landscapes and living environment. Spatial quality through integrated design can lead to more feasible and accepted solutions for the water problems. Living with water in the 21st century is to design solutions that lead to integrated interventions and to create attractive and inspiring Dutch landscapes.

Introduction

The Netherlands has been living with water for ages. This is visible throughout the landscape. Big parts of the landscape are naturally shaped by and adapted to the water system that was present. The major rivers have formed the land. Large parts of the coastal area consist of natural dunes that protect the land against floods. At places the local water tables or water quality offer the perfect circumstances for unique ecosystems. Next to that many features of the Dutch landscape are manmade in order to deal with the water system. The landscape is designed to live with water. Primary flood defences, like dikes and dunes, prevent 65% of the country from being flooded on a regular basis. Cities were built on strategic places, where rivers and streams could serve as an economic factor. The landscape of the deep polders that have been reclaimed from the sea and lakes is known to be typically Dutch: long, small pastures separated from each other by ditches and canals. Next to that we must not forget that still one sixth of the country's surface area is covered by water.

Like in many delta areas, the population and economic activities in the Netherlands have been steadily growing. This poses the challenge to use land in an efficient way. For many years the water system has simultaneously been adapted to the intensive land use. However, by the end of the 20th century it became clear that this was not a tenable approach Politicians and general public realised that the rather technocratic approach of continuation of dike reinforcement and draining the land could not persist. More room for water became the leading principle and the existing water policy was (and is) gradually changing into a more integrated and adaptive policy for water and space. This also announced a shift to a broader group of actors that is involved in water management. Water is no longer solely the concern of water boards and the Ministry of Transport, Public Works and Water management (V&W). Spatial actors like nature conservationists, building corporations and infrastructure companies are more and more involved and take water into account in their daily decisions. The skills of spatial planners and designers are increasingly appreciated in processes of finding integrated solutions to living with water. This paper will provide insight in how water policies are changing to a more integrated approach to water and space. Therefore it will first give a brief overview of the physical, historical and organisational background in the Netherlands. This is followed by a description of the Dutch water policies and the most important changes in the last decades. After that some inspiring examples are presented of 'spatial designing with water'. They show how close cooperation of water managers and spatial architects can lead to solutions that are practical and beautiful at the same time.

Historical and institutional context

Until the late Middle Ages Dutch people more or less accepted the power of water. To prevent damage they build their houses on artificially raised hills (mound or 'terp') or they only used the pasture close the rivers during summertime. This was followed by centuries in which the more technical approach of keeping the water outside got the upper hand. By building dikes and creating 'polders' the people created more space for living and working. Many old windmills still remind us of those times. Still, the Dutch history is scattered with small and bigger disasters related to water. This has always affected the way people dealt with water in the Netherlands. The most significant disaster of the last century was the flooding of the province of Zeeland and Zuid-Holland in February 1953. The dikes breached at many places and many people and livestock lost their lives. This event was the reason to create the so-called Delta Works, a set of major waterworks and dike reinforcements that protect the southwest of the Netherlands from future floods. Two other major events in the last century were the occurrences of extreme high water in the main rivers. In 1993 and 1995 the water got up to a level that the decision was made to evacuate inhabitants of the deepest river basin. Luckily no breaches occurred, but it was the incentive to start a new way of thinking about water management. This awareness was underlined by the increasing frequency of excessive rainfall that the Netherlands was facing by the end of the twentieth century. Next to this more periods of drought have occurred in the recent years. The most recent climate scenarios (2006) produced by the Royal Netherlands Meteorological Institute (KNMI) forecast a rise of temperature between 1 to 6 degrees Celsius by the year 2100 (base year 1990). The rainfall will increase as well, with less frequent but more extreme showers in summer and longer periods of rain in wintertime. The sea level will rise between 35 and 85 cm. This is an absolute rise, which does not take into account the effect of soil subsidence in the Netherlands that is caused by the continuous drainage of the marshy land consisting of peat and clay.

Just like water has influenced the Dutch landscape, the water system and the institutional structure have also influenced each other throughout the ages. The water boards are the oldest democratic institutions in the Netherlands. They originate from local communities electing community members that were made responsible for taking care of the dikes, ditches and flumes in their area. The water boards play a big role in water management and flood protection at regional level and they execute delegated national tasks as well. The local water management is shared with the municipalities. Those are responsible for the discharge of rainwater and sewage water in urban areas. Municipalities also have spatial tasks. The twelve Provinces make up the intermediate level. Their role is to make sure that regional and local parties implement the national and provincial policies on water and spatial planning. An important feature of this task is the co-ordination of the different sectoral policies, such as water, environment, housing, and economics. The coordinating party at national level is the Ministry of Transport, Public Works and Water Management (V&W). It is responsible for the preparation of the national policies on flood protection and water management and for supervision of the implementation. Rijkswaterstaat, the implementing directorate of the ministry existing since 1798, has the task of operational management of some waters and waterworks of national interest, like the big rivers and the primary dikes and dunes. The other ministries that deal with part of the water issues are the Ministry of Housing, Spatial Planning and Environment (VROM) and the Ministry of Agriculture, Nature Management and Food Safety (LNV).

Water management in the 21st century - General principles

The shift in thinking about water management triggered by the earlier described events got tangible in a new policy paradigm named 'Water management in the 21st century', better known under the Dutch abbreviation WB21. The basic principles of WB21 have become a connecting thread for the choices made in the Dutch water management. Starting point is that water must be allowed more space, before it takes it for itself. For centuries rivers were being narrowed and straightened, ditches were filled up and areas with an impermeable surface were increasing. Today's trend of increasing river discharges and more extreme showers might force the streams to break out from this tightened system, finding its own way and taking its own space. Therefore WB21 is based on three basic principles. The first principle is to anticipate instead of reacting to changes in the water system. This notion gives water a more prominent role in spatial decisions. The second principle is to combine technical solutions with smart use of space, for example multiple-purpose use of space like houses on water. The third principle is the preferred order of measures retain-store-discharge. Preference goes out to retaining water in the area where it falls, for example by making it possible to soak into the soil. The storage of water in the area or in a different area (e.g. by maximising capacity of existing canals) is the second-best option. Discharging water to another water system has the lowest preference, as it is a way of shifting the burden to another area.

Flood safety policy

These principles of finding more spatial solutions for water problems have not only set foot in regional water management. Also the national flood safety policy is undergoing a change. First example is the project Room for the river, in which plans are made that give more space to the river instead of reinforcing the dikes. If raising the dikes would be the only measure taken, this would implicate a rise of 30 cm of all primary river dikes to deal with river discharges that are to be expected by the year 2050. This would be undesirable, as higher dikes also mean bigger impacts in case of a dike breach. Next to that the project has set itself a goal to find solutions improving spatial and landscape qualities at the same time. This has also led to participative planning processes in which landscape architects, spatial planners, engineers, and stakeholders together seek for the most desirable solution. The national government only sets preconditions, for example the minimum lowering of the water level. Another new feature of the flood safety policy is that it is no longer focussing on probability alone (i.e. setting standards for flood defences) but it evaluates how we can take into account the possible consequences of floods as well. Looking at consequences broadens the scope of finding solutions. In some cases more spatial solutions might prove to be more suitable. For example creating areas as compartments for controlled flooding or adapting the design of buildings and dwellings to floods. Also in coastal safety policy one can see a change in policy. In the ten so-called Weak Links (the ten most urgent spots) of the Dutch coast safety is no longer seen as an independent objective. Solutions had to improve spatial quality as well and thus creating space for other functions like nature or recreation. Starting point is to have 'soft' measures where possible and 'hard' where necessary. This means that preference goes out to solutions that are movable, like strengthening with extra sand, above building immovable structures, like a dike. Reason behind this is that dynamic measures would increase flexibility in future scenarios.

Adaptation to climate change

This adjustability of measures also fits in the reasoning behind the more forward-looking approach to climate change that is now being developed, under the programme Adaptation Space and Climate (ARK). The governmental bodies involved in spatial development, including the Ministry of V&W and the water boards, work together to develop a concrete vision on what needs to be done to make the Netherlands climate proof. Starting point for the programme is the notion that climate change is inevitable. However, it is not exactly clear to what extent the temperature will rise, the rainfall will increase, and the sea level will rise. Therefore ARK is looking for ways to have a flexible and robust spatial planning that makes it easy to react on the foreseen and unforeseen changes. This asks for a new governmental approach as well, that coincides with the changes in water management. Leading principles in this approach are: adaptation to climate change is leading in spatial developments; make use of natural processes, like the sand dynamics in the coastal areas, and risk prevention, which asks for minimisation of possible effects.

Water quality

Also water quality policy has eye for the spatial impacts and opportunities. To tackle water quality problems a mix of spatial or natural solutions next to more technical solutions is chosen. Many regional parties have started restoring brooks, creating more natural banks, and making use of natural processes to improve water quality. One quite recent change in the institutional arrangements on water management is the introduction of a river basin district approach, which stems from the requirements of the European Water Framework Directive. The boundaries of river basins not fully coincide with those of the existing administrative bodies and this has lead to new networks of co-operation between parties in the (sub)river basins. Through this approach it is easier to work together on integrated solutions and it tries to create synergy between solutions for water quality and quantity problems.

In 2008 this broad range of water policies assemble in a new national Water Plan. This plan will constitute of a vision on spatial developments structured by water in the Netherlands in 2100, a target image of 2040 and an execution programme for the period until 2015.

Inspiring examples

As stated earlier, the Dutch way of living with water has always influenced the landscape. Polders, dikes and terps but also major waterworks like the Afsluitdijk or Oosterschelde flood barrier have determined the image of the Netherlands. This process will continue in future. As a result of the shift to a more integrated approach of water and spatial developments other actors get involved in water management. On different aspects of water management we see several successful examples of the involvement of spatial actors, planners and designers, that lead to solutions that are more spatial, more integrated and better fit into the landscape. Such solutions are generally more accepted and thus more likely to be implemented. One example of a local project where several problems are simultaneously tackled is in Apeldoorn. The reconstruction of a system of brooks will contribute to not only water quality and quantity problems, but it will also restore and preserve nature with some special species. Next to that the design of the plan enables some firms to expand their business; it will provide for recreational sites; historical artefacts will be restored, and it improves the spatial quality for inhabitants of Apeldoorn.

Another local project, in which a major spatial intervention brought different objectives together, is the historic city centre of Breda. Economic decline of a

The Afsluitdijk. (Photo: Theo Baart).

part of the city centre gave rise to the idea of bringing back the water in the filled up part of the old harbour. Breda now has a beautiful new spot that attracts tourists and residents. Bringing back the historic water also creates more space for water, which is needed to meet the local goals for adaptation to climate change.

The earlier mentioned project Room for the River has also lead to some successful experiences of integrated design and planning. For the river IJssel, a guidebook Spatial Quality was made on how to deal with existing landscape features. This guidebook helped the planners in the case of Westenholte in their search to meet the conditions of spatial quality. A 'quality team' under direction of the Government Advisor on Landscape supervised the process and advised on the outcomes. Chosen options will soon be executed.

Another promising process has taken place in the rural area around the brook Essche Stroom in the province Noord Brabant. Here the water board has taken the initiative to explore the historical water elements and water use in the area in order to use this inspiration for the design of future water measures. The close involvement of inhabitants, designers, and historians lead to surprising outcomes and broad support for interventions in the area.

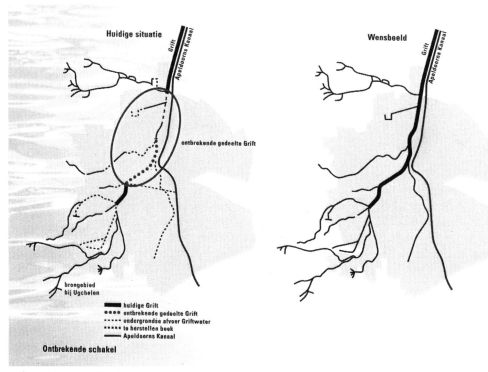

Grift zone: missing links, perspective.

Conclusion

At the moment we are facing big challenges in water and spatial development in the Netherlands. Above examples show that combining the competences of water managers, planners, designers, and stakeholders in an area is a promising direction to deal with this challenge. It illustrates the mutual relationship between water and spatial quality. Water is a key factor in creating climate proof cities and landscapes. Regarding the Netherlands with our rich culture in spatial planning, water is also the major component in designing tasks when it comes down to urban and landscape planning issues.

Water can improve spatial quality, by bringing back historical values, giving space for nature development, or by just creating a pleasant, spacious place to live and recreate. On the other hand spatial quality and design can contribute to better solutions for water problems that are generally more accepted and thus more likely to be implemented. Spatial design helps actors to broaden the scope for finding solutions, a broadening in space, subjects, and time. Spatial design helps to switch between spatial levels: local, regional, national, international to find solutions. It can combine different stakes within one design. And it helps looking backward and forward in time, using important inspiration from history and translate it to current tasks. These competences are of great importance as we still have a lot of tasks ahead. For example in the Randstad, our most densely populated and low-lying part of the Netherlands, where living, working, recreating, agriculture, etcetera, are fighting for place and the pressure on the water system will increase as a consequence of climate change. Or in the big lake the IJsselmeer, where flood safety, freshwater availability and nature preservation need to be guaranteed in future. Living with water in the 21st century is to design solutions that lead to integrated interventions and to create attractive and inspiring Dutch landscapes.

1.2 Living with Water – Talkshops

Talkshop: Transforming with the Arid - planning

(Abstract) Revitalizing Qanats in Post Disaster Period - The Bam Experience in Iran
~ Amir Semiari

(Abstract) Cultural Landscape Characterization in a Desert Area Generated by an Ancient Ditch Irrigation System - Tilcara, Argentina
~ Miguel Martiarena

(Abstract) Ordos Dongsheng District San Tai Ji Reservoir Landscape Design, Baihongju River Reservoir Design and the Surrounding Streets Conceptual Planning and Design
~ Hu Jie

Talkshop: Transforming with the Arid - heritage

(Abstract) Water System in Historic Gardens of Southern Europe - Portuguese Case Studies.
~ Cristina Castel-Branco, Ana Luisa Soares

(Abstract) Use of Water in Historic Moorish Gardens
~ Katrin Hagen, Richard Stiles

City, Stream, and Environmental Values - Shiraz City Stream
~ Mohsen Faizi, Mehdi Khakzand

(Abstract) Gardens depend on Water - The History of Water Management and Preserving Scenic Beauty in Japanese Gardens in Kyoto
~ Hidefumi Imae

Talkshop: Transforming with the Rains - Discharging Rains in Public Space

(Abstract) Tropical Metropolitan Rain Gardens
~ Paulo Pellegrino

(Abstract) Storing Water in the Poelpolder
~ Ben Kuipers

(Abstract) Transforming Landscape Character with Sustainable Development - case study the Royal Project at Fang, Chiengmai, Thailand
~ Apinya Limpaiboon

Transforming with the Arid – planning

Revitalizing Qanats in Post Disaster Period

The Bam Experience in Iran

~ **Amir Semiari** ~ Post Graduate Student in Landscape Architecture at SBU,

Iran ~ Abstract

In some parts of the world the necessary access to water and setting up of a system of transporting water, is an unavoidable practice that results in making up complex traditional disciplines and ordering systems to allocate fair opportunities for water utilization.

The characteristics of water balance in arid regions between drinking consumption and agricultural purposes, is the critical point in distribution and transformation of water in hot and dry climates. Therefore its patterns have changed under the influence of natural phenomena and human activities. Such influences have caused environmental changes in both positive and negative sense by changing the circulation and distribution of water, and these changes take place regionally, especially in arid lands where water is the key factor of the environ-

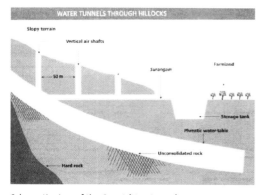

Schematic view of the Qanat (Haeri-2003).

Current water transport system in rural context.

ment. Besides, need for water has resulted in about one-third of the world's land-mass being irrigated by groundwater; in the U.S 45 percent of cultivated land is irrigated by groundwater, while percentages for Iran, Algeria and Morocco stand at 58, 67, and 75 percent respectively (Salih-2006).

Scarcity of water supply in Iranian marginalized settlements in the vicinity of the desert in hot and dry climates pose a significant case study. For instance, in Kerman province cultivated fields and palm gardens, surrounding the citadel of Bam, cause indigenous practices to rise in importance, in order to solve the problem giving sustainable and nature-based solutions.

The amount of annual average rainfall in Iran is approximately 242 millimeters which is less than one third of the global average annual rainfall (approximately 860 mm) and even this little amount of precipitation is not the same throughout the country (Haeri-2003). Therefore, technically solving the problem nationwide is achieved through dams, underground channels - called Qanats, and wells. Environmentally, however, Qanats have more advantages over other techniques.

The Kariz (-Qanat) system is a remarkable technique which was invented by people of the plateau of Iran. It is specific to Iran and is a typical feature of Iranian scenery that can be described as the greatest contribution made by Iranians to hydraulics. This system must have been started at least 5000 years ago in Iran. The Kariz system is usually found in central Iran toward the east and southeast (Mehraby-2007)

For centuries, Kariz as an eternal system for harvesting underground water in Iran, has been the source of inspiration for other nations which reflects widespread dissemination of the technology across ancient trading routes and political maps.

In 26 December 2003, the catastrophic earthquake of Bam, the famous, ancient city of Kerman province, left hazardous effects on the Qanats system. A great human heritage related to sustainable management of groundwater in arid zones, including the development of a sophisticated culture of rational resource allocation was damaged. Prior to the earthquake, the Qanats of Bam played a major role in groundwater transport and irrigation of the area, providing over 50

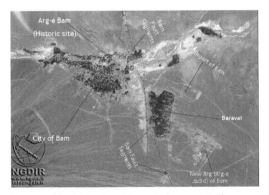

Demographic distribution of Bam city (www.ngdir.ir).

IKONOS satellite image of Bam one day after the quake.

percent of the annual water requirement. The earthquake caused extensive damage to many parts of the Qanats system (Salih-2006). Regarding the fact that the cultural landscape of Bam is an outstanding representation of the interaction of man and nature in a desert environment, using the Qanats, the system is based on a strict social system with precise tasks and responsibilities. It has been maintained, and in use until the present, but has unfortunately become vulnerable to irreversible change (Unesco-2008).

Consequently, the water transport system was completely destroyed by earthquake, along with the rest of the city and its environments which are now listed by UNESCO as part of the World Heritage Site entitled "Bam and its Cultural Landscape".

According to the priorities for revitalizing of these quaint endowments, the proper approach is to achieve participatory association between local populations, NGOs and executive administrations. As an essential and integral part of ancient Iranian lives, Kariz has played a key role in forming many aspects of culture within the community. Because of this, the present paper is concerned with appropriate use of indigenous knowledge and skills in close collaboration with the international center for Qanats and historic hydraulic structures and the Iranian Ministry of Agriculture in order to define a holistic strategy for maintaining the Qanats of Bam which could be seen as a pilot for other regions and countries. Consulting with the conscious locals and affording elaborate profession for restoration and future management of the Qanats is an indispensable part of these partnerships.

In any way, Kariz still remains to be the principal, and in some cases the only, source of irrigation and domestic water supply in many parts of the world. Eventually, revitalization of this heritage in the post-disaster period can be used as an educational facility for students, technicians, professionals and researchers as well as the public, and could be an initiative measure for optimizing our living with water.

Deformation of Qanat opening caused by the earthquake force.

Cultural Landscape Characterization in a Desert Area

Generated by an Ancient Ditch Irrigation System, Tilcara, Argentina

~ **Miguel Martiarena** ~ Magister Landscape Architecture, Universidad

Católica de Córdoba, Argentina ~ Abstract

Certain small towns and urban peripheries contain into their limits subsystems which allow designing strategies to obtain a better sustainability. These subsystems are fragile and could be lost due to city densification if they are not protected. This is occurring with the ditch irrigation system in Tilcara, a small settlement in the north of Argentina, after the region was declared as World Heritage by UNESCO in 2003. A new highway was opened, connecting with Chile, a convenient exchange rate favored international tourism, and the absence of a formal heritage protection plan and Estate control, came to demonstrate the vulnerability of the system.

The settlement of 4000 inhabitants, with pre-hispanic origin and incaic roots, is located on the East Andes, on a corridor that connects the desert High Plateau and the Yungas´ Tropical Forests, at 2480 meters over sea level and has an average annual precipitation of 140 millimeters (Image 1).

A distinct characteristic of this town is the presence of this ancient ditch irrigation system allowing the existence of green urban spaces, small productive areas, and a political and social organization that makes an effort to maintain it as a sustainable system against the desert environment. This research-work considers the ditch web as a complex system in evolution, composed by physical, environmental and social elements, expressed by the presence of many land cover class-

Image 1. Irrigation ditch System Tilcara.

Image 2. Irrigation ditch System Tilcara, close up.

es, creating spatial patterns that could be identified and quantified through the process of aerial or satellite images (Image 2).

An approximation of the statistical conformation of the landscape was made using Geographical Information Systems (GIS). This allows constructing a curve that shows the land cover class proportions identified in the aerial photograph in relation to the distance to the irrigation web. In this way, landscape patterns that conform a gradient in relation to the distance to the water were characterized (Image 3)

For the results validation, 13 random placed urban transects were surveyed and the land cover classes, vegetation species, and their corresponding uses were ordered by their distance to the irrigation ditch. Also an inquiry has been made into the irrigators on the cultural meaning assigned to the ditches, the vegetation and the Irrigators Society structure, which is the political and social organization that controls the ditch irrigation system. Finally, the most fragile sectors of the web were detected with a simulation using the developed model.

The irrigation ditch system is an important resource that affects the 23% of the citizens. Not only the water, but the low construction density near the ditches and the presence of crops and urban forests – amongst other characteristics -, define the town landscape. The irrigation system is really an essential component of the local culture. Tilcara´s irrigation web offers a range of services that outweigh the old original function of watering crops and orchards. It is necessary for its conservation that the citizens discover the new meaning that the ditches have acquired throughout the centuries: it is a complex system extended 50 m to both sides of the water path, it is related with a social structure and cultural behavior, and it is controlled by formal and informal institutions (Image 4).

The system is revealed as a strong gradient of green land cover classes, whose proportion decreases in a logarithm behavior with the distance to the ditches, in opposition to naked soil and constructed land cover classes. The goal of this gradient quantification is that it will serve as a guide for directing a protection plan of the urban forest and crops in relation to the distances to the water paths.

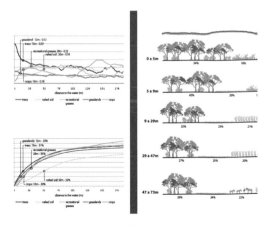

Image 3. Landscape patterns form a gradient in relation to the distance of the water.

Image 4. Tilcara.

Ordos Water City

Ordos Dongsheng District San Tai Ji Reservoir and the Surrounding Environmental Landscape Design, Baihongju River Reservoir Design and the Surrounding Streets Conceptual Planning and Design

~ **Hu Jie** ~ Landscape Department of Beijing Tsinghua Urban Planning & Design Institute, China ~ Abstract

Ordos is located in central and southern part of Inner Mongolia Autonomous Region, the city has a total area of 86,700 square kilometers. Nowadays, Ordos has a rapid growth of social and economic development, meanwhile Ordos also faces many ecological crises such as natural environment destruction, water resources shortage,etc. How to synchronize the rapid economic growth with the local cultures and natural landscapes to provide a higher quality of living environment, and promote the development of regional tourism, is the primary and ultimate goal of Ordos Shan Tai Ji Reservoir and the surrounding environmental landscape design.

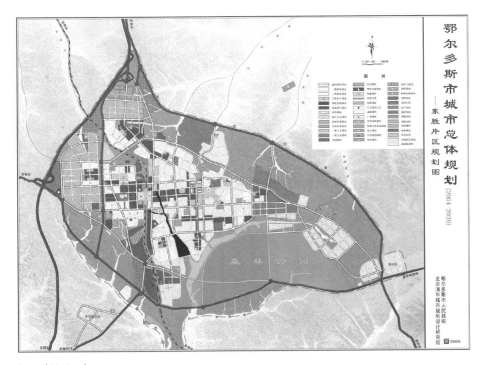

General Masterplan.

Shan Tai Ji reservoirs is located in the center of Dongsheng District, running through the old city commerce and residential area towards the southern city residential area. The South East part of the reservoir and the nearly completed Forest Park is adjacent. The central and southern cities main stream is an important urban greening landscape corridor. The water has the main function of drainage and sewage. The reservoir maximum storage capacity is 30 million cubic meters. With water treatment technology, using used water as resources to build an important city water park to improve the quality of city, at the same time also to promote the surrounding real estate development projects.

Our Design Goals

• Creating an ecological leisure services Water City: Prominent Green - Water - Sun – Life, are four major characteristics, and create beautiful natural scenery of the North Waterfront and high standards of leisure base. Provide an attractive space environment and projects to the public.
• Value the importance of landscape and ecological relationship, to reflects the

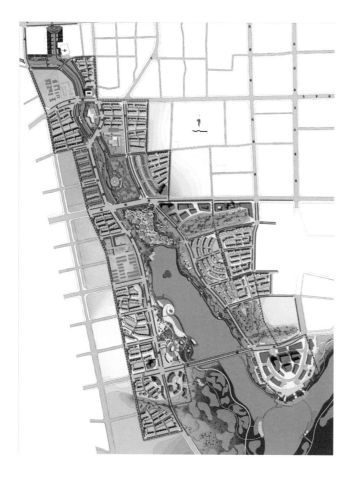

Masterplan of SanTaiJi Reservoir

natural ecological river: The whole city should emphasize the ecological characteristics image, and create efficient utilization of water resources in water-saving model of the city and landscape.

• Keeping a good relationship between the environment and the city, to respect and reflect city cultural background: Construction and open space should reflect balance the characteristics of simple and gorgeous layout, also build a natural growth in the urban area, creating rich characteristics of Ordos Water City, an important node in the design of the prominent display of a city's image landmark buildings.

Ecological Water Treatment Strategy

River and reservoir act as a major source for city water treatment facility, but the water quality could not reach the landscape water standards. Through the design of integrated water management, the use of wetland, and blasting techniques such as oxygen-enriched air purifying water quality to meet the requirements of water quality and create a natural ecological environment for the water landscape.

Bird Eye View of Ordos.

Talkshop

Transforming with the Arid ~ heritage

Water system in historic gardens of Southern Europe

Portuguese case studies

~ Cristina Castel-Branco ~ Ana Luísa Soares ~ Instituto Superior de

Agronomia (Lisbon, Portugal)

"History is a continuity. Though it is mostly a restless impatient being. It looks into tomorrow as it looks towards yesterday… tradition is a progress that had success. The highest role of tradition is to pay progress, the courtesy that it owes him – allow progress to oustant from tradition just as tradition has sprout from progress" (Miguel Veiga in Marcas do Tempo 2004).

Water systems in heritage gardens, and the ancient economy of water and design give an inspiration for today's sustainable concepts.

Since the 90's we have been restoring gardens and learning the immense lesson of tradition in garden design and maintenance. The wisdom of some solutions in historic gardens allows for progress in contemporary design, as they are ecological, simple, well built, solid, and the time has given them a medal of consistency, authenticity and longevity. Water systems are part of this lesson from the past, and inspiration for the future. Water is a scarce element and an essential feature of Portuguese garden-making, historic gardens in Portugal are a lesson of water sparing but also of water design as in many southern climates. The present project, financed by EEA Grant's Norway, aims at restoring this rich Portuguese heritage of historic, private and public gardens that belong to the Portuguese Association of Historic Gardens and Sites; the Association has won a one million euro subsidy (co-financed 60% by the EEA Grant) to restore their irrigation systems. Twelve owners have the same objective: to recuperate their ancient hydraulic systems and thus reduce the amount of water losses and incorrect consumptions within these gardens. A side benefit will be to restore and give life to areas of the garden such as channels, fountains, reservoirs and jets that have long been silent! Walls and trails are also part of the implemented works for they usually play a crucial role in the water collective and a distribution system. Improving biodiversity habitats through the availability of water elements is also taken into account for historic gardens are havens for many species relying on water for ecological processes.

In Portugal the hydraulic system is a structural and defining element of the garden because the four months of hot summer coincide with no rain, and there is a need of storing water for those high temperature and full-sun summer months. These hydraulic systems are usually associated with other built structures such as subterranean channels tapping the underground natural springs, walls that have imbedded channels, trails, fountains, tanks and jets. These were considered part of the hydraulic systems and will be the subject of restauration work. Each garden's hydraulic system allows it to work and survive as a separate entity, a real lesson of sustainability but it also uses water as esthetic features in the garden such as reflecting pools. Many gardens associate water features with superb esthetic productions of so-called azulejos, ceramic tiles in a technique leaning on the Islamic traditions, that are since the 10th century rooted in southern Portugal. Nowadays these historic gardens don't make full use of the water that is available, and free of charge in their subterranean ancient water systems; this leads not only to increased maintenance costs but also, very often, to a waste of natural resources, which in turn leads to unnecessary energy costs, such as for the pumps that replace the gravity systems and the old lessons in water sparing. Usually gardens are built in slopes allowing to make terraces, and the water comes from above, running along open stone channels, then collecting in large reflecting pools, and at lower levels used as jets and fountains with sculptures. Finally the lower terraces are used as orchards and vegetable gardens using the water in a gravity system of channels along a square system of irrigation.

The 20th century's strong trend to consider natural resources to be inexhaustible, led to the underrating of traditional systems that collect water from springs and underground aqueducts, channels on walls, animal-powered wells, waterwheels, wind mills, and collection tanks. All projects are made by members of the Historic Gardens Association and supervised in order to follow the restoration principles set out in the "Florence Charter", signed by all the countries represented within the Scientific Committee for Parks and Gardens of ICOMOS (UNESCO) in 1981. Those principles consider historic gardens as monuments and in fact all these 12 gardens associated for this subsidized project are real monuments from the north to the south of Portugal, therefore the restoration and preservation works will follow the Heritage Laws.

These include the recovery of ruined water structures, involving their cleaning, insulating, and rebuilding where necessary, so that the collecting system and distribution channels can be set to work again, reservoirs can be re-filled, and fountains can spring water as in the original design. According to the Florence Charter, these original structures can be coupled, invisibly and discretely, with distribution systems using high technology, such as camouflaged watering pipes for drip irrigation, programmed irrigation, fountains, and closed circuit waterfalls using re-pumping. The original attribute is apparent in the fact that the project seeks to recover traditional water usage techniques, promoting a rational use of water and thus avoiding wastage and unnecessary energy costs. With this project involving owners and landscape architects the Assocation of Historic Gardens intends to return the garden's original identity and nature so it will be prepared to be open to the public and enjoyed by many. The project will run from 2007 to 2010 and we present here four gardens which were the first to invest and will be ready this year. The works have started in Quinta das Lágrimas in Coimbra (10 ha from the 14th, century on), Coimbra Univeristy Botanical Garden (14 ha from the 18th century), the Fronteira Palace Gardens in Lisbon (6 ha from the 17th century), and José do Canto Garden (4 ha in S. Miguel island in the Azores from the 19th century). All four will be ready by the end of 2008. The project is on progress with the next four that will be finished by 2009, and the last year will see the end of the project with the last set of four smaller ones being restored and the launching of a book explaining the learning process of restoring historic gardens.

Quinta das Lágrimas (Coimbra)

Quinta das Lágrimas' gardens are of rare historic value due to the number of events that took place there, and which are undeniably part of Portugal's history. Inês de Castro's passion with the Infant of Portugal D.Pedro in the 14th century is almost a pioneer announcement of Rennaissance love stories such as Tristan and Isolda or Romeo and Juliette. The difference here is that the love story is documented here in this farm, garden and fountains, giving to the place a magic attraction and a permanent flow of visitors. This historic value associated with the natural springs within the farm, also stems from the structures built over the centuries, giving the place a rare authenticity: supporting walls, springs, fountains, tanks, and channels. The first building of which there is a record is the pigeon loft which gave the estate its name as late as the 13th century when it was owned by the Order of the Holy Cross. In the 14th century Queen Isabel ordered the building of the Cano dos Amores, a 500m long aqueduct. The water from Fontes dos Amores (Fountains of Love) was supplied to Saint Clare's Monastery and the Queen's Palace, while the Friars were supplied with water from Fontes das Lágrimas (Fountains of Tears) (Fig. 1). Here a triple channel built around 1650 led water to a mill, to feed the palace and at lower levels to a large area of irrigation. In the 19th century, Dom Miguel Osório Cabral e Castro undertook restoration work on the house and began the building of a romantic garden, comprising lakes and irregular shaped beds of bambus, Araucarias and camphor trees. In the 1990s the palace was transformed by the family into a Hotel, now Hotel Quinta das Lagrimas Relais & Chateaux, and the restorations in the garden have been successful as visitors reached this year 50.000 entries. The works are expected to be finished by June 26th 2008.

Coimbra Botanical Garden (Coimbra)

The Garden was founded between 1772 and 1774 by order of the Marquis of Pombal and is located in the old part of the city, near the University. Coimbra Botanical Garden (CBG) covers an area of around 13ha and is divided into two distinct parts: the Formal Garden and the "Arboretum". Nowadays the CBG also calls attention to nature conservation and environmental education, promoting activities that raise public awareness generally and motivate children in particular. The activities also call attention to the importance of nature and the urgent need to protect and preserve it, encouraging citizens to learn and adopt a civil and cultural behaviour (Fig. 2).

Fronteira Palace Gardens (Lisbon)

The Marquis of Fronteira's Palace and Gardens were built around 1669 to mark the restoration of Portugal after 60 years of Spanish rule. Set at the foot of Monsanto hill, the garden is one of the most beautiful and well-preserved examples of 17th century landscaping. Tanks, fountains and statues abound. The most

Fig. 1- Quinta das Lágrimas.

Fig. 2 - Coimbra Botanical Garden.

remarkable is a large tank topped by the tiled King's gallery, which houses the busts of Portuguese sovereigns in its recesses (Fig. 3).

José do Canto Garden (Azores)

The garden covers approximately six hectares and it was first completed in 1845/46. Its construction required a continual expansion of the park and its botanical wealth continued to grow for over half of the 19th century, until 1898. Rich in terms of the quantity and diversity of its plant life, the garden retains its original form. In the 19th century it was considered one of the finest private botanical gardens in Europe and it played a major role in the restoration of the Coimbra and Lisbon botanical gardens (Fig. 4).

Fig. 3 - Fronteira Palace Gardens.

Fig. 4 - José do Canto Garden.

Use of Water in Historic Moorish Gardens

~ **Katrin Hagen** and **Richard Stiles** ~ Technical University of Vienna, Austria

~ Abstract

Does the use of water in historic Moorish gardens have lessons for how future landscape design should respond to climate change?

The future impacts of climate change have risen close to the top of the political agenda, and its effects on the landscape and vegetation are already beginning to be visible in many parts of the world. However, it could be argued that climate change of this type is nothing new, and that at least one type of landscape has been adapting to it for some two centuries. Urban areas have long had modified climates which are characterised by, amongst other things, the so-called 'heat-island' effect. In Europe this has been the case ever since the explosive growth of cities which was stimulated by the industrial revolution, and in particular through the associated burning of fossil fuels.

The heat island effect and not just the horticultural introductions of urban dwellers, has meant that the vegetation of towns and cities has long become differentiated from that of the natural regions in which they are situated. For example, tree species which thrive in urban areas, both planted and the spontaneous, tend to be originally from bio-geographic regions which are both significantly hotter and dryer than those in which they grow in the urban context. One way to consider the future impacts of climate is in terms of a further step in this already familiar direction.

It is not just the urban areas themselves, but also landscape designers who have a long history of manipulating the (micro)climate in order to modify the growing conditions of plants to achieve desired effects, such as the creation of Mediterranean or sub-tropical gardens in cool northern climate zones. In the light of the likely effects of climate change, in the future the desired effects are

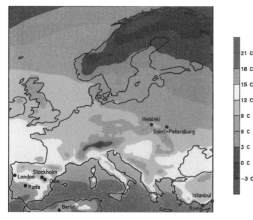

Fig.1: Current climate analogues of the future climates of several European Cities on temperature background of the current climate (HALLEGATTE, KOPF, HA-DUONG, 2007).

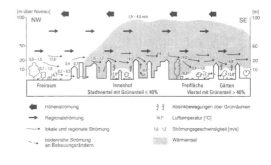

Fig.2: City profile at summer night-time showing the heat-island, wind structure and temperature of different urban situations (ZIMMERMANN, 1984).

more likely to involve the creation of parks, gardens and green spaces characteristic of cooler rather than warmer (micro)climates. In this context, the role of water in the manipulation of the micro-climate is likely to be critical. The use of water in the urban areas of the future to manage the micro-climate and create new landscapes for the new climates of future towns and cities will provide an important challenge for landscapes architects in coming years. However, now is the time to start facing up to these future challenges, and one important starting point is to see where lessons can be learnt from past experience.

Several centuries ago, in Moorish Spain, a sophisticated garden culture developed in which it was possible to create gardens, not only of great beauty, but above all ones which had microclimates which provided environments of a high degree of thermal comfort for humans despite the extreme macro-climatic conditions in which they were located. This paper argues that it is time to re-evaluate the garden culture of Moorish Spain from a new and contemporary viewpoint, namely that of the lessons which they can provide for the work of today's landscape architects in contributing to the adaption of our urban landscapes in order to meet the future challenges of climate change. The role played by water in Moorish garden design, as exemplified for example by the Generalife in the Alhambra is central in this context and can provide inspiration for the increasing use of water in the design and planning of cities in the future. Anyone who has passed by the "water stairway" in the Generalife will remember the freshness caused by the falling water both sides of the steps and the effects of its peculiar sound. The challenge is to consider how to re-interpret such knowledge and examples to meet future needs.

Fig.4: Water Stairway in the Palace Gardens of the Alhambra in Granada, Spain (RUGGLES, 2000).

Fig.3: The twelfth-century garden in the Seville Alcazar, Spain (RUGGLES, 2000).

City, Stream, and Environmental Values

Shiraz City Stream

~ **Mohsen Faizi** ~ Assistant Professor ~ **Mehdi Khakzand,** Ph.D. Candidate

in landscape architecture ~ Iran University of Science and Technology (IUST),

Iran ~ Abstract

Man has allways tried to destroy the landscape, anywhere. On the other hand there are three factors defining landscape in Ian Thompson's theory: Ecology, Community and Delight. Following his theory, a stream in Shiraz-Iran which is called: 'Dry stream' is defined as landscape because of the first factor Ecology: the city Shiraz is located in the hot and dry climate, however the two other factors of Thompson are not fulfilled. The main goal of this article is to find a way to revive Community and Delight in this environment.

Although it is a seasonal stream, it has a great role in Shiraz ecology. It originates from Nahr-e-Azam and conducts Shiraz flood water into the Salt Lake outside of the city. During rainy seasons this mechanism saves the city from the danger of flood.

Like a narrow line this stream divides the city in two parts. There are many offices and residential buildings on each side of it, so the community of people in any time of day and night make the site along the stream, dry or not, into a lively urban space. From the aspect of aesthetic (Delight), this urban space has the potential to become a beautiful landscape by creating a partnership of light, pavement, water and of course attendance of people. Unfortunately, the terror of automobiles nearby (by definition of speedy highway) on one side, and the process of subway construction on the other side, reduce this stream that is worthy to be a landmark of the city - this divine blessing is going to be lost by the gradual attacks of technology.

This article describes a case study namely Cheonggyecheon Seoul project in South Korea, similar to the Dry Stream in Shiraz-Iran. This stream in Seoul had similar conditions but now, it not only revives the city but also defines functions for each part.

Furthermore, its scenic value, landscape, and ecology make it into an impressive part of Seoul urban space. By these understanding the similarity of the two streams in Shiraz and in Seoul, especially in physical feature, Cheonggyecheon Seoul project can be a good pattern for us to think deeply about our stream landscape and urban design in Shiraz. To do research, in order to create a rich and great landscape and urban space along the Shiraz Dry Stream, and increase its environmental value as an important landscape element.

Introduction

Man has always been cruel to the nature around him. This cruelty gets worse when it comes to existing nature in big cities, like their valleys and seasonal rivers. Naming them as floodways we have prepared ourselves for their destruction, particularly in Shiraz where the river is named "Khoshk" meaning "Dry". This river flowing from the mountains to a plain and linking the Nahr-e- Azam to the salt lake (Maharlou), has created green valleys which could penetrate through the city as wide green arteries and keep nature's liveliness and freshness in the city. On the contrary, not only the shore of the river, but also the river itself, is under construction and therefore from its landscape almost nothing is left, and the river is only considered as an inundation place. In order to prevent accidents and passersby's falling into the canal, in some places the edges are made too high to even see the river easily. Existence of different garages and building rubbish shed into the river is another destructive element of its landscape which damages the ecosystem of the environment too. Thompson adds to the meaning and context of landscape the component delight(s), increasing the complexities of decision making process (Thompson, 2000). It is obvious that delights have a key role in giving identity to the urban landscape. This assumption means that landscape aesthetic and its enhancement should be considered beyond its visual aspects, in combination with other dimensions of the urban environment. Aesthetical values can be assessed through different approaches and motivations. Current wide literature and materials comprise different approaches that concern these purposes through a professional and expertise point of view. Other approaches are driven from the social sciences framework, namely from environmental psychology, integrating behavioral studies in relation with aesthetical and public perceptions (Kaplan 1989, pp.509-530). Thompson discusses the effect of community and presence of humans in landscape of which culture is one of the features of this community. Nevertheless, the balance between natural environment and human societies has always existed in societies; and searching for delight and aesthetics, delight and balance of human tasks and their environmental relationship, has always been considered in a such way that man can live comfortably with nature. From Thompson's point of view 'Ecology' is one of the

Fig 1: Khoshk Stream Landscape.

effective elements in landscape. Prior to many other experts, Garrett Eckbo has paid attention to the key role of ecology in a healthy environment. He believes that public needs the designs ecologically responsive (Eckbo, 1998). As mentioned before, inattention towards these issues about the Shiraz Khoshk stream has even caused damages to the human environment, particularly to residents living along the edge of the river. Paying attention to the natural element of ecology should enhance the human environment quality and as a result prepare welfare for him. McHarg has called the architectures for designing with nature and he also reminds the effect of factors in nature in designing (Mc Harg 1992). There is no doubt that streams and rivers as urban natural corridors have key roles in many cities; and as we know, by connecting various areas and different cultures with their social approach, streams and rivers form many of these cities. Importance of these rivers is because of passing of time and their historical and monumental aspect (as cultural heritage) and giving identity and also their wonderful effect on the ecology and quality enhancement of the environment.

Description of the case

When the population of Shiraz city was around 300,000, the valley of Khoshk stream passing through the city did not play a big role in space occupation. However, its ecological role was not felt much either. But soon the population of the city amounts to 2 million. The lands around the valley, all located in the downtown and south of Shiraz University and within and beside the Ghasr-e-Dasht gardens, are not insignificant any more. In order to enhance the welfare level, cultural and urban activities, these lands should go under urban planning again, if not only because of efficiency. There is no doubt that this efficiency comprises public welfare, suitable and beautiful access to it, and it also takes away the low-spirited and exanimate from the city. Although necessity of preparing an organization plan for Khoshk stream has been approved by municipal council and Contemporary Designing Organization, it is not clear why these studies have not been continued or achieved any result. One of the reasons is lack of a comprehensive plan for rivers in urban and regional planning. Since Shiraz is

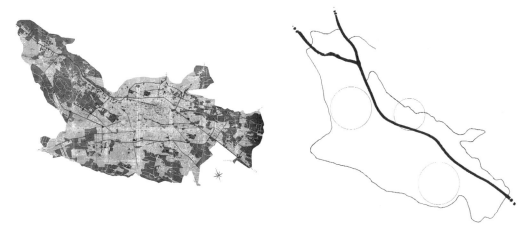

Khosk stream as a natural axis with relation to various zones of Shiraz City.

not in a desirable condition due to the entertainments and parks and because Khoshk stream owns potential facilities in entertainment services, it seems necessary to make use of this opportunity in a convenient manner.

Khoshk Stream

This natural body of river cum valley, which follows the whole linear length of the city from its west to the east, links the great canal to the salt lake, and has left significant ecological impacts on the ecosystem and ecological qualities of Shiraz city. Moreover, it had strongly affected the quality of artifact environment and the city perception. As it can be understood by the name of the Khoshk (dry) river, this river is dry about half of each year, and in the rainy seasons, from the middle of fall to the middle of spring, it carries the flood streams to the salt lake. In years of drought, the river is dry most of the times. Khoshk stream has attracted a long length of the city constructions around itself, while the floods of the river are a threat to the city and its high water level can enhance the visual aesthetic quality of Shiraz. Moreover, if we pay attention to landscape designing of its low water level, it can efficiently improve the current conditions. Besides, haltering the flood water it can be used for the development of green spaces of the city. Furthermore, preparing a continuous flow of living water in the river and developing phreatic water within it would increase the ecologic area and the landscape quality of the city as a whole (Poormokhtar 1380, thesis, Shiraz University). In areas near the river (such as Chamran axis) where landscaping is considered, the river itself has not been used. As Bagh Boland of Chamran, the linear park alongside the Chamran Boulevard in the river bank and close to the existing gardens own ecological capabilities, but none of the potential capabilities of the river has been used. On the other hand, the many various restaurants have granted a revivification and a special urban life to this part of the city, increasing its social capabilities, but the capabilities of the river have not been used for the improvement of community quality. Finally, though in designing Chamran axis it has been tried to use natural delight elements, the potential aesthetics of the Khosk River have not been taken into consideration.

Fig 3-4: Chamran axis as a designed landscape.

Natural Elements Feature in the Enhancement of Landscape Quality of Khoshk Stream

Natural elements of urban landscape play a key role in the enhancement of the environment quality. Water is one of the most important ones in human life. Water is considered a key natural resource in sustainability and landscaping, and plays an important role in the (urban) open space environmental quality (Hough 1990). The city/water relationship is a complex one which can be described with Thompson's point of view as ecology, society, and delight. The existence and crossing of Khoshk stream in Shiraz city develops different characteristics in urban environment, that should be taken into consideration. However, beyond the historical, geographical, and morphological contexts of Khoshk stream in Shiraz, other aspects can be mentioned, such as water quality, flood vulnerability, and accessibility that will be discussed briefly in this article. But what concerns the authors of this article is paying attention to the increased delight and landscape value of this seasonal river and its contribution in increasing the urban attractiveness. As a result, water quality and even quantity improvement, and having it flow in the current valley of Khoshk stream should be considered in the enhancement of urban landscape.

Urban Regulations, Positive or Negative Factors in Khoshk stream Landscape

Many newspapers and magazines about Shiraz city in recent years focused on the destruction of Khoshk stream landscape by urban constructions. Naturally one of the problems about this river is contravention of municipal rules and regulations and other respective organizations. On the banks of the natural axis, that is Khoshk River, high buildings have been constructed (including Sara Grand Hotel and Farhangian residential complex), while structure with lower height on the bank should result in a better reinforcement and improvement of the river's landscape.

Fig 5-6: Effect of construction on stream landscape.

Inattention towards this problem is obvious in the residential buildings alongside the river. Considering the presence of Khoshk stream as a cultural heritage that contains the public's memories of old days (as a mental sign), it possesses a social aspect, hidden from the authorities. It is obvious that place identity can play an important role in the perception of environmental changes and problems. Damaging an old construction is considered as a criminal act. But developing bypasses, overpasses, subway tunnels, and their installations, that destruct an identity that gives even an ecologically valuable natural-historical axis is not only never considered a crime, but is also confirmed by the authorities every day (Poormokhtar 1380, thesis, Shiraz University).

Studying Landscape and Waterfront of Khoshk Stream through Thompson's Viewpoint

Actually the waterfront of Khoshk stream can be divided into the following categories. The first two categories are natural and the third one is artifactual:
- The main river bed area where the river passes
- The natural waterfront of the river which are either abandoned or tree planted, etc.
- The riverside, changed highways for cars passing fast

Considering the presented data, the river landscape and the natural and artifact waterfronts of Khoshk stream with the above mentioned features are analyzed in the following.
- Ecology: Considering the necessity of confronting the environmental challenges in today's world and eliminating them in the format of various expertise, emphasizing on the main bed of landscape profession which means the nature and its inevitable role in protection and sustainability of the environment, the professional value of ecologic approach inside the architectural landscape activities and projects should be taken into consideration in all aspects: designing, planning, and managements (Roshani 1374 Tehran). As it can be seen in the pic-

Fig 7: Old bridge on Khoshk stream as a cultural landscape potential.

Fig 8: Khoshk stream cross section.

tures except the becket gable wall, many parts of the river length have remained natural. Unfortunately, inattention of the authorities towards protection and purgation of this natural axis and also the carelessness of public in keeping this ecosystem clean has brought risks to it, which can be resolved by a little attention. However, some actions such as pine planting plan performed alongside the river are movements in order to help the ecosystem of this environment. Nevertheless, sometimes these actions did not have an appropriate rationality. For example, in some western parts of the river abundant in gardens and trees, this plan is performed but in western parts, poor in trees, not much action has been taken.

The pollution of Khoshk stream is general because of the swages, garbages, construction materials and agricultural drainage that includes various chemical materials organic materials and different poisons. On the other hand in many parts of the river length except becket walls we can observe a establishment of bypass highways, overpasses and subway tunnels and their respective installations which cause pollutions due to the cars and subway (and its installations in future) that can be considered as a threat to this ecosystem itself.

• Community: Landscape architecture can play a worthy role in the creation of a part of social and public spaces of environmental systems. Since a general part of social interactions of man forms in open spaces, considering community values that can enrich such spaces is necessary (Thompson 2000). Public contribution in creation of these spaces can help this important issue. "Public river landscape perception" is the process of extracting meaning from stimuli and important events encountered in river landscapes. It is obvious that environmental perception depend on the physical elements in the scene (landscape) and their spatial arrangement (importance); furthermore the individual (i.e. cognitions, feelings and behaviors of users), cultural, and social features have an important effect on it. It is also important to consider the human activities in the riverfront since when the human contact with the river gets more intense, the possibility of interactions between these two increases too. The riverfront accessibility and visual preparation are the prerequisites of public utility, society and landscape

Fig 9: Effect of pollutions (visual & environmental) on stream ecology and landscape.

Fig 10 -11: The effect of car and technology existence on Khoshk stream landscape.

issues which should be answered by some arrangements. However, this problem is not true about moving cars - and their view to the river should be controlled. Thus, in order to use the river landscape properly, other convenient solutions should be suggested for the transit of cars and people and reduce the traffic in the river's axis by a rational design. Though, controlling the altitude or height it can be designed in a way that the pedestrians would have enough view to the inside of the watercourse while the car drivers would not have this possibility.

According to Mannina, if the river is considered an important focus and generator of events, we must investigate the problem of major urban roads using the river as a corridor attentively since this problem causes disruptions in the city and may become devastating.

• Delight: Delight and aestheticism is an innate tendency of man existing in him from the first moment of his birth and lives within him all his life. The effect of this natural tendency can be seen in all aspects of man's life including his manual artifacts. Landscape designing as the man's interference in the nature for meeting some parts of his material and spiritual needs is not an exception in this regard and it should always contain aesthetic values (Thompson 2000). The presence and crossing of the river in the city can bring an additional quality enhancement and aesthetic to the environment. No need to say that the riverfront that remain more natural are more potential to present aesthetic. Express by-passes, overpasses and subway tunnels and their installations including articraft edges that weaken the river's capacity for presenting its aesthetics. However, articraft environment of Khoshk stream landscape can be used in a way so that its natural features be presented to the public. The same activity can be seen in Seoul. Accordingly, the total topics for studying the landscape features of Khoshk stream are as following:

• Biological components in ecological areas.
• Typology of human movements and visual contacts in social areas.
• River morphology in delight factors.

Fig 12: Khoshk stream and human visual relations.

Table-1. Effective factors in the evaluation of river landscape.

Effective factors in landscape	Related Features
Ecology	Biological diversity
	Water quality
	Environmental pollution (air, noise,..)
	Diversity of (green spaces) plants and trees and their quantity
Society	Modes of man's transportation in the riverside and defining walk ways
	and bike ways
	Formation of public events
	Visual permeability (the depth and width of views)
	Worthiness of the river as a cultural heritage
	Physical relationship of man with the water
	Defining leisure and tourist units beside the river
Delight	Passing of the river
	Attractiveness of Riverfront
	Arrangement of the biodiversity
	River dimension in width and length
	Passing of bypasses and overpasses, etc. and the quality of man-made environment

As it can be understood from the table above, several factors affect the landscape of Shiraz Khoshk stream that changing each can present a different landscape.

Research Procedure

This research was designed on the basis of an approach that includes the effect of three factors of ecology, society (people), and delight. In this context Khosh river is considered the material (natural) world and the center for this article, and according to Ian Thompson's theory, "society" and people, "ecology", and finally "delights" are its three effective factors (Fig 13). These three poles can have fundamental effects on the landscape quality of this urban body (Khoshk stream).

A Foreign Case Study (Seoul experience)

Cheonggyecheon project in Seoul is an interesting experience very similar to the Khoshk stream project in Shiraz. This project was designed and performed by four Korean landscape architectures when the expertise and the municipal authorities of Seoul found out that even if constructing roads, tunnels, and bridges alongside and over the main river of this city could be a little help to the problem of city traffic, it brings irreparable losses for the future of Seoul. This river, like Khoshk stream in Shiraz, possesses a significant position in the physical and ecologic structure of Seoul city (www.City Mayors Seoul development.htm, December 2007).

Actually, restoring a six-kilometer river in the heart of Seoul that has been covered by expressways and overpasses for fifty years is not an easy task. The task is even more difficult when the river meanders through one of the largest and most densely populated cities of the world. The project of Cheonggyecheon, or the Cheonggye river restoration is without question the most famous urban renewal scheme to have ever been undertaken in the history of Seoul. Typically, four aims have been defined for this project. The first aim of the project, restoration of the Cheonggyecheon river, completed in 2005, was to rectify the problem of expressways in terms of public safety that threatened to downfall and collapse at any moment; the second aim was to address Seoul's deteriorating environmental conditions by creating a citizen-centered friendly environment in the centre of this city; the third aim was to praise and respect the history of the 600 year old Korean capital; and the fourth aim was to encourage redevelopment in the surrounding neighborhoods (at that time lagged behind) in the city centre. In order to fully understand the importance of the Cheonggyecheon river project to the Korean people it is necessary to know a little bit about Korean history, particularly the parts that relate to Seoul. The Choson Dynasty, led by Emperor Taiju, choose the land on the banks of the Cheonggyecheon near its intersection with Han River (Korea's capital in 1392). Monk Muhak, on behalf of Taiju, chose the site after a two year search for a location that satisfied the principles of feng shui. According to Muhak, the land possessed a high energy that was enhanced by (four) prominent mountains. These mountains were exactly to the north, south, east, and west of the site. In Syngman Rhee's years of presidency, Cheonggyecheon river was covered by concrete overpasses and in 1968 a multi leveled expressway was established overtop of the river. On July of 2003, Seoul's mayor (Lee Myung Bak) who was elected as the president later, established the renewal of the river. This was a big deal which not only aimed at tearing down the overpasses and expressways, but also compensating all years of negligence (apparently in order to develop) that resulted in the dry up of the river. It is said that during these years 120.000 tons of water was pumped into this river each day. In September 2005, the river was opened for the public and it was praised as a great victory in renewal and beautification of the city. Though there was a sig-

Fig 14-15: Cheonggyecheon stream landscape and new constructions.

nificant contrast at the time of the former mayor, Goh Kun, in comparison with the current conditions. In those days, unfortunately, the municipal governors sold the river's surrounding neighborhood for building shops, economic agencies, and commercial activities. The cost of the project was approximately assessed to 900 million dollars. Moreover, in about 12 trillion won (US$12 billion) is expected to be invested to re-develop the 792,000 square meter region near the stream into a major commercial and residential area over the next five years. Some Korean environmental organizations have criticized the project for its high costs, calling it purely symbolic and not really beneficial to the city's eco-environment. A main part of this seasonal river, Cheonggyecheon, facilitating the relationship of water and landscape of the river (developing wide terraces) was designed in two parts on both sides of the river (as it can be seen in the picture). Walls in the sides are made of the stones in the region in masonry structures (Hwang 2003).

Eight major attractions of the river are designed in the central space of Seoul. Cheonggye is a public space in the beginning of the restored axis of Cheonggyecheon. The second one is Gwangtong-gyo repaired bridge which is developed and used as a space for celebrations and events by Choson Dynasty. Jeongjo Banchado was the third, a ceramic wall picturing the great rulers of Choson Dynasty. The next attraction was called the cultural wall which cultural works were illustrated on it. The fifth one had restored the old laundry near the river. The wall of wishes was the sixth one and it constituted 10x10 centimeter tiles where people can carve their wishes on them. The next is a very interesting one including piles of the bridge and the foundation of an old tunnel which has been designed to revive the feelings of the past. The eight attractions were

Fig 16-17: Cheonggyecheon stream landscape and effects on human existence.

designed as an environmental friendly urban park wherein the history, culture, past, present, and future are combined.

Landscaping of the river and the arrangement of the plants and trees alongside the street is done in a way that links the two sides of the river in terms of space. In order to perform this task, constructed guard walls and terraces and the lands near the river were used perfectly. The trees alongside the street are made to add to the attraction of the artifact edges of the river and underground water pipes are used for protecting them. The environment and the natural riverbed and ecosystem friendly are created for teaching and experiencing real nature. In order to protect the ecosystem the followings were allocated: 3520 square meter to willow marsh, 17074 square meters to terraces for man and nature relationship, 12589 for the habitat of birds, 7316 square meters for habitat of fish and 29 places for rapids and swamps (www.Wikipedia,the free encyclopedia.htm December 2007).

Data Analysis

A brief review on Seoul's experience not only familiarizes us with a better management of the city (landscape) problems, but also concerning what is formed, makes us look more cautiously at the remaining environmental and natural values of our cities not just through Thompson's principles but through any analytic look. The following table contains the comparison and contrast of the Khoshk stream's current condition and the condition of Seoul's river in the past. This table can notify us of the worthiness of Khoshk stream in terms of different factors and its high potentials for the landscape quality enhancement. It also illustrates how a desirable landscape could be achieved for Khoshk stream of Shiraz, considering the aforementioned potentials and values.

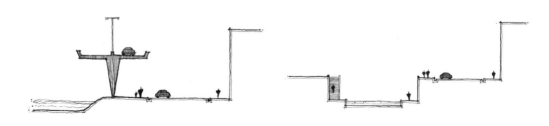

Fig 18-19: Cheonggyecheon stream (old & new) cross section.

Table-2. Comparison of the current condition of Shiraz River and Seoul River's condition in the past through Ian Thompson's threefold viewpoint.

Effective factors in landscape	Related features	Common points	Different points	Evaluation
Ecology	Biological diversity	*		Biological diversity is almost equal in both projects.
	Water quality	*		It seems that the water quality of both rivers are similar with no significant difference.
	Environmental pollution (air, noise,..)		*	It can be said that environmental pollutions in Seoul (because of its higher population and machinery) is more than Shiraz.
	Diversity of (green spaces) plants and trees and their quantity		*	It seems that Shiraz River possesses more capabilities in this regard. This can play a better role in landscape designing of the river.
Society	Modes of man's transportation in the riverside and defining walk ways and bike ways		*	According to the current evidences, the traffic and the road ways were more convenient in Seoul.
	Visual permeability (the depth and width of views)		*	There is more visual view to the inside of Seoul River and it is not so about Shiraz river which reduces the relationship of the public with the landscape.
	Worthiness of the river as a cultural heritage		*	Seoul river have overcome more historical evolutions in comparison with Shiraz river and therefore it possesses more capabilities for becoming a cultural heritage.
	Physical relationship of man with the water	*		Both rivers (because of their location) could have the same condition.
	defining leisure and tourist units beside the river	*		Both rivers have the same condition (except in Chamran region that the constructions are in a distance from the river).
Delight	Passing of the river	*		Passing of both rivers in their beds are similar.
	Attractiveness of Riverfront		*	Though the riverfronts of both rivers are similar, it can be said that the attractiveness of Shiraz river in its margins is more. (because of the existence of more open spaces)
	Arrangement of the biodiversity		*	Plants and trees arrangements of Shiraz river possesses more diversity which causes an enhancement in landscape and increases the possibility of landscape designing.
	River dimension in width and length		*	Shiraz river is longer and wider than Seoul river and therefore it developes more possibility for designing.
	Passing of bypasses and overpasses, etc. and the quality of man-made environment		*	Because of its higher techniques and technology, the constructed artifact surrounding Seoul project has a better condition than Shiraz constructions.

Conclusion

From Ian Thompson's viewpoint, landscape evaluation can be considered as a parallel process with analysis of ecology, community, and delight. Ecologic analysis starts with one point and with earth, topography, and geology of lower levels but then in landscape evaluation, dominant cultural layers are usually studied (that can involve social views), while in ecologic analysis, vegetations, wild life and ecosystem processes are discussed. On the other hand, aestheticism of man (in community) makes him tend to high quality landscapes (even visually). Although most probably the source of landscape changes are of human and not nature, our evaluation in this article includes landscape changes process too. However, in order to achieve the above mentioned qualities in landscape area, many points should be considered, as following: Biological diversity, water quality, environmental pollution (air, noise,..); diversity of (green spaces) plants and trees and their quantity (in the ecology); modes of man's transportation in the riverside and defining walk ways and bike ways; visual permeability (the depth and width of views); worthiness of the river as a cultural heritage; physical relationship of man with the waterfront; defining leisure and tourist units beside the river (socially); passing of bypasses and overpasses, etc. and the quality of man-made environment; river dimensions in width and length (aesthetically). Furthermore, other results could be obtained considering this research:

• Avoid a single one way judgment in landscape evaluation. Thus, different effective factors was tried to be used in the evaluation of Khoshk stream.

• Treat landscape considering theoretical and detailed criteria. Thus, in this research Thompson's principles were applied in the landscape evaluation.

• An actual experience could be very efficient. Seoul project and its similarities with Khoshk stream of Shiraz was an interesting example. However, Seoul experience illustrates the high potentiality of this river for its landscape quality enhancement.

Gardens depend on Water

The History of Water Management and Preserving Scenic Beauty in Japanese Gardens in Kyoto

~ Hidefumi Imae ~ Kyoto City Cultural Properties Section ~ Abstract

Prologue

Japan is a country blessed with some of the best water conditions in the world. But from ancient times to the present, the people of Kyoto have been very much concerned with preserving their environment. Since ancient times, water has been the most important element in the continuing tradition of Japanese Gardens. But water environments can change suddenly and drastically. As the quantity and quality of water decreases, maintaining gardens becomes more difficult. If a garden loses enough water, it will eventually be destroyed. Therefore, preserving water resources is very important for keeping gardens alive.

Kyoto, due to its long history as a cultural center for traditional Japanese gardens, has had a lot of experience handling water crises. After each crisis the people who lived here, developed new garden designs and invented new ways of managing water. Recently, water scarcity and quality has become a major problem throughout the world. It is in this light that I share in this presentation ideas based on Kyoto's responses to water crises in three historical periods prior to the pre-modern era. Our predecessors in Kyoto devised a unified and multipurpose system for water management, and our modern gardens depend on this system. In my opinion, there is a lot people can learn from historical water management system in Kyoto about avoiding and dealing with water crises.

Heian Era (Ancient Times)

Recent archaeological investigation has discovered the role that sheer chance, the original landscape, Heian politics, and architectural and urban design ideas during the Heian era had on the placement and style of traditional gardens in that period. A lot of gardens in the ancient city Heiankyo, in the center of what is now Kyoto, depended on springs and natural rivers. Heiankyo, whose model was an old Chinese castle city, was established in 794. Before it was built, the area around it had many hills, springs, and forests. When the main roads for the castle city were built, many of these were cut down and filled in, but natural areas remained in the area between those roads. The residents of Heiankyo used these when they built their gardens. Since especially water resources were so useful, house lots that included these grew in value. The position of traditional garden elements and structures was determined to some extent by where these water resources were. If someone was fortunate to have easy access to a natural spring, hill, or forest it was easy for them to build a beautiful and creative garden. For others it was slightly more difficult. We know that people shared water and our best guess is that they paid for the right to use other people's water and used horizontally cut pipes as canals. Unfortunately, there aren't any examples of this type of garden using hill, forests, and spring still in existence. However, there does exist one similar type of garden, using just natural springs, in the House of Icho near Shimogamo Shrine. Urban design ideas during the Heian era adhered to a strictly established code that emphasized symmetry while reflecting political prerogatives. This affected the design of traditional gardens as well. For example, in the city center, house lots were laid out in the city on a rectangular grid. The emperor's house was in the northern central area, and the higher nobilities' houses were in the grid blocks closest to the emperor, while the lesser nobles' houses were in the more southerly and distant grid blocks. Correspondingly, the landscaping within the individual house lots was also based on a similar grid design, typically with a main house in the rear, symmetrically placed smaller side buildings behind or to the side, an open area in front of the main house, and a pond and garden area in the very front. On the one hand, the natural location of water resources such as springs and so on, didn't always fit in with the mandated style. On the other, a noble's position in the grid block was not of his own choosing, but assigned to him by royal fiat. Therefore, in the city center, there was a significant element of luck, which was viewed as a gift of nature, not social standing or design, that determined whether a give noble's house would be located near suitable resources for building a beautiful garden. High-ranking nobles built homes and gardens in the countryside as well. In this case, they were freer to build them more closely to where they could use natural resources. However, they didn't use the water directly. They built simple dams to control and channel the path of the rivers so they would flow to their gardens. One can still see an example of this type of garden at Daikakuji temple. In the early Heian era, there the city was composed mostly of nobility. There was little stress on water resources. Eventually, however, as more people gathered in Heiankyo and water use grew, developing and maintaining gardens became more difficult. Furthermore, the size of house lots became smaller. There were fewer large houses. This also made it more difficult to follow the traditional style and for people to build new gardens in that original style. Together, as the Heian era came to a close, these factors created the first water crisis.

The Kamakura and Muromachi Era (Medieval Times)

In the ensuing Kamakura era, the changing culture and the ensuing water crisis led to the creation of garden designs more suited to the times. For example, in the cities, Zen priests began using stones and sand to imitate and express the feeling of water. This design made it possible to build gardens in small places and with less water. This unique style, now famous and admired throughout the world, is called "Sekitei." The most famous examples are Ryoanji temple and Daisenin temple. The Heian era had been very peaceful. Power, as well as the greatest interest in and ability to build gardens, had resided with the aristocracy. As Japan entered the Kamakura and Muromachi eras, the Samurai class gained political power and were also interested in building gardens. They built gardens in the city and in the countryside, as had the nobility, but developed a style more suited to the life of a Samurai. The Samurai class, often called to endure the horrors of war, prized a simple and peaceful lifestyle. Their houses were smaller and simpler, so their gardens were too. They went deep into the countryside to find secluded and peaceful locations for their gardens. One reason for this was that it was easier to get water and stones there than in the city center. In addition, it was the custom to use these houses in the countryside to entertain important guests. In mountains and countryside, using sand and stones to create gardens could cause landslides and would not be safe. Rather, garden builders cut terraces into the side of the mountain, creating "hideaways". At the base of these, near the protected edge of the mountain, they could dig sand pools, and built hermitages and houses near them on the outer edges of the terraces, overlooking the mountain. As rivers, while they are flowing in the mountain are generally smaller, these were usually sited near the junction of several rivers. The design of the garden was an integral part of creating these terraces and hideaways, with an active control of the landscape to use the natural scenery around to create a beautiful effect. Two examples of these types of the garden now are in Kinkakuji-temple and Ginkakuji-temple.

Edo Period (Pre Modern Times)

In 1603, the most powerful general, or "Shogun," seized power and established a government in Edo (now known as Tokyo). This marked the beginning of the Edo Period which lasted about 300 years, when society was very peaceful and static. The people's living in the Edo Period was enforced with a system of social position. In the Edo Period, the growing population and changing culture increased the agriculture and commercial need for water. Power and wealth spread into other parts of society. Water had become a more complex and multipurpose resource. New means for using water evolved naturally out of the original garden management practices. These new uses remained linked to the original purpose and developed into a unified system. I will present several examples of this. In the prior eras, along the inner edge of mountain terraces, Samurais and nobles had built simple mountain pools and used simple dams at the juncture of mountain rivulets. In the Edo period, improved technology allowed them to build more effective dams. They were now able to safely create larger garden ponds along the outer edge of their hideaways in the mountains. In addition, there was increased use of land for agriculture, and the most valuable land was near the available water, for example in the land in between rivers. Farmers built their farm in these areas and used canals to channel the dam water for their fields. Since they lived close to the water and their livelihood depended so intimately on it, they knew it was important to use it carefully. There is an example of this type of the garden now at Shugakuin-Rikyu. Further downhill, in the city, the water flowed underground, and people built wells to access it. Artisans such as tofu makers, tea houses, laundries, and clothing manufacturers, who required the water for their livelihood, gathered near the locations with the best wells creating integrated neighborhoods specialized for these uses. The spread of wealth and power meant that merchants and others were now also wealthy enough to build small gardens in their houses. These gardens were built for the purpose of bringing light, clean wind and green areas inside the urban landscape. These types of gardens, called "Roji," imitated the atmosphere of a hermitage at the bottom of mountain. Usually these gardens did not have ponds, but needed outside water for watering. For this purpose they used well water. In this time skill at digging a well was not what it is now. They could not burrow deeply, so they took good care of the wells in order to maintain the water level. Many teahouses in Kyoto still have surviving examples of these types of garden. From gardens high in the mountains, to terraced fields, to urban craftsmen, each was directly linked to and had an interest in, preserving and protecting the water resources, creating a unified system of water management.

Epilogue

In contemporary Japan, it has been only recently that landscape design has become integrated into architectural planning from the outset. Until recently, there was a separation between building construction and other urban design elements such as embankments and canals. Moreover, construction was focused mainly on the function and strength of the given structures. However, in the Heian Era to the Edo Period, form and function were closely tied to the aesthetic beauty of the structures themselves, and of the surrounding natural landscape. We should focus at present again on water preserving systems from ancient period to the present in Kyoto. Japan is a country blessed with some of the best water conditions in the world. But from the ancient period to the present time the people who live in Kyoto have been very concerned with preserving our environment. Our predecessors in Kyoto devised a unified and multipurpose system for water management, and our modern gardens depend on this system. In my opinion, there is a lot people can learn from historical water management system in Kyoto about avoiding and dealing with water crises.

Acknowledgements: In writing this presentation I received much support from a lot of people. I must thank David Crespo and Imex Language Institute for their support in helping me transfer my ideas in english. Also, I want to express my appreciation to my co-workers for their support and forbearance.

Transforming with the Rains - Discharging Rains in Public Space

Tropical Metropolitan Rain Gardens

A radical change in how rainfall and nature are managed in

Sao Paolo, Brasil

~ **Paulo Pellegrino** ~ Professor of landscape planning and design at the

School of Architecture and Urbanism of the University of Sao Paulo, Brasil ~

Abstract

Occupying a sedimentary basin 800m above sea level, formerly crossed by meandering rivers, bordered by marshes and rain-forested hills, Sao Paulo is now the 3rd metropolitan area in the World with 20 million inhabitants, covering 3.100 sq miles, with a GDP of US$ 99 billion, where millions of cars try to move under the most crowed air space in the southern hemisphere, with the highest per capita helicopter ownership. Amid mushrooming skyscrapers, we viewed an opportunity in two new landscape design projects to explore how to gather, transport, store and release the rainwater. And, at the same time, reveal what happens if the natural precipitation -an average of 1.550mm/year, concentrated in the warmer months -provided to the city is not taken away as much as fast as possible by the existing stormwater-drainage piping system.

Capturing and using rainwater gives us not only an opportunity to rethink how we design and manage public and private open spaces in order to improve their environmental and aesthetic quality. But mostly trough reducing the demand for water, the effects of flash floods and a treatment for the runoff, Landscape Architecture could assume a key role in restoring natural processes and making the City more livable. These examples explore the different ways in which rainfall can be captured from buildings and other sealed surfaces and then stored and released in the landscape. They show exactly how the concept has been applied in two different settings along one of the City's main river, the Pinheiros, which is now one of the main arteries for transportation and corporate location in the City. Once part of its flood plain, it used to accommodate the flood waters from the huge basin, both sites are located facing the heavy traffic of multi-lane freeways, a rail line, power lines and the built channel of the river, that characterizes today this landscape.

The first landscape design discussed here is for a high-end offices tower, built in a narrow strip at a point of high visibility. This new tower was meant to be a green building, what allowed us to introduce some of the principles of natural drainage, in a way that could more efficiently match the city standards for runoff detention, in a more ecological way that could even permit the re-use of the water. In this project we also used the roof tops as integral part of the water conservation landscaping, enhancing the climate comfort and energy consumption.

The second example is a public park that is under implementation on a remnant flood plain spot that was representative of the informal soccer playing fields that used to be very popular in these settings. That was the reason for its preservation, after a litigious ownership battle, and than its denomination as a heritage site. The area was stripped-off of its original hydrological features by the various playing fields implemented early. Now with a program for a new educational park viewed as an arboretum displaying new plant collections of native and exotic species, we were involved for applying a natural drainage system that could gather, transport, store and release the runoff as a storm water chain that could be easily read by its users. The scheme developed for this site is shown here, with its goal in retain, detain and treat all the runoff prior of its release in the river. A key feature of each of these schemes is the enhanced role of runoff catchment and infiltration associated with surface modeling and planting design.

Locations of the two examples.

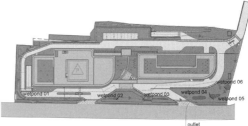

Runoff catchment on site of example .1

These examples enable us to test some of new ways of working with water in this urban settings, in a way that allow us discovering how water might behave naturally in this surroundings, and working as hard as possible to allow and enable it to do. They represent a more environmentally-friendly and positive approach to tackling the increasingly frequent water-related problems that affect the City. These big issues are mainly dealt by engineers and politicians, but as landscape architects we think that we have a very effective contribution to give, because to some extend this is also an instance where even small-scale designs could do a difference. This also meant a challenge to bring to the specific conditions of our environment, climate and cultural uses some of these natural drainage systems that started to confront the old paradigms of urban drainage in this huge humid-tropical metropolis.

Birds eye view of the public park (second example).

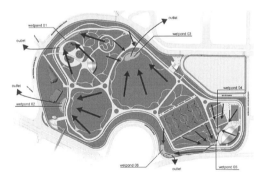

Storm water management of the public park.

Storing Water in the Poelpolder

~ **Ben Kuipers** ~ Landscape architect, Netherlands ~ Abstract

The Westland area that accounts for 3000 hectare of glasshouse horticulture is even according to Dutch standards an extreme landscape. Once a landscape made by creeks behind the dunes, it is nowadays a landscape of glass. A landscape in which the rain cannot reach the soil, because it pours directly from the glass roofs into the ditches.

Recent floods, whereby many hectares of glasshouse horticulture were inundated, made us more aware of the necessity to take measures. The biggest challenge for this area is the question how the excess water that pours down in this area, in increasingly extremer weather conditions due to climate changes, can be collected and drained off.

The spatial pressure in this region is very high. This part of the country is below sea-level and very densely populated as a result of which there are no idle spaces that can be used for temporal storage of water. The drainage canals collect the water and lead it to the sea. It's an extensive branched network but without sufficiant buffering. In case of heavy and sustained rainfall the water level rises above the limit of tolerance of 35 cm., which leads to flooded land. At the same time there is a need for irrigation water in dry periods. For that reason water is presently stored in basins. Land is expensive is this Intensive used area. So the growers are applying innovative solutions, such as floating greenhouses and cellars underneath greenhouses for storing irrigation water. The national policy is aiming to increase the capacity of the land to store the peaks of heavy rainfall temporarily, in order to prepare the country for climate changes. This is done by enlarging the system of drainage canals and by creating lower areas for temporarily peak storage of water.

The aim to prepare the Westland area for changing climates is linked to other goals, such as increase the recreational and ecological quality of the area and to make the area more attractive to live in. This led to the 'Poelzone Project'. The drainage canal Poelwetering is to be enlarged to collect the water and lead it to a new pump house at the seaside. At the same time, the Poelwetering will be provided by green banks to turn the Poelwetering into an ecological and recreational corridor from the river Maas to the North Sea. A strategic element in the Poelzone Project is the 'Poelpolder'. A lower part of the area of about 60 hectares with its own regulated water level, surrounded by dikes and now still covered with greenhouses. The project aims to remove all the glass houses from the Poelpolder to change it into an ecological green area, which can also serve as an temporarily storage of water in case of emergency. In a situation of heavy rains which is foreseen to happen once in a period of 15 years the Poelpolder must be able to store 75.000 m3 water. To raise the money to realize the project, also about 1.200 houses will be developed as real estate in the Poelpolder. Development Company 'Het Nieuwe Westland', composed of local and regional administrators and the polder board, commissioned us to design a Masterplan.

We first tried to design a basin of about 7,5 hectares, which can be filled with water once in 15 years and which could also serve as an attractive park. In times of heavy rains the park would be covered with water with a depth of 1 meter. After the water is pumped out, a layer of mud would be left behind. Not a pleasant situation from a recreational or ecological point of view.

To decide where to locate the basin, a map showing elevations and levels was used. The map showed that breaking the dikes would lead to a lake of about 40 hectares. This gave us the idea to change the polder into a lake; after all, a lake could be used for temporarily water storage too! With a limit of tolerance of 0,35 meter in water level, a lake measuring 22 hectares of water could store the 75.000 m3 water as well. So we changed the assignment into creating a lake, which can serve water management ecology, recreation and housing. By doing so, a lot of opportunities and advantages were created:

• The lake can be used 365 days a year for water storage, instead of once in 15 years, making the drainage canal system more solid.
• There is no more need for pumping water out of the polder and maintaining the dikes around it.
• It is more easy and safer to build houses on heightened land instead of near dikes.
• The new houses will be situated at an attractive lake, which can be reached by boat without the uses of sluices. Living with your yacht in the back of the garden.
• The lake and its banks give many opportunities for recreational use.
• The ecological potential of a lake including wetlands is very high.
• The lake will increase the quality of the water in the water system.

The Masterplan contains the following ingredients:
• The whole Poelpolder is considered to be a park, with place for recreation, living and nature, with the lake is the central theme.
• Housing will partially be provided by creating densely built area with canals and canal houses, like many Dutch fortified cities.
• The west bank will be arranged as an ecological corridor.
• The east bank will contain a promenade with housing in low density.

The Poelpolder (inside red line) in the Westland area.

• The west side will join the adjacent area, which will serve as a green area.
• Living on the water will be possible, not only in new style house boats but alsoon floating platforms.

A design competition generated a number of architectural solutions for the housing concepts.

Realisation of the Poelpolder project is sponsored by the national government. Innovation will be the key word for the development. For instance, research will be done to see how the energy surplus of the greenhouses in the surrounding can be recycled to heat the dwellings. Also geothermic energy will be applied for heating and generating energy.

Study for floating houses in 'the fortified city'.

The Poelpolder Project, masterplan.

Possible future images.

Transforming Landscape Character with Sustainable Development

Case study the Royal Project at Fang, Chiengmai, Thailand

~ Apinya Limpaiboon ~ Instructor in Planning and Landscape Design, School of Architecture and Design, King Mongkut's University of Technology, Thailand ~ Abstract

On October 2006 a big flood hit Northern part of Thailand, more than 40 provinces were damaged by massive water, thousands of villagers along both sides of rivers and streams lost their homes and their farmlands. The dramatic force of water accumulated from the northern mountain range, flew through flood plain area and agricultural land to Chaopraya River Basin, before disposing to Ao Thai Bay. An extreme force of water flow was evidence of earth un-balance, caused by deforestation and critical changing global climatic conditions. In the north high up in watershed mountainous area, one so-called Royal Project was also affected by the fierce stream.

The Royal Project is the project initiated by the King of Thailand, His Majesty the King Bhumibol Adulyadej, to help curb opium production in Thailand's highlands, preserve nature and watershed areas, and develop the socio-economic conditions in the highlands through the agricultural research and implementation of development programs. (www.royalprojectthailand.com/general/english /main.html). All Royal Project products are marketed under the brand name Doi Kham, which in Northern dialect means Golden Mountain. Doi Kham Food Products Co., Ltd. was founded in 1969 as a leading manufacturer and exporter of agricultural products. It is this Doi-Kham factory at Fang, Chiengmai, that was also destroyed by flood: 6 factories and most areas were covered by water, and the project had to be closed down. Employees and workers in the project were immediately unemployed.

This paper is to discuss about how to transform this old factory site, that formally speaking was built unplanned, into more suitable use according to natural constraints, so it can help preserve watershed and be able to adapt with excess water in rainy season. The project and the site are significant not only in terms of water-sensitivity, but also for historical and social value. It is the first factory built under His Majesty's initiative to promote and develop the agricultural products in order to support the rural living standard. The task was to re-open the factory as soon as possible, so production lines would not stop too long. So the study of proposed new land use had to be done almost at the same time as reclamation and re-construction processes. New development programs must be formed in response to natural-social value, as well as reflect the Royal Project's concept and objective. Thus, communication and co-ordination between key bodies is important to find appropriate solutions. The study has been conducted through the analysis of site physical contexts and the participation of local people to preserve and rebuild the local landscape character, which will be the most achievement of the project and community as a whole. Collaboration program between policy makers, villagers and project management team should be set in action to make the development possible.

This case study shows the site which was destroyed by water and how we can take this opportunity from the disaster to rethink about suitable usage. After reading the landscape and water flow system, we proposed that the reclamation plan should not scope only at the site itself but also extend to the adjacent community and agricultural land. New planning will take an advantage of water usage, at the same time be able to adapt to high stream flood as a retention area, so some portion has to be left un-built and this is the matter to challenge engineer and researchers to bring in innovative technology for the production line. The new master plan will be a place for Living Museums, research fields, and innovative preserved fruit processing factory where people can observe and receive training by seeing and learning from real-life examples. It will be a live-long learning center for various interest groups which will benefit to Thai society in a vast scale. Economically, it will attract tourists to visit study and appreciate Thai culture and buy local high quality products.

Even though the project is small in size, if implemented successfully, it will be an example of sustainable development to show that people (society), nature (water), and economy (policy) can developed together. The development plan demonstrated in this study would support the most significant objective of Royal Project, which is enhancing people's quality of life along with environmental awareness. In conclusion, this work demonstrates how landscape character would change to transforming with water and how Landscape Profession could contribute to society and nature.

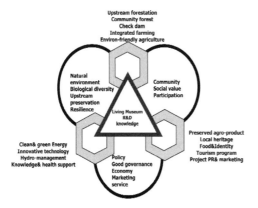

Scheme of sustainable development used in Doi Kham project.

The project site after the flood.

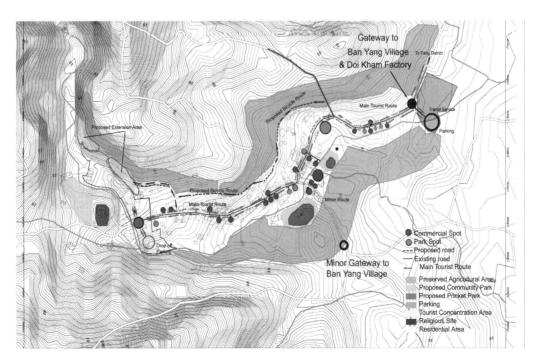

The conceptual master plan.

Day Two, July 1, 2008

2

Land meets Water

Land and water are two opposites, like a yin and yang that produce growth and prosperity when they come together. The world's oceans surround our continents. Coasts are everywhere. There are serene beaches of limpid water and white sands, or dynamic places of wind and dramatic erosion. Sheltered inlets have harbors, deltas are heavily populated landscapes, coasts attract tourism; people always want to profit from being near the sea. Inland lakes are valuable resources of nature often with precious fish. Lakes can be man-made to provide fresh water supply. Shores attract development.

When land meets water our imagination is captured, but shores and coasts can also be places of worry and concern. Globally the claim of humans on coasts and shores is increasing. Sea levels rise and lakes are shrinking. The dividing line between land and water is always dynamic and dramatically changing: sometimes because of the will of man; sometimes because of the land or the sea; sometimes just because of unpredictable disaster. Shores and coasts are more and more a place of focus for landscape architects, waterfront development is globally a challenge. How to deal with lakes and coastal regions in a way that sustains the landscape, increasing our safety and quality of life?

Dynamic processes of nature often appear where land meets water. These processes can be turned into mechanisms for landscape planning and development.

Processes of barrier sands are orchestrated with a seaward march of sand-catching pods that makes the landscape grow in Louisiana.

Understanding the waterfront as a site of dynamic landscape forces, both urban and ecological, and see it as a machine with which landscape architects can develop new design models is illustrated with projects from Holland, New Zealand, and China.

An environmental analysis to minimize future loss and damage, and how this should influence decisions, gives thought for rebuilding a sustainable Gulf Coast after Hurricane Katrina.

Not rarely, waterfronts define the identity of cities at a seaside. How to deal with the urban waterfront when major changes are taking place? The success of Venice is reduced to a kitsch spectacle based on mass-tourism gazing on a drowning empire – but with a paradigm shift processes of landscape can be exploited to a new response within its Lagoon landscape. Landscape design with water helps in rebuilding a sense of community after the disastrous earthquake in Kobe, from the small neighborhood stream to large scale urban waterfront. Water unites not only cultural and natural systems, but also global and local organizations that find a location in El Chorrillo waterfront development in Panama City.

2.1 Land meets Water – Papers of Morning Sessions Day Two

Key Note: Landscape Literacy: Reading the waterlines
~ Anne Whiston Spirn, School of Architecture and Planning, Massachusetts
Institute of Technology

The Seaward March: the Pod and the Buoy
~ Cathy Soergel Marshall and Kristi M Dykema, Assistant Professors of Landscape
Architecture, Louisiana State University, US

The Gulf Coast: Rebuilding a Cultural and Ecological Infrastructure after Hurricane
Katrina
~ James L. Sipes and Anne Kirn Rollings, Landscape architects and environmental
planners, EDAW, US

Littoral machines: How Waterfronts become Coasts
~ Matthew Bradbury, Senior Lecturer Landscape Architecture, Unitec Institute of
Technology and Frank de Graaf (Consultant DHV), New Zealand

Venice is Not a Modern City
~ Jorg Sieweke, Landscape architect and urban designer, Ass. Professor, TU Berlin,
Germany, Co author: Anna Viader, Landscape Architect and Architect, Berlin

Community Design around Kobe City to Live with Water
~ Mayumi Hayashi, Associate Professor, University of Hyogo, Japan

Recapturing a Waterfront: Panama City, Panama
~ Ken McCown, Urban Designer, Arizona State University and Design Workshop,
US

Landscape Literacy

Reading the Waterlines

~ **Anne Whiston Spirn** ~ School of Architecture and Planning,

Massachusetts Institute of Technology ~ **Abstract**

Human survival depends upon adapting ourselves and our landscapes – cities, buildings, gardens, roadways, rivers, fields, forests – in new, life-sustaining ways, shaping contexts that reflect the interconnections of air, earth, water, life, and culture, that help us feel and understand these connections, landscapes that are functional, sustainable, meaningful, and artful.

This is no new task. The power to read, tell, and design landscape is one of the oldest and greatest human talents; it enabled our ancestors to spread from warm savannas to cool, shady forests and even to cold, open tundra and hot, arid deserts. But, now, our ability to transform landscape threatens human existence. Having altered virtually every spot on the planet, humans have triggered pertur-bations that have changed it irrevocably and dangerously. And, now, at a time when we need to rapidly adapt lives and landscapes in creative ways, most peo-ple have lost the ability to read the stories that landscapes tell. Signs of hope, signs of warning are all around, unseen, unheard, undetected. Most people, for

Waves and harbour wall shape dark depths and light shallows – two sides, one surface. Fairlight Pool, Sydney Harbor, Australia. Photo: Anne Whiston Spirn

example, can no longer read the waterlines in landscape: whether they live in a floodplain, whether they are rebuilding a city or planting the seeds of its destruction, whether they are protecting or polluting the water they drink. This inability to read and understand landscape is a form of illiteracy, one that makes it hard for individuals and societies, for humanity, to address effectively the environmental challenges that face the world today.

To be literate in landscape is to recognize both the problems in a place and its resources, to understand how they came about, by what means they are sustained, and how they are related. It permits us to perceive pasts we cannot otherwise experience, to anticipate the possible, to envision, choose, and shape the future. We can "see" water underground in the tree along a dry creekbed, in the cracks of a building's foundation, the slumps in pavement in a city; or "see" the connections between buried, sewered stream, vacant land, and polluted river, and imagine rebuilding communities while purifying water. And we can imagine poetry.

Designers are storytellers. Among all the materials with which landscape architects craft their storylines, water is among the most powerful, both figuratively and literally. Water is a source of life, power, comfort, fear, and delight, a symbol of purification, of both the dissolution of life and its renewal. Water flowing – tapped to irrigate crops, to drink, to carry wastes – orders the landscape of human settlement. Flows of water and capital, interacting, produce landscapes of affluence and poverty. "The next war will be over water," it is said in many parts of the world.

Meeting the environmental and social challenges posed by water in the coming century will demand landscape designs and plans that combine the pragmatic, the poetic, and the political, that reframe old stories and tell new ones. The landscape architect's task is also to make the landscape's waterlines tangible and legible, to teach others to read landscape and to understand those readings so that together we may speak new wisdom into the landscapes of city, suburb, and countryside.

The Seaward March

The Pod and the Buoy

~ **Kristi M Dykema** ~ **Cathy Soergel Marshall** ~ Assistant Professors of

Landscape Architecture, Louisiana State University, US

"Theories need myths as much as myths need theories. If theories illuminate myths, myths confirm theories" (Segal 10).

In southern Louisiana, water and land disappear into one another creating a golden carpet of hydrological and ecological systems: barrier islands and coastal wetlands whose primary charge is buffering the inland territory from weather-related tidal surges. The crown jewel of Louisiana's barrier system is Grand Isle, serving both the state's tourist interests and the US Army Corps of Engineer's ongoing research of barrier restoration.

Data from Grand Isle indicate that the relative sea level is rising at a rate of 0.4 inches per year (1.03 cm/yr; Penland and Ramsay, 1990). This is the highest rate reported along the contiguous United States. Subsidence and rising sea level are largely responsible for both shoreline erosion and the transgressive nature of most of the barrier islands in Louisiana. The historical decrease in size and increase in segmentation of Louisiana's barrier system, as well as the rapid loss of the wetlands, has greatly increased the vulnerability of the mainland areas during major hurricanes. "Since the 1956, coastal Louisiana has lost over 1.2 million acres of land (485,830 ha; Barras et al. 2003). It is estimated that coastal Louisiana will continue to loose land at a rate of approximately 6,600 acres per year (2,672 ha/yr) over the next fifty years" (State of Lousiana, 2004, App. D-29).

The water approaches

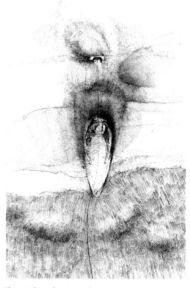

The pod: orchestrated accumulation.

The Story: water meets land

"The structural meaning of a myth is both noncumulative and interlocking. It is noncumulative because the myth contains a series of resolutions of the oppositions it expresses rather than a single, gradual resolution. Its meaning is thus cyclical rather than linear, recurrent rather than progressive.... Each cycle...represents not the consequence but only the 'transformation' of its predecessor" (Segal 119).

Adopting the perception of Grand Isle as an ideal laboratory dedicated to the future recovery of lost territory, this paper introduces a speculative, artificial process to reclaim intercessory landscapes. Between water and established land, shoreline dunes and nascent barrier islands are built up, orchestrated through the deployment of ephemeral devices marching seaward in search of that which has been given over to the rising ocean. Hundreds of devices (soil deposit pods) are planted in unison, inland from the existing shoreline. Singularly and collectively, they await moving wind and water, catching and piling the shifting sands, trudging ever outward towards the ghosts of former shorelines.

In resolving the design of the pod, this project aims equally at the pedagogic and the plausible. This project looks at growth as a process of accumulation and loss. It looks at landscapes as syncopated rhythms of time, landmass, and fluctuating weather. Seen didactically, it uses the story, the speculation, to illuminate opportunities for growth and outline strategies that operate on the land at multiple scales over long cycles of time.

Phase one

Storms gather and dissipate while dancing on the delicate line where water meets land. It is a contestable line and one subject to constant revisions. The Gulf Coast shoreline humbles itself to wind and erosion, lying-in-wait while the negotiations, instigated by shifting weather, find a temporary stopping place. Shapeless, moving sands and wind-blown debris locate moments of respite on the fragile shores, but can collect only briefly before being washed or blown elsewhere.

 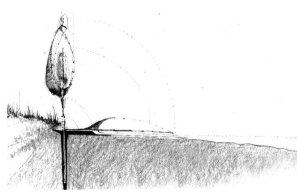

Phase one.   Phase one.

Marking the inception of an impending reclamation, phase one begins with the planting of the pods. With the goal of reaching the lost barrier dunes, the first planting of the pods is sited at the high-tidal edge. They are staked into the sand and positioned upright. Their first task is to provide safe harbor to the wind-bound particles of sand and debris. In unison, they are raised as sails to the wind so that they might catch that which drifts away, causing it to fall, instead, onto the tidal edge. Slowly, the pods score the various tempos of wind deposition and manufacture at their feet nascent dunes.

Standing at attention each pod transforms the shoreline through its porous, fabric netting that catches and slows the airborne velocity of the wind-bound particles. The netting sifts the particles, slowing their flight and causing them to fall into piles accumulating behind the device. The piles sort themselves according to particle densities, such that the heaviest debris falls closest to the pod and the finer particles are cast outwards in arrays moving away from the device. Not unlike the curving ridges of unassisted dunes, these newly formed mounds of debris emerge in rhythms along the high-tidal edge.

Over time, the deposited dunes close in on the device. The accumulating weight pushes on the upright pod, causing the stem to break and the pod to tip and fall to the ground. This marks the first seaward step. The, fabric netting and aluminum frame fall to a rest in front of the tidal edge, awaiting water-carried debris to wash through and accumulate.

Phase two

The resting pod gently responds to the constant fluctuations between high and low tide. In search of an intermediate landscape of stasis, the pod shifts back and forth. During this phase, the pod transitions between soil accrual at low tide and seaward scouring in high tidal events. The pod's exploration of the intermediate edge allows its average dormant state to uniquely evolve within the median tidal range.

As the device's transient range narrows, it settles into a comfortable dormant state and is anchored into the land. The tidal pressure pushes the pod into its station point, grounding the pod by transforming the stem into an anchor and lodging it into the newly accumulated dunes. The pod resumes its role as accumulation device, catching and arraying the washed-up soils.

Once sited, several fabric panels are resurfaced with photovoltaic material. The pod will generate sufficient energy to provide a diffused glow in the evening terrain. By day and by night, the anamorphic process of rebuilding the shoreline will be visible.

Phase three

This is a device for construction. It is also a device for remembering. To move forward on this shoreline, the pod must also look back. As the impetus for accumulation builds around the pod, so does the impetus for extraction. Embedded within the belly of the pod is a buoy that, when released into the Gulf, will mark the accumulation destination: the 1956 shoreline. With 1.2 million acres to reclaim, the first task of the pod is to enable the release of the buoy.

The high tide water washes through the pod and a tidal trench is scoured from its underside. Opening to the Gulf, the trench will slowly reach a depth and length that invites the entry of the low tide. Eventually the carved inlet widens, allowing the pod to be flooded repeatedly. When water consistently floods and stands within the belly of the pod, the interior cavity will release a buoy. The released buoy floats within the emptied cavity of the pod, awaiting launch.

The tidal draw will eventually pull the buoy from its cavity. Tethered to its parent pod by means of an incandescent dragline, the buoy moves seaward into the Gulf of Mexico. The glowing dragline traces the Gulf floor, registering subterranean topographic escarpments. The buoy and dragline are secured to the sea floor at the location of the 1956 coastline, connecting the past and present coasts as the new shoreline develops.

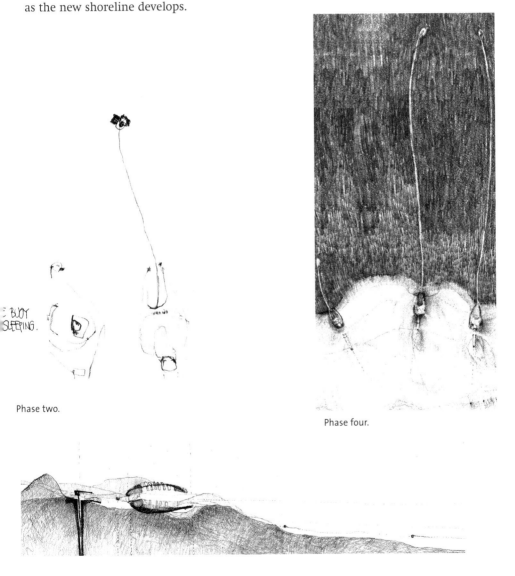

Phase two.

Phase four.

Phase three.

Phase four

With the buoy released, the pod can enter its final stage: a mature soil deposit station ensconced in the shore and capable of more rapidly stimulating dune creation. In time, the nascent dune landscape is able to support emergent beach plant communities on the backs of the dunes. More consistently, wet areas can be found between the dunes, nurturing rich and diverse ecosystems.

The pod surrenders to the landscape as new shoreline typologies are born. Consumed, it retires to the earth, a mechanical host no longer needed by its once dependent body. In some cases, the retired pod can be extracted, reconstituted, and reinstalled. But, most often, the retired pod holds its station point interminably, now marking the point of progress instead of regression.

Waves of pods are stationed along the coast. As the accumulation process marches seaward, new high-tidal edges are identified and marked for stationing. The pods, whether recycled or first-run, and their associated buoys can be seen moving back and forth with the rise and fall of the water, with the escalation and deceleration of the wind, with the shifting of the sands. The process begins again, and then again, marching towards a balance between decay and growth.

The seaward march

"The sublunary world is divided into three kingdoms: the mineral kingdom, the vegetable kingdom, and the animal kingdom…. The rhythm of the animal kingdom is that of everyday existence. The rhythm of the vegetable kingdom is that of the year. The rhythm of the mineral kingdom is that of the ages, of life calculated in millennia. As soon as we contemplate the thousands of years of existences for metals, cosmic dreams come to us" (Bachelard, in Jackson 11).

By introducing a device that both stimulates and catalogues the accumulation process, the life cycle of land reclamation can be made theatrical and occupiable. The re-established land evidences traces of those impacting environmental forces and makes spatial the memory of the march towards lost land. The device enables a landscape where visitors occupy the forces of change over time, decay and weathering, and growth.

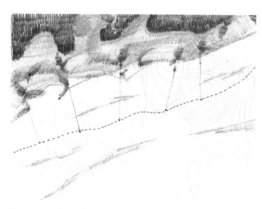

The seaward march.

The seaward march.

Transforming the Gulf Coast

Rebuilding a Cultural and Ecological Infrastructure after

Hurricane Katrina

~ **James L. Sipes** and **Anne Kirn Rollings** ~ Landscape architects and

environmental planners, EDAW, US

If you ask the people along the Gulf of Mexico Coast what "Transforming with Water" means, you may get very different responses. If you asked before August 29, 2005, you may have heared about ripples being created when waves wash over a beach, the shifting sand dunes, or even how the coast is being reshaped by the loss of barrier islands. But if you asked after that date, you would probably hear a horrific story about the devastating force of Mother Nature, and about Hurricane Katrina.

Hurricane Katrina

On August 29, 2005, Hurricane Katrina slammed into the Gulf of Mexico. At landfall, it had winds of 140 miles per hour, a storm surge of more than 30 feet, and impacted an area that covered 108,000 square miles. When levees and flood-walls failed, parts of New Orleans were inundated with over 20 feet of water. It left 527,000 people homeless, resulted in 1,299 casualties and caused well over $250 billion in property damage. A few weeks later, Hurricanes Rita and Wilma also ripped through the area. By late December, the Federal Emergency Management Agency had taken 2,530,657 registrations from hurricane victims (Steiner 2006).

The hurricanes wreaked havoc on the region's natural resources, sweeping away more than 30 square miles of Louisiana wetlands and 25 percent of Mississippi marshes. These losses contributed to a longstanding environmental problem. Since the 1930s, the Louisiana coast has lost about 1,900 square miles of marsh and swamp making it increasingly vulnerable to hurricane and storm surges. Furthermore, as is well-known, New Orleans reaped the results of this ecological damage when its levees and floodwalls failed; inundating the city with water as deep as 20 feet in many places (Steiner 2006).

On September 15th President George W. Bush pledged to rebuild the Gulf Coast and do whatever it takes to bring back New Orleans and southern Louisiana. In a 2006 speech, former New Orleans Mayor Marc Morial said that the challenge "is not only about rebuilding New Orleans and the Gulf Coast, it is about rebuilding a culture, a human system" (Steiner 2006). Rebuilding, though, has proven more difficult than most imagined.

A Legacy of Devastation

The Gulf Coast has been battered by major hurricanes for as long as human beings have settled there, and the results have been devastating. Katrina is just one example. Past trends of natural disasters are expected to continue in the future. A major hurricane has hit the Gulf Coast every year since 1994, and, in 2005, the area experienced 26 named storms and 14 hurricanes, 7 of hurricanes were considered to be major. In 2006, even before the start of the hurricane season, experts predicted that warm water temperatures in the North Atlantic would make it worse and estimated an 81 percent chance of a major hurricane hitting the Gulf Coast.

The destructive impact of Hurricane Katrina was due in large part to the development patterns that have been occurring along the Gulf Coast for the last century. When the French sited New Orleans in the early 18th century, they respected the Mississippi Delta's ecological constraints and settled on the highest ground behind the area's natural levees (Lewis 2003, Barry 1997). New Orleans thrived as a result of that wisdom. Later, outside forces, often at odds with natural systems, altered the developmental patterns of the region and the city (Lewis 2003). Taken together, contemporary and historical teachings could begin to light the path towards the creation of truly resilient and sustainable cities and regions.

Several million people currently live in coastal communities along the Gulf of Mexico, a 350 percent increase since the 1950s. At the same time we have been building homes, we have been destroying barrier islands, marshes, and wetlands that once served as natural buffers that absorbed the impact of high winds and storm surges. Every new hurricane that hits the Gulf Coast makes the problem even worse. Southeastern Louisiana lost more than 100 square miles of marsh because of Hurricane Katrina and Hurricane Rita, and the Chandeleur Islands lost more than half of their land mass as a result of Katrina.

The Mississippi River has been straightened, tributaries dammed, channels dredged, wetlands filled, areas that were originally part of the floodplain have been cut off, and hundreds of miles of levees, dikes, and pumps have been built in the region to accommodate development. Collectively these systems have

Fig. 1 Map showing paths of hurricanes that have hit the Gulf Coast since 1851.

changed the natural flow of water. Although they help protect some areas from flooding, they increase flooding in other areas. The impact on the natural process along the Gulf has been devastating.

As a result of environmental damage, the Gulf Coast is more exposed, and minor storms that had little impact 20 years ago, cause significant flooding today. Unless development patterns along the Gulf Coast change, this trend is going to continue, and future damages will continue to set records for level of destruction.

Context for Disaster

The devastation that resulted from Hurricane Katrina did not happen in a vacuum. The Gulf Coast megalopolis plays an important role in the national economy especially in the energy and trade sectors. For example, the Port of South Louisiana is the largest (in tonnage) US port and fifth in the world. It has annual exports of 52 million tons (corn, soybeans and wheat) and annual imports of 57 million tons (crude oil, chemicals, fertilizers, coal and concrete). Geopolitical analyst George Friedman offers a succinct summary: "a simple way to think about the New Orleans port complex is that it is where the bulk commodities of agriculture go out to the world and the bulk commodities of industrialism come in" (Friedman 2005, Steiner 2006).

Navigation channels and canals have had a significant impact on natural resources in the region. There are nine major shipping lanes and more than 13,000 kilometers of canals through Louisiana's marshes. They are directly responsible for up to 30% of the state's current wetland loss and indirectly

Fig. 2 Photograph showing the flooding that occurred in New Orleans after Hurricane Katrina.

responsible for even more because they have significantly changed the hydrology of the marsh (Zinn 2006). The Mississippi River Gulf Outlet, frequently referred to as Mister Go, was built to make it easier for large ships to access New Orleans. Unfortunately, one result is that freshwater marshes have turned brackish, and there have been massive die-offs of cypress trees as a result.

Despite the impacts of the navigation channels and canals, there are continuing efforts to expand these facilities. Proposals for port and navigation improvements along the Gulf Coast would cost an estimated $50 billion, but these improvements will have no impact on environmental sustainability or reducing the potential impacts of future hurricanes (Dickey 2005). The U.S. Army Corps of Engineers (Corps) is considering spending up to $14 billion on projects, where they were considering $1.1 billion for activities prior to the hurricanes (Zinn 2006). One question, though, is how to spend that money.

Everyone seems to agree that improving natural barriers is most important, and not just because of Hurricane Katrina. Louisiana alone contains 40% of the wetlands in the contiguous United States, yet accounts for 80% of wetland loss in the Lower 48 states. At this rate, even with current conservation projects under way, another 1800 to 4500 square kilometers will vanish under the Gulf in the next 50 years.The impact on public resources, including fisheries, wildlife habitat, navigation, flood control, and hurricane protection, has been estimated at more than $37 billion. Construction of massive levees that channel the Mississippi River, dredged canals and flood control structures, commercial and recreational boat traffic, forced drainage to accommodate development, and agriculture have all contributed to the wetlands deterioration and loss.

Louisiana's 3 million acres of wetlands have borne the brunt of human activity, population increases, and natural processes for decades. As the barrier islands disintegrate, the formerly sheltered wetlands are then filleted like fish, exposing the soft underbelly of their forests, marshes, and ecosystems to the full force of open marine processes such as wave action, wind, salinity intrusion, storm surge, tidal currents, and sediment transport, which then exponentially accelerate their demise. Critical for planners, landscape architects, and professionals in the industry of the built environment is the understanding of the life cycle of wetlands... they are not a stagnant land mass, and they will not automatically regenerate themselves like re-dividing cells; nor are they islands, or ruled by something as simple as the predictable tides alone. Models and studies showing how nature intended the barrier islands / wetlands system to work and protect will help design professionals to take our cue from nature as to the evolution of the system, rather than persisting in the engineering practices that have proven totally damaging and unsuccessful in the past. Geologic and coastal reparation input regarding models for mitigation strategies should be a part of any planning process in the Gulf Coast.

Impact of Demographic Change

In addition, the rebuilding of the coast is also having an impact the resources of the region. According to the US Census Bureau, after Hurricane Katrina nearly 300,000 people moved away from coastal areas between Texas and the Florida

Panhandle. The losses were most pronounced around New Orleans. The City lost half its population — about 229,000 people — between July 2005 and July 2006. Neighboring St. Bernard Parish lost three-quarters of its 65,000 residents (Heath, 2007). The area also lost many of its jobs. According to state Labor Department figures, metro New Orleans area also had 113,300 fewer non-farm jobs in June 2007 than in June 2005, two months before Hurricane Katrina hit the City (Dunbar 2007). Some people moved away from the region, but many moved to other towns, cities, and rural areas throughout the region. In the 22 coastal counties in Louisiana, Mississippi, Alabama, and Florida that were declared disaster areas by the federal government because of Katrina, population dropped by more than 10 percent virtually overnight. The rate of population growth doubled in nearby counties after Katrina (Heath, 2007). This hurricane diaspora has put tremendous pressures on communities as they try to accommodate this growth. Perhaps no other city was affected more by the hundreds of thousands of people who fled New Orleans after Katrina hit, than Baton Rouge. Within days, Baton Rouge, an inland city of 225,000, was an overwhelmed mass of about 500,000. Many evacuees were just passing through, but city officials say that today, Baton Rouge's population remains 275,000-325,000. Baton Rouge's population has reached the mark that pre-Katrina projections estimated for the year 2030. Government officials say their planning for a range of projects has had to be accelerated by up to a quarter-century (Johnson, 2007). In Baton Rouge, $5 billion in construction in 2008 and 2009 is much higher than past years for the Capital Region, and the 35,000 permanent residents gained after Katrina represented a 5 percent population growth, something that typically would take several years to mount, Scott said (Perilloux 2007). According to new Census Bureau state population estimates released at the end of 2007, the Gulf Coast region has rebounded, having gained 50,000 residents as of July 1. The estimates for July 1, 2006 were the first broad measure of the hurricane's impact on demographics in the region. After the storm hit in August 2005, the Bureau estimated the State lost 250,000 residents. Despite the most recent gain, the State is far from returning to its pre-Katrina population level of 4.5 million (Dunbar 2007). Absorbing many of the people who fled Katrina were places such as Tangipahoa Parish, La., northwest of New Orleans, where the population grew five times as fast in the year after the storm as in the year before. The 149 counties within 100 miles of the coastal area hit by Katrina added 270,000 people from mid-2005 to mid-2006, more than twice as many as the year before. Many parts of the Gulf Coast were inundated with a decade's worth of growth in a year, and that has resulted in significant impacts to schools, traffic, housing, and other aspects of urban and rural infrastructure. It is likely that some coastal communities, indeed parts of cities such as New Orleans, will decline or even disappear. This process may have already begun before the hurricanes, and it is clear that many residents will not return to some areas (Dickey 2005).

Planning for the Future

There has been no shortage of plans for restoring the Gulf Coast. Discussions of how to rebuild the Gulf Coast range from suggestions to just do it the way it was before, to more aggressive proposals that would take years to implement. For example, some proposals to restore coastal marshes and wetlands involve some combination of giant channels, valves, and sluice gates. One idea is to build a pipeline to carry 70 million cubic yards of silt to the coast, while another wants to divert one-third of the flow of the Mississippi River to start a new riverbed. Do we strengthen the levee system and build more levees, focus on restoring barrier islands and wetlands, or perhaps both? Can we design new communities that can withstand the impacts of hurricanes while still protecting our natural resources? Do we need to stop development along all or part of the Gulf Coast? Previous planning efforts have had mixed results. The 1972 environmental movement resulted in requirements that state governments develop comprehensive plans, and in the Gulf Coast region, these plans addressed specific requirements for coastal management. The State and Regional Planning Act of 1984 and the 1985 Omnibus Growth Management Act also were steps in the right direction in regards to addressing the impact of growth on natural resources. According to a report released by the National Research Council (NRC), we still have not stopped the loss of wetlands in America despite more than 20 years of progress in restoring and creating wetlands. According to the NRC, the contiguous United States has lost more than 50 percent of its wetlands since the 1780s. Even though 1.8 acres of wetlands were created or restored for every acre lost during the past eight years, the United States still lost wetlands. Section 404 of the U.S. Environmental Protection Agency's Clean Water Act requires those who want to discharge materials – such as soil or sand – into a wetland to get permission from the U.S. Army Corps of Engineers before doing so. It also requires individuals to provide "compensatory mitigation" – such as creating a wetland elsewhere – as a condition for issuing a permit (NRC, 2001). Are Section 404 of the Clean Water Act and other efforts having a positive impact on reducing the loss of wetlands, or are we just running out of wetlands? The answer to that is debatable, but it is obvious that our current efforts are not enough to help restore the kind of environmental balance that is needed to help stabilize the Gulf Coast region. One problem is that a lot of the created or restored wetlands are poorly constructed,

Fig. 3 Map showing Societal Risks along a section of the Gulf Coast. Societal Risks refers to the portion of the population that is the most vulnerable, such as those who live in poverty, over the age of 65 and under the age of 16, those without a car, etc.

Fig. 4 Map showing potential risk of storm surge along a section of the Gulf Coast.

and as a result they do not function as intended. Previous attempts to help the state's wetlands led to passage of the 1990 Coastal Wetlands Planning, Protection and Restoration Act, which was sponsored by Senator John Breaux (D-LA). The "Breaux Act" currently funnels about $40 million to $50 million annually into the state for wetlands restoration projects. Congress directed the Corps to develop options for a post-hurricane rebuilding plan called the Louisiana Coastal Protection and Restoration Plan. In this plan, announced in the March 3, 2006 Federal Register, the Corps identifies four combinations of structural and non-structural measures that would protect coastal Louisiana against a Category 5 storm. Central issues include (1) what role(s) would restoration projects play in such a plan, (2) how would restoration projects be integrated with structural measures, and (3) how could projects to protect the New Orleans urban area and to restore coastal Louisiana be most effectively integrated to minimize damage from future storm events (Zinn 2006).

The Coast 2050 Plan is one of the most recent and ambitious series of coastal management and restoration plans that have been proposed for the Gulf Coast. The Coast 2050 Plan, which was released in 1998, is led by the Corps. It provides recommendations for 77 "restoration strategies," to be completed over 50 years. The strategies would be distributed along the entire Louisiana coast, but is concentrated in the central coast. The anticipated result from fully implementing these strategies was to protect or restore almost 450,000 acres of wetlands (Zinn 2006). Under Coast 2050, Louisiana's barrier islands would be restored or maintained using the most cost-effective means. This would most likely include beach nourishment with dredged material combined with marsh creation projects on the bay side of the islands, although hard structures such as sea walls and groins are also being considered. But even under the best of circumstances, the array of projects in a complex program like Coast 2050 could not be completed for decades. In the aftermath of the 2005 hurricanes, the ecosystem restoration goals may be in competition with other demands for federal resources in coastal Louisiana. These demands include flood protection, economic development associated with navigation, and housing. However, the reality is that it may be too expensive to fully support all these goals at the same time. (Zinn 2006) Too often in the past, insufficient attention was paid to the interactions between engineering structures, which extensively modified hydrologic regimes, and the physical and biological environment. One result was that extensive engineering efforts for managing the Mississippi River and numerous large-scale coastal navigation and storm-damage reduction projects caused widespread, ongoing changes in wetlands and barrier island stability, some say magnifying the storm damages that were realized in the recent hurricanes. Many of these changes either were not foreseen or, if anticipated, were considered to be an acceptable cost of progress on other fronts (Dickey 2005). Some hurricane protection projects may have adverse effects on navigation access or on the coastal landscape. Restoration of the landscape in one area may claim river sediments that could have built land elsewhere in the coastal region. But there may also be project and program complementarities. A navigation channel may serve as an excellent conduit for moving sediment-laden water to areas where a wetlands restoration project is being proposed; in turn, that wetland area may help moderate storm surges and reduce storm damages (Dickey 2005).

A Sustainability Analysis Model

One approach is to strengthen the environmental resources that once provided a natural buffer from hurricanes, tropical storms, storm surges, flooding, and other natural disasters. 'What If?' the Louisiana and Mississippi wetlands had not been so depleted and maneuvered by coastal development that they could have provided more of the natural protection of the coastline they inherently provide if left on their own? What if we can restore these resources?

Being able to determine which areas are most likely to be impacted by hurricanes, storm surges, flooding, and other natural disasters will assist decision-makers in preparing for and minimizing their impacts. EDAW worked with the National Consortium to Map Ecological Constraints to develop a Sustainability. Analysis Model that can be used to map environmentally-sensitive areas of the Gulf Coast Region and to classify potential risks associated with natural disasters. This model, which takes a holistic approach founded on the idea of sustainable resilience, provides guidance for today's rebuilding and tomorrow's land development. EDAW is leading the effort, supported by a voluntary national advisory committee of geologists, landscape ecologists, transportation planners, urban designers, architects, landscape architects, water resource specialists, demographers and regional planners (Steiner 2006). EDAW's Sustainability Analysis Model integrates and expands the work being done from the Environmental Protection Agency (EPA), Federal Emergency Management Agency (FEMA), National Hurricane Center (NHC), National Oceanic & Atmospheric Administration (NOAA), NOAA Coastal Services Center (CSC), and Coastal Data Development Center (NCDDC). Among the factors being addressed in the process are historic hurricane tracks, high wind risk areas, storm surges, flooding, significant flooding events, rise in sea elevation, lose of wetlands, marshes, and barrier islands, economic impacts, demographic vulnerability, and growth patterns (Steiner 2006). By combining these factors into one comprehensive model, the resulting analysis can then be used to create public and private sector policies that reduce impacts from future hurricanes and severe storms.

One reason that Hurricane Katrina caused so much damage is that more than 10 million people currently live in coastal counties along the Gulf of Mexico. This is 3.5 times the population that lived there in the 1950s. Much of that growth occurred because of a lull in severe storms along the Gulf Coast over the last couple of decades. Another dimension of the random brutality of a major storm is the disproportional impact upon the human resource. Some members of society are more vulnerable than others. Even before Hurricane Katrina hit, Mississippi and Louisiana suffered from some of the highest poverty rates in the USA. High risk populations include a high percentage of people over the age of 65, single parents with children, people living in poverty or on public assistance, having no vehicle, living in rental units, or living in older structures build before 1970. These factors are combined to create a societal risk map using data from the Coastal Risk Atlas (CRA). CRA is a project operated by the NOAA Coastal Data Development Center (NCDDC) in collaboration with the NOAA Coastal Services Center (CSC). The CRA can be used to identify high-risk demographic areas, as well as those that are vulnerable to storm surge, flooding, and high winds (EDAW 2006). To forecast and track hurricanes and severe storms, mathematical models can be used to simulate the characteristics of a storm and the potential impacts it will cause. These include the Inland High Wind Model, which was developed by researchers at NOAA, and is used to estimate how far inland strong winds extend. This map is generated with FEMA's HAZUS-MH software. HAZUS-MH is a risk-assessment program from FEMA that is used to analyze potential losses from floods, hurricane winds, and earthquakes (EDAW 2006).

According to the 1989 Congress Report on Climate Change, 20 percent of the US coast, including the Gulf Coast, will be impacted by sea level rise. Scientists predict that in the next 50 to 100 years, we can expect the sea level to rise 21 inches to 44 inches. The EPA produces "Maps of Lands Vulnerable to Sea Level Rise on the Gulf Coast," which identifies areas in danger of being inundated. This map illustrates land along the coast that is below the 1.5-meter contour, and below the 3.5-meter contour, since these areas are the most likely to be impacted by a rise in sea level (EDAW 2006). Being able to predict storm surges along the Gulf Coast is critical. The greatest potential for loss of life related to a hurricane is from storm surges. One of the most common software packages used to model storm surges is Sea, Lake, and Overland Surges from Hurricanes (SLOSH), which was developed by the National Weather Service. The shallow coastal bathymetry along the Gulf Coast has a significant impact on storm surge potential. Currents and tides are controlled by the basins and ridges that make up this undersea terrain, so a thorough consideration of these maps is essential in any planning process (EDAW 2006). FEMA's Q3 floodplain maps indicate flood risks for a specific area based on local topology, hydrology, precipitation, and measures to provide flood protection. Q3 Flood Data product is designed to serve FEMA's Response and Recovery activities as well as to provide the foundation for flood insurance policy marketing initiatives. Many areas along the Gulf Coast, such as this section of the Florida Panhandle, are susceptible to flooding in low-lying areas (EDAW, 2006).

The goal is not to create science, but to employ data-driven environmental analysis to minimize future loss of life and property and protect public health, safety, and welfare. With all of the available data, the key is to assess the data and determine how it should influence decisions about rebuilding a sustainable Gulf Coast.

Littoral machines

How Waterfronts become Coasts

~ **Matthew Bradbury** ~ Senior Lecturer Landscape Architecture, Unitec

Institute of Technology ~ **Frank de Graaf** ~ Consultant DHV ~ New Zealand

Introduction

Waterfronts are one of the most important urban developments in the last 30 years. Transforming the 19th century port infrastructure of the European and American city into a new urban topography of personal consumption has developed into a global model of urban development, the generic 'port town' that Rem Koolhaas so accurately skewers (Koolhaas 1995). This paper argues that we need to change the present model of waterfront development, from the generic, to a new understanding of the waterfront as a site of dynamic landscape forces, both urban and ecological. The authors, an academic and landscape architect in New Zealand and a practicing urban planner in the Netherlands, explore the implications of this idea and use several design case studies in Holland, New Zealand, and PR China to illustrate this proposition. The authors start by 'renaming' the waterfront as a littoral, the biogeographic region between the sublittoral zone and the high-water line and sometimes including the supralittoral zone above the high water line.

The implications of this new definition for urban waterfronts is that they can no longer be seen as narrowly defined terrestrial margins, but rather fluid zones, subject to forces and circumstances, often the result of specific landscape conditions, deep in the hinterland or sea. The littoral is the zone in which these forces are most actively engaged. We argue that the future for the contemporary waterfront lies with this rethinking, the opening up of new design possibilities through an understanding and privileging of the different hydrological forces at work in the littoral zone. For this reason we have named this region a 'machine', a device that applies force, changes the direction of a force, or changes the strength of a force, in order to perform a task. We like the idea of this edge being more than a passive zone, which simply receives the dictates of real-estate demand or engineering calculations. The concept of treating the waterfront, and by extension the city, as a landscape is generated by the idea of Landscape Urbanism (Waldheim, Charles. ed. 2006). Landscape Urbanism (LU) is a conceptual framework that uses the landscape to organise urban conditions, rather than architecture. Some of its most important and useful concepts are derived from landscape ecology. This body of work posits that we are all living in a constantly moving environment of many open-ended networks. These networks encompass both the environmental, such as, water flows and plant and species diffusion, and the social, such as human movement systems. LU offers a new way of critiquing the city; LU reconceptualizes the city as network system with non-particular inputs and outputs, a system in which we can observe the potential interaction of other systems. Since this hybrid ecology is not fixed and is always changing, the designer's role is to expose network systems, to encourage and activate environmental systems that are often elided by the development and to suggest new social systems that combine social and environmental goals. The materiality of these systems can be visualised by specific computer software such as GIS, which can both map existing systems and model future possibilities.

Waterfront reinvention continues to be an important part of the redevelopment of many cities around the world. Our paper offers examples of waterfronts that are being specifically transformed by an understanding of different hydrological conditions. The paper offers a technique, GIS mapping, as a way of both understanding existing landscape and urban conditions and representing design strategies. The implication of this work for landscape architects, designers and planners are particularly important when seen in context of global sea level rise. Rethinking the waterfront as an evolving landscape system, rather than a static urban ensemble helps designers to see sea level rise as part of the changing ecology of the city and helps suggests dynamic landscape procedures to allow for these changes.

The author's look at four different water conditions, freshwater, salt water stormwater, and brackish water, and examine the implications, when these elements intersect with contemporary urban development. The authors explore the implications of these hydrological systems by looking at a number of case studies. The first looks at Holland, a country whose terrestrial integrity is generated by the relationship between water conditions. The next study looks at a waterfront development in Auckland, New Zealand. This design examines techniques for re-conceptualizing an urban waterfront as a landscape, and then looks at a specific problem, the provision of a stormwater wetland/public park on the waterfront. The third study is a new city development in the Bohai Delta, PR China. This design deals with the huge water problems, both with fresh and salt water, caused by the rapid urbanization of North China.

Holland

Holland is located on one of Europe's largest river deltas. The natural supply of fresh water within this coastal region presented an opportunity for the Netherlands to manage the fresh water countryside within artificial coastal barriers. Over many years, the Dutch have developed a fresh water economy based on a polder system, new land which is located 5 meters below sea level. Living below the sea level has meant the provision of a strong coastal defense system to keep the salt water out, to prevent flooding and environmental damage. However a contemporary belief in a more sustainable natural coast is changing the Dutch approach towards urban planning and water management. The traditional 'hard' engineered environment is now changing into one that is more attuned to environment and ecological processes within the river delta. The result of this new thinking has lead to 'water transparency', a change within the coastal zone, from a strongly defined division between fresh and salt-water areas, into a situation of more ecological diversity. A different water management strategy is changing part of the Dutch context into a more natural European river delta. A brackish water zone, managed between the tidal sea and fresh water polders and rivers is part of a new thinking about coastal barrier systems. This has lead to new waterfront development, with cleaner tidal water systems and an inland salt-water fishing industry. The more naturally managed water system contributes to both a diversification of ecological systems and a new urban environment.

Afsluitdike – Holland

The Afsluitdike is an example of a coastal dike that closed down the IJsselmeer Lake from the sea and made a direct separation between a fresh/salt water system. The fresh water lake is now part of a water system that can buffer and support rural activities. The old coastal dikes that surrounded the lake are being transformed into polder dikes, which will sustain a more urban openness towards the water. This is possible because the coastal dikes are higher and more stable and able manage high waters, waves and high tides. Enclosing the lake, 1927-1933 was a strategic decision that changed the regional water environment. Not only the water quality was affected, but also the urban waterfront and port of Amsterdam that now faced the new lake instead of the open sea.

Bergen Op Zoom – Holland

Bergen Op Zoom is an example of a historical coastal city that has changed into a fresh water city because of the Oesterdam construction. The city water-

Closing the Afsluitdike, Holland, 1932.

front is now facing the river, and is not affected by tides, or connection from the port of Rotterdam to Antwerp. However the city is now returning to salt water based urban waterfront. The reason, because fresh water is harder to manage, for example it is liable for algae blooms, which affect the water quality and the adjacent urban water activities (www.bergsehaven.nl/).

The urban and landscape development of the Netherlands has been driven by a clear desire to separate salt water and fresh water systems. These two projects start to demonstrate what urban and landscape implications are generated by water management strategies. Brackish water zones, mixtures of salt and fresh water, instead of strong separated water systems, have a strong functional value. These zones are supplied by tidal sea and fresh water systems and protect the land against high seas and big waves. Examples of the infrastructure of these water systems are for instance, the `Oosterschelde Kering` a transparent dam that can protect (be closed) and minimize the environmental effect of the brackish water zone, coastal ecology and existing water systems. The economical value of ports and waterways can also be managed and protected. The innovative coastal barrier at Rotterdam (Maeslantkering) is another example how urban river deltas can be protected, two gigantic arms close the whole river from storm surges. Modern techniques and engineering solutions can contribute to integrated planning and sustainable ecological river deltas.

Auckland – New Zealand

Auckland, New Zealand's largest city is located on an isthmus between two harbours, the Manukau and Waitamata. The centre of Auckland is situated on the southern side of the Waitamata harbour. The Central Business District (CBD) is located around the central street of Auckland, Queen Street. Queen Street lies in a valley, a typical feature of the topography of this area, which is made up of a series of undulating bays and headlands, connected to ridges and gullies running from north to south (Bush, 1971). Queen Street runs north to the harbour. Auckland's waterfront can be divided into roughly two parts: to the west, a mix of marinas, ships industry, and storage facilities; to the east, the extensive wharf infrastructure of a modern working port. Like many waterfront cities in the world, Auckland is experiencing the slow but sure transformation of a heavily industrialised and polluted harbour into a lifestyle zone of apartments and marinas. It is in the centre of the waterfront, in the lower Queen Street area, that new, non-port developments have begun. The first of these was the development of Princes Wharf in the early 1990s. The overseas terminal and port warehouses were converted to an apartment and hotel complex. To the west of this wharf the fishing boat harbour was located. The second waterfront development was the transformation of this area into the Viaduct Basin, a complex of apartments, restaurants and bars. Future plans for the Auckland waterfront confirm the west/east separation on the Queen Street axis. Port development and activities are to continue to the east, while a new waterfront of apartments and offices is planned to gradually occupy the western part of the waterfront. However, the Auckland waterfront is a highly contaminated landscape. Untreated and heavily polluted stormwater enters the Waitamata from the three catchment areas of the

CBD: Freeman's Bay, Queen Street and Parnell. After heavy rainfalls, highly visible and toxic plumes can be clearly seen from in the harbour. There are also areas of major site contamination. The most polluted areas are the petro-chemical contamination of the Tank farm, an area within the Western Reclamation. The other major site contamination is polluted marine sediment, the legacy of over one hundred years of antifouling and other ship industry detritus. The contemporary Auckland waterfront presents a number of issues; the transformation of an industrial marine environment, the requirements of real estate development, the public desire for genuine public space, and the necessity for a remedial environmental infrastructure. The author has developed a design project, which starts to address these disparate issues by avoiding contemporary urban design solutions, such a the use of 19th century street and square configurations. Instead, the project starts by reconceptualizing the Auckland's waterfront as a landscape. To rethink the waterfront as a landscape necessitated an analysis of the existing topography of the CBD and Port. The project found three landscapes: the first is the existing landscape of ridges, valleys, and the reclaimed land of the waterfront infrastructure; the second is the hydrological landscape of freshwater, stormwater, and saltwater, governed by tidal movement and rainfall; the third is the historical landscape of native ecotones (Morton Ewen 1993). To make these landscapes visible, necessitated finding a way to represent them, their possible manifestations and any congruencies with environmental operations. Using a GIS programme, ArcView, the project redrew the Auckland waterfront as topography, both terrestrial and submarine. This analysis revealed a fundamentally different view of the city than that revealed by conventional urban design analysis

Wynyard Point Park – New Zealand

This is a large reclaimed industrial site, occupied by a tank farm, a collection of large industrial tanks used mainly for storing petrochemicals. The ground under this area is heavily contaminated. This quarter is gradually being redeveloped as an urban waterfront. Peter Walker and Associates designed the first master plan. They proposed the extension of the existing grid with two major axis, a north/south line, which linked the site to Victoria Park, and an east/west line, which links the redevelopment with the Auckland CBD. A new city park was proposed at the end of northern axis. The Wynyard Point Park project starts by carefully considering the serious environmental issues that are present on this site, notably the heavily contaminated ground under the tanks, and the presence of a major stormwater outfall from the Freemans Bay catchment. The question the project posed was: is it possible to clean the contaminated stormwater, remove the contaminated soil on the site, and make an enjoyable and useful public space at the end of Wynyard Point? The use of constructed wetlands for stormwater treatment was explored (Dickenson 2004). A well-established model for stormwater treatment in Auckland subdivisions, was established (Shaver 2000), we experimented with enlarging this model to an urban scale. A process was established were the functional requirements of the wetlands intersect with the termination of the various Tank farm leases. As the leases come up, the contaminated soil is removed and stockpiled. The excavated sites are stabilised and stormwater from the Freemans Bay catchment is gradually diverted into the first of the receiving ponds. Wetland planting starts to be established, gradually as the leases terminates, greater and greater areas of land are freed up. As the physical requirements for the treatment capacity of the Freemans Bay catchment stormwater exceed the amount of land available, the investigation explored ways to increase the receiving pond area. We investigated using the excavated contaminated fill, stabilised with concrete, to form new reclamations, making in effect, a new landscape. Faced with the functional requirement of different pond sizes and the establishment of a new topography to accommodate the wetland structure, the project began to transform the existing reclaimed landscape at the end of the Wynyard Point. From an industrial apron, protected from tidal movement, the site was transformed into a more fluid world, caught between the fluctuating tides and seasonal rainfalls. Topography and plant species are adjusted and modified for this new, fluvial landscape. A social programme is gently inserted into this new topography. The typical urban typology for Aucklanders is not the street or square, but the more relaxed zones of beach and bay, informal intersections of land and sea, swimming, sailing, sun bathing, bbq, and football. Informal and fluid transects, where activities match topography.

With the gradual cleaning of the polluted stormwater, the social topography of the wetlands also changes, becoming more relaxed and convivial. From a relatively hard urban quality nearest the apartments, the landscape changes to a freshwater marsh, then finally a new urban beach, as the fresh water meets the salt.

PR China – The Bohai Coast Development.

China's rapid urban and architectural development is leading towards an ecological conflict within the regional coastal zone. The coastal area of North China is vulnerable to the need for urban and industrial fresh water and the threat of the rising sea level (www.giwa.net /areas/reports/r34/causal_chain34b_ giwa_ r34.pdf).

Existing rivers are drying out because water is claimed by cities and industries. Ground water is being exploited for agricultural use, and many water systems are also being polluted by rapid development. This process is developing towards a water crisis if the citizens don't change their present development-driven water policies. New sustainable urban-engineered development strategies in North China could contribute towards a better global environment for people and wildlife. Landscape architects and urban planners have a great responsibility to plan and sustain future urban ecological developments. There should be a focus on avoiding water conflict, by creating urban environments in harmony with there surrounding. A new urban water perspective is needed for planners and architects to sustain the global environment, by starting with sustainable water systems in the coastal zone.

The Bohai Delta, located in North China, is one of the areas where urban development is booming. In Tianjin, urban expansion and the deep-sea port are creating opportunities for local and regional economies. The redevelopment is rapidly spreading along the coastal region.

We have learned in Holland that water management is a major part of coastal development. A strong knowledge of different water conditions is required to manage and sustain new urban development. In the case of the regional development of Tianjin, we start with a perspective informed by this knowledge to find the right strategy for urban development. Safety, ecology, identity, economy are the key points for urban water management, creating value for city development. The coastal development of the Bohai Delta is located in a river delta and requires a strong coastal defense system to prevent flooding (www.unep.org/dewa /giwa/areas/reports/r34/regional_definition34b_giwa_r34.pdf). We have learnt from Dutch examples that a flexible coastal defense system, where salt and fresh water can mix, will have less negative effect on the natural ecology and environment. Some of the critical issues that face this project are: dehydration of the rivers and the rising global sea level that will increase the penetration of seawater inland. A strong coastal border can stop the movement of salt water but create water quality problems. Clean salt water is easier to manage than the scarce fresh water. A higher water quality could generate a higher urban waterfront value because of the many water recreational activities. One of the tasks within the Bohai Coastal area is to keep the salt water clean and on the move. The tidal differences of the coast are an opportunity to flush and generate clean water. Sustainable environments control the fluctuation of the water within the dikes. Less fluctuation means more integration of land and water. People then are able to approach the waters edge. Ecological development on a coast which lacks fresh water like the Bohai Delta is a difficult question. Strategically planned fresh water areas within high-density urban zones that are directly accessible to the public are critical in any development. Fresh water is a life source for the city and surrounding rural areas. Sustainable technologies, to reduce fresh water consumption, fresh water collection and treatment are probably not enough to meet

Tianjin Coastal Development.

the rising water consumption within the developing coastal delta. Most of the fresh water problems in the delta are caused by the unsustainable rapid development occurring upstream. A water management strategy should help designers to challenge the Delta development in China. Urban planners and landscape architects are on the frontier of design development, they have the opportunity to contribute to a better living environment. Designers should not only focus on the water issues within the coastal zone but more efficient water management development on a national level. An urban water plan could generate new perspectives of waterfronts, ecological and sustainable development for a better living environment.

Tianjin Binhai Tourism Service Area – Delta Diamonds, PR China

Tianjin is a city of 10 million inhabitants located 250 km from Beijing and 50 km from the Bohai Sea. The Port of Tianjin is located to the west of Bohai Bay and in the estuary of the Heihe River. It is 170 km south east of Beijing and east of Tianjin City. It is the largest man made seaport and river port in Mainland China. TEDA (Tianjin Economic Development Area) is built around the port. The Bohai Sea is a delta region, heavily polluted, a very salty and shallow water body with a 4.5 m tidal difference. The supply of fresh water is slight, coming from both river outfall and rainfall. North of the Port is the TEDA area of urban expansion. One of the development projects is 42 square kilometre reclamation: the Delta Diamonds project, a competition entry by DHV and partners. The concept is to develop a land reclamation based on the natural morphology of a delta, the rivers, lakes, islands and waterfronts and the presence of different kinds of water; fresh and salt. The design principle is pragmatic, based on Dutch land and water reclamation practice. The first move is to control the seawater by building a sea defence enclosure dam, separating sheltered enclosed saltwater from the saltwater in the bay. The dam is similar to a Dutch dike. The land level within the dike can thus be significantly lower. The supply of fresh water is achieved by storing rainfall underground in a fresh water lens above the saltwater ground table. The water supply is topped up by run off from houses, roads and industry, after suitable filtration. The reclamation is configured as islands, separated by saltwater 'rivers' that are controlled by sluices in the perimeter dikes. The final urban form is almost like an inside-out city: the perimeter is a dike, inside, a series of islands are surrounded by saltwater bays. The exterior waterfront is protected against the tidal range by a saltwater landscape, a wetland garden. The waterfront conditions inside the dike ring are much more varied, with a controlled tidal level. There is great variety of urban edge conditions, park, marina, promenade, road, housing, and civic buildings. This construction strategy has the possibility of engendering a different urban character to each of the different islands.

Conclusion

By privileging water based infrastructure systems, we have shown an understanding of the ecological operation of a coast that can transform a waterfront. Exploiting environmental systems, such as wetlands, can enhance coastal storm protection infrastructure. It is possible to create new urban configurations without falling into conflict with the ecological water environment. Acknowledgment of changing water systems through global warming can be made. Waterfront development can be related to water typology and networks. Sustainable urban and agricultural fresh water systems can be co-jointly developed. An urban ecology can be developed based on water networks. Urban typologies can be developed based on local conditions and systems.

In this paper we have shown that water infrastructure can be the main ecological, environmental and urban drivers within a coastal zone. A better understanding of water systems will not only provide more sustainable developments but also opportunities to create more dynamic and responsive waterfronts. Clean water and water control will generate a different kind of waterfront than the one we have become used to over the past 20 years. It is a waterfront that is located within its own particular world, its ecology, and environment. By engaging with the particularities of the site, designers can avoid the generic, and engage with the making of new and unique urban conditions. Through an understanding of these systems and networks, landscape architects, architects, designers, and planners can develop new design models for waterfront development which transform waterfronts into responsive ecologies.

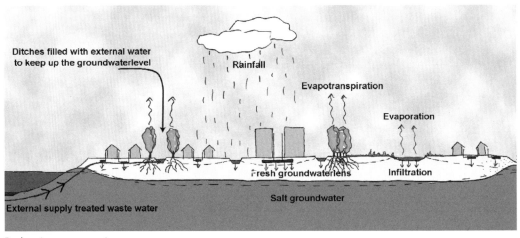

Fresh water management

Venice is not a modern city

~ Jorg Sieweke ~ Landscape architect and urban designer, Ass. Professor, TU Berlin, Germany ~ Co author: **Anna Viader** ~ Landscape Architect and Architect, Berlin

Introduction

The genealogy of Venice can be understood as a role model of cultural adoption processes to water-bound conditions. The successful integrative system of Venice was based on its local setting in the lagoon. In the past century it was struck by the measures of scale and speed imposed by modernism. Venice lost its ability of further adoptions of culture to the local requirements. Today its success is reduced to a kitsch spectacle based on mass-tourism gazing on a drowning empire. Venice was a laboratory of civilization; by what means can it be reinvented?

A nonlinear history

Venice was conceived as a detached entity, fitting perfect in its time and environment. The entire structure of the archipelago is consequently modeled along pre-modern conditions. Within the process of founding Venice a number of brilliant solutions were invented to make the impossible location hospitable. Due to sparse resources most infrastructural requirements were tight fit. For example rainwater was collected on the campi and stored in cisterns below, serving the appropriate sweet-water supply quantity to the residents of the neighborhood. The network of this underground invisible water system has determining the size and scale of the urban fabric.

Transport was organized water bound. The urban system was optimized and integrated to the needs of the time within a local and regional scale and pace. The decentralized structure made the city independent. Independence was the key to success. Transport was largely by water therefore the archipelago was accessible and also protected by the lagoon from the sea.

Critical functions like graveyards and industry of the time were outsourced to neighboring islands in the lagoon. Venice adapted perfectly to the ecology of the lagoon in terms of trade, defense and representation. It was taking advantage out of its territorial condition. This made the city a symbol of proud representation of a culture going along with the natural system.

Modifying the geomorphology delta, sea or lagoon

The specific territorial location of Venice at the mouth of three rivers, the Brenta, Sile, and Piave, exposed it to the dynamic natural processes in a geological scale. During the time of the early settlement the lagoon had a tendency to become a delta with the river mouths silting up the the lagoon that became more shallow year by year. The rivers were redirected already in the 16th century to avoid the basin becoming part of terra firma.

Today the lagoon is facing a reverse threat; it is endangered to become part of the sea. The largest measure proposed today is the flood barrier project to save Venice from sinking. The entire lagoon is meant to be taken under technical regime and control of M.O.S.E. It is in doubt if this strategy may succeed in the long run. The technical mega-structure wants to impose a flood control on the entire lagoon. The consequences of the impact cannot be foreseen yet. Dynamic feedback loop of the lagoons hydraulic ecology can only be predicted and have been subject of surprise before.

Infrastructure

In pre-modern times the lagoon itself was utilized for infrastructural purposes. It was providing transportation and defense and many other means. In modern times the railways and roads based transportation represented accelerated networks of traffic and trade. The frequency of people and goods increased significantly. Venice was still bound by water, bound no longer in the sense of being supported, but in the sense of being delayed by it. It became too slow; its detached structure did not allow to incorporate modern infrastructure systems. Venice could not speed up. The splendid isolation resulted in a strangled isolation.

Modernism imposed Venice to be connected to its accelerated terms. Very late a bridge/dam finally linked the city to terra firma like a protheses. The archipelago is attached to the centralized infrastructure systems of traffic and supply today. The harbor was relocated to Marghera leaving the lagoon city behind. The ferry terminal welcomes the largest cruise ships like the Queen Elisabeth II. Digging deep navigation channels brings another massive measure to the aquatic system resulting in further sinking of the ground the city is founded on. In order to accommodate the demands of acceleration and centralization massive interventions were imposed neglecting the geological setting. Drinking water could not be provided for the large demand of tourists by the traditional cistern rainwater system. Therefore groundwater was pumped out of the aquifer beneath the city. As a result approximately half of the sinking rate of the territory in the past 50 years is a long-term man-made side effect of exploiting the aquifer. Venice is not only threatened by the rising water level but by physical drowning of the territory itself. Therefore aqua alta is not an outside condition, but a direct result of misreading and mismanaging the lagoons hydraulic system.

Nostalgia of a static artefact

Venice forgot about its own concept: Although founded on unstable ground, the culture of the city was always embracing nature and the sea. The Marcus Square located at the canal front is an iconic and symbolic gesture of a city facing and living with the water. The predominant cultural ritual is the cities annual espousal with the sea. The traditional ceremony represents an understanding of treating the water in harmony and respect instead of dominating and forcing it.

"Venice is born from the sea; at the same time Venice is a wonderful expression of human creativity.

Although it is committed to the water it is a product of human fantasy, inventiveness and determinedness. Venice is the utmost expression of our capabilities and vulnerability."?

The city was located within the regime of the lagoon. Living in Venice was bound to a continuous process of adoption to the changing cities necessities towards the lagoons requirements and limitations.

Paradigm shift

Today the city is a static cultural artefact that is not able to adapt to changes of its environment anymore. Raising water level, sinking ground level and bad water quality are turning the lagoon to hostile setting that endangers the cities further existence. The cliché image of Venice is cloned several times in the world: Las Vegas, Los Angeles, Dubai and China. Venice is understood as an image, not as an emerging cultural-natural system.

The more successful the image of the city was the more the lagoon -the immediate local environment has been neglected and rendered invisible. The success of exporting the image of the lagoon city destroyed the elaborated resilient system the city emerged of.

The predominant idea of adapting cultural systems to the natural regime and resources reversed to a technical regime that is taking control over the natural system of the lagoon in order to freeze a cultural state of nostalgia. In terms of a future development we may ask: „Is this what Venice is about? Would it not be more promising to understand and reflect the long tradition of symbiotic conditions of culture and nature in the lagoon city?

Venice reached a bifurcation point. Venice will either drown or must reinvent itself. Most residents already left the island behind to leave it to the faith of mass-tourism. This raises the question to our concept of modern culture today. Modernism should be reflexive as Ulrich Beck suggests, understanding the consequences of each measure taken. Cultural heritage should not be considered in the sense of a static nostalgic postcard, but as a pool of references based on the ingenuity of sophisticated pre-modern techniques and strategies (see also: Reflexive Modernisierung (2007) Ulrich Beck, Anthony Giddens, Scott Lasch, Suhrkamp, re-print).

Redefining measures of control to measures of negotiation and adaptation

Since Venice will not win the race of catching up with other regions in terms of late-fordism modernism, it might be better of to reconsider its local condition and immediate environment. It seems like an old person, trying to run without having ever practiced it before. The lagoons water and marshland condition can no longer be neglected. If trade and defense were the advantageous requirements in the beginning, what might be the contemporary condition of a water bound civilization? "Venice has been punished in contemporary time, it was struck by modernism. The city could not reinvent itself since it never was a modern city. Venice is limited by old bonds but challenged by new constrains." (Mayor Massimo Cacciari in MARE: No. 18 Venedig/ Venice (2000) Interview by Thomas Schmid).

The urban structure of Venice is not laid out to carry a centralized infrastructural system. Centralized systems are hierarchic and static in their layout, they either function well in their logic of dimension and hierarchy but they must fail in the next adoption process. In order to succeed as a knot in a postmodern global network of city regions Venice must respect the limitation of its local environment again. Future concepts should re-engage measures of decentralization, deceleration, diversification instead of measures that impose control and dominance (Fig 1).
We are interested in developing an understanding of nurturing the lagoon as a

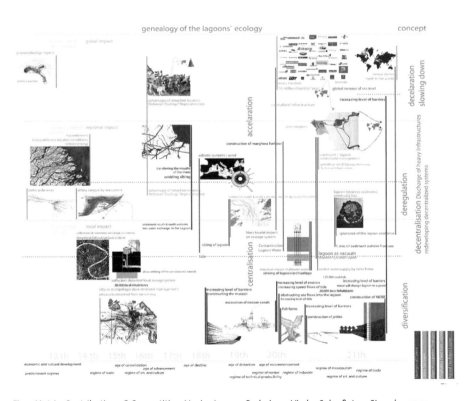

Fig. 1 Matrix; Contribution 2G Competition. Venice Lagoon Park. Anna Viader Soler & Jorg Sieweke. 2007

park. The lagoon itself is the outcome of larger forces of natural dynamics. We are interested in understanding these forces and their physical expression in the dynamic system of the lagoon. Wind, currents, sedimentation rates, temperature – in water and in air, change during the course of the seasons (Fig. 2). Mapping the complex system of the lagoon can identify a variety of locations with specific ecological parameters and comfort zones.

Proposals

The projects leave the city of Venice to the tourists and establish a new dimension of being Venetian: developing modes of operating with and not against the natural order of the lagoon.

The proposals suggest a network of attractive milieus based on decentralized, decelerated infrastructure. The identified comfortable conditions can be utilized as potential recreation spots. Heavy industry in the lagoon, mass-commute, precarious condition of the canals; all these impacts of the city cannot be solved by measures of control in the usual modernist manner but have to be negotiated and refined by understanding the fluid condition. Venice may rise again in the postmodern age. The coming era of post-fordism (after mass production) might be the second renaissance of Venice. It may return to cultural and natural values that might be established easier in the information age. The lagoon has been too slow; now going slow is no longer a failure but the target to become Venetian again.

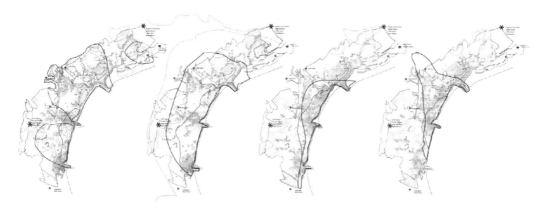

Fig. 2 Four Seasons; Contribution 2G Competition. Venice Lagoon Park. Anna Viader Soler & Jorg Sieweke. 2007

Park near Fusina

Through the superposition of a new accessibility system at the marshland near Fusina, the influence of nature processes can be identified as foreground for the development of the project. With the strategic position of only some new objects, the reading of the place and the understanding of its changing condition will be perceptible. The design of the Park takes on a minimum of design measures. Concrete footways, some kilometres long, enable to enjoy the diversity of this environment at the south of the future Fusina Terminal. The "Micro topography" profile of the ways appears and disappears with time. The, at first glance homogeneous and undifferentiated, landscape converts in a quiet but variable surrounding soon. Within the infinity of this vast landscape every little detail becomes significant. An effort is required to appreciate this quality and the precision to keep an eye on any small change. It implies a deceleration of the everyday life, getting used to a different speed of the site. This intervention means a new response about the sensitization within the Lagoon landscape. (Fig 3)

Archipelago ex poveglia.

Nowadays, some of the smallest islands of Venice Lagoon are being reconstructed in their original form. They were once important strategically positioned defence points that now became completely obsolete. Some of these islands are disappearing recently, because of the stronger currents from the sea and because of a lack of maintenance. Near the "Malamocco Port" we find three of these islands: Podo, Ex Poveglia and Fisolo. The first one and the third one are not real-

Fig. 3 Norman Harzer & Claudia Köllner. Student work. WS0708 TU Dresden. Institut für Landschaftsarchitektur. Professur für Landschaftsarchitektur. Prof. Ch. Schonhoff. Assistant: Anna Viader Soler

ly recognizable anymore and will withdraw shortly. The proposal for a new treatment for Ex Poveglia suggests a reflection in how to deal with historical heritage through new approaches.

On a bigger scale, bringing new uses to places that have become "peripheral" means a decentralisation within the Lagoon. Moreover it focuses an alternative offer for leisure uses. Slowing down. Like the tentacles from a Medusa, the existing island Ex Poveglia, will be surrounded by a new archipelago. The island will not be reconstructed one to one as it was before. The existing will be protected, but also transformed by new accesses. The former topography of defence remains in its actual "deformation" as one of the highest points in the Lagoon. The vegetation grown up in the past years means also a potential for a further process. Static and dynamic elements (Marina, floating island and "new land") are the stimulating forces for the development and protection beginning at the Ex Poveglia Archipelago. (Fig 4)

Fog Catchers

Fogcatchers are proposed: these re-introduce a decentralized infrastructure prototype, namely to collect sweet water as an autarkic natural resource. Meshes of high-density polyethylene take accumulated water drops out of the fog. The Fog Catchers are located on the sandbanks and salt marshes and can collect significant amounts of drinking water. The water is collected in catchments canals on the ground and stored in cisterns. On foggy days and nights they may collect 4-15 Liters per square meter mesh.

Fig. 4 Tobias Gellert. Student work. WS0708 TU Dresden. Institut für Landschaftsarchitektur. Professur für Landschaftsarchitektur. Prof. Ch. Schonhoff. Assistant: Anna Viader Soler.

Community Design around Kobe City to live with Water

~ **Mayumi Hayashi** ~ Associate Professor, University of Hyogo, Japan

Kobe is a city in Hyogo Prefecture, which lies in western Japan near both Kyoto and Osaka. The Great Hanshin Awaji Earthquake struck this area in 1995, killing more than 6400 people in Kobe and neighboring cities. Kobe is a city with the Rokko Mountains to the north and the sea to the south. The water that flows from there is used for drinking and daily use. After the Great Hanshin Awaji Earthquake, with the cooperation of the national government, Hyogo Prefecture, Kobe and other cities, a Green Belt Strategy was planned to comprehensively manage sand defense dams, forestation, forest recreation and ecological conservation.

In the urban area, along with projects that deal with cleaning rivers, artificial streams and biotopes were made on neigborhood community level. Many of these projects have been conducted with citizen participation, and I have been involved in a number of them.

Finally, for the seashore, we are discussing the view of the new waterfront, including the view from the mountain and the view from the seaside. In particular, community design using historical warehouses is being promoted to create an important landscape point along the seashore. The artificial stream from Matsumoto flows into the nearby Hyogo Canal. The canal has been restored with cleaner water, and it now hosts a canoe regatta competition. We are conducting community design in many places dealing with water through cooperation between citizens and governments.

Fig. 1 Map of Japan (Google Map).

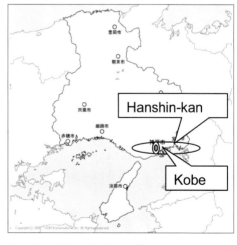

Fig. 2 Map of Hyogo Prefecture (Google Map).

Introduction

The city Kobe is in Hyogo Prefecture, which lies in western Japan near Kyoto and Osaka. The city lies with the Rokko Mountains to the north and the Seto Inland Sea to the south. The eastern part of Kobe and the cities to its east, including Ashiya and Amagasaki, are collectively known as the Hanshin-Kan area. This area with its abundant greenery is one of the most popular residential areas in western Japan. Kobe is a large city with 1.3 million people and is a government ordinance-designated city (Fig.1 & 2).

In this paper, I analyzed the process of reconstruction of the Hanshin-Kan area, which has rich water resources, after the 1995 Hanshin Awaji Earthquake. While introducing projects that I have been involved in, I consider the meaning of water and waterfront areas in Kobe and the Hanshin-Kan region.
Rivers pass through the Hanshin-Kan area from the mountains in the north to the seashore in the south. The water that flows from the Rokko Mountains supplies drinking water and water for other daily uses. Springs from underground rivers also provide clean water that benefits the Japanese sake makers in the area. In addition, the rivers offer beautiful scenery and places for recreation. On the other hand, because of the steep slopes, serious tragedies have occurred, including floods from heavy rains and landslides from earthquakes. For these reasons, many dams to prevent erosion and other water control measures have been built in the mountains.

The Earthquake and Renewed Recognition of the Blessings of Water

This Great Hanshin-Awaji Earthquake struck the Hanshin-Kan area and neighboring cities in 1995, killing more than 6400 people. The earthquake occurred on January 17 in the middle of the cold winter, and many people lost their homes and had to seek shelter.

Fig. 3 Earthquake damage (Mainichi newspaper publishing company, 1995).

Fig.4 Earthquake damage (Mainichi newspaper publishing company, 1995).

Fig.5 Earthquake damage (Mainichi newspaper publishing company, 1995).

The traffic was paralyzed and people could not use communication tools or get enough food (Fig.3-5). The Earthquake not only robbed many people of their lives, it also destroyed the foundations for the lives of the survivors, including the roads and the supplies of electricity, gas and water. Reconstruction of the cities was necessary, and people waited several months to return to their usual lifestyles. Waterfront areas also suffered significant damages. Immediately after the earthquake, citizens realized the blessings of water and greenery again. Rivers were important for getting water for daily use and spring water was used for drinking. Many people have said that they felt consoled by the green of the mountains and at waterfronts by rivers and the seaside. I personally went to the riverside to get water for daily life and drew water from wells (Fig.6).

The Rokko Mountain Green Belt Concept and the Eco Road Network of Water and Greenery

The conservation of green areas and slopes on Rokko Mountain, where landslides and other great damage had occurred, were reexamined. As a result, after the Great Hanshin Awaji Earthquake, a green belt was planned through cooperation among the governments of Hyogo Prefecture, Kobe and other cities, as well as the national government, to manage erosion prevention dams, conduct reforestation, and promote forest recreation and ecological conservation comprehensively (Fig.7). As a result, at Rokko Mountain, efforts have been made for mountain management and the reconstruction of rivers, as well as the design of disaster-resistant communities. I managed workshops in Ashiya City, which is to the east of Kobe, to consider what types of disaster prevention are suitable and how

Fig.6 Rokko Mountain.

to conserve rivers and mountains as good places for the recreation of residents and the environmental education of children. We delivered the conclusions of these workshops as a proposal to the national government and the city council. In this proposal, we divided the area at the foot of the mountains in Ashiya into four zones and considered construction and management in each of them. These zones include the entrance zone from the urban area, a zone that has historical sites, the Koza waterfall area that has waterside sites and precious plants, and the deeper mountainous area where hiking roads should be improved.

After the workshops, I used questionnaires to survey the residents. The community residents evaluated the workshops highly and they expected to undertake conservation and recreation activities in the mountains. Since then, citizens have been leading practical mountain management activities.

Workshops for Community Design with Water

Just after the earthquake, there were many fires in urban neighborhoods. Almost seven hectares of the Matsumoto district in the Hyogo Ward of Kobe was destroyed by fire. The damage was severe because fire trucks could not come quickly and there was no water even after they arrived. In March 1995, two months after the earthquake, plans for land readjustment and redevelopment for 24 districts in Kobe and other cities were announced, but the planned area was only 4% of the devastated area. A construction plan was announced for Matsumoto as a land readjustment district, and a community design committee for that plan was founded to consider a blueprint for reconstruction. I became involved as a consultant for this district and dealt with the planning process for

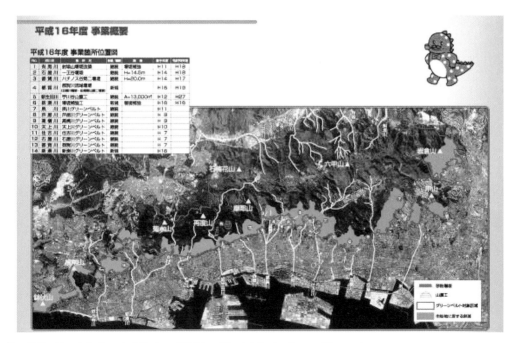

Fig.7 Rokko Mountain Greenbelt Strategy (Ministry of Land, Infrastructure and Transport

streets, parks and community roads, including the creation of a streamside road.

They proposed a streamside road in Matsumoto because the area had been burnt extensively after the earthquake. As a result, part of the readjustment of the lands planned in this area was a major road next to a stream linking from park to park. Many discussions in the community design committee resulted in a consensus among the residents for the design of the stream and the plan for its maintenance. The water in the stream was planned and is now maintained by the citizens. The Matsumoto community design proposal was delivered to the city very early, making it the second district to make a proposal to Kobe in 1995, the same year as the earthquake. This proposal was not the usual type of proposal in which land changes were negotiated one by one with local citizens by government agencies and other organizations. This proposal for community design determined the positions of the roads and the parks, and the forms and ways of use through the agreement of everyone. We had discussions in the community design committee and subcommittees every week for several years. In particular, the residents advanced the plan for the stream with their strong will. The Kobe municipal government division responsible for sewage proposed a detailed plan to allow 2000 tons of highly treated water to flow through this stream daily. Citizens, however, asked, "Even if we clean the stream in the front of our homes, what should we do if some neighbors do not clean their parts?" Some responded, "Isn't thinking about that community design?"

To examine technical issues, we showed cross-section plans of a stream that could handle a 2000 ton flow and considered the planning design comprehensively, including the speed of the water flow, the whole design, and the coming and going of cars, especially in balance with residential parking. The residents also took excursions to see other areas. The plan for the stream was prepared

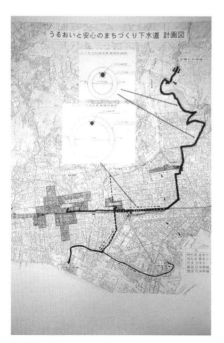

Fig.8 The stream concept.

Fig.9 The stream design.

through discussions with mutual respect among the residents, government, and professionals, which is a rare occurrence in big cities (Fig.8-10).

Efforts to Make Biotopes in Schools

In urban areas, efforts were made to make embankments and other riverbank-protection works more accessible and enjoyable for citizens. The idea was to make the rivers, which were used out of necessity at the time of the earthquake, more familiar to the citizens. In addition to projects that dealt with cleaning rivers and planting trees after the earthquake, we created artificial biotopes, which are natural habitats designed to support a variety of wildlife. Many of those projects have been led by citizens, and I have also been involved in a number of these projects (Fig.11 & 12).

For example, since the earthquake, many primary schools have been developing biotopes for environmental education for urban children with the support of the environmental bureau of the Kobe municipal government. I was involved in a project at the Mikage Primary School from the beginning and in biotope construction projects at several other schools. The goal of a biotope is to reconstruct habitat for plants and animals as it might have been before the location was developed. In many of these projects, biotopes have been made by children, members of Parent-Teacher Associatons (PTA) and community residents in partnership. At the same time, wells and water reservoirs were also dug, and in many schools wells and water reservoirs were also constructed as disaster countermeasures. At Mikage Primary School, where I was involved, the science and home economics teaching staff, along with the principle and vice principle, made the

Fig.10 The stream.

Fig.11 School biotope plan.

Fig.12 School biotope.

main plan together. We had discussions in a workshop format and we planned and constructed the biotope as a place for environmental education. During the construction, in particular, children of the school, PTA members, residents, professionals and experts worked together in adjusting the terrain, placing rubber liners for water-retention, putting in clay, installing timber and other landscaping features and planting native plants. Furthermore, since construction of the biotope, we have continued monitoring the biotope to consider what types of maintenance are suitable and to act as interpreters to explain the natural ecosystems of animals and plants to the children. Through this monitoring, we are trying to spread methods of environmental education for children and maintenance techniques for biotopes to more people. The monitoring includes verifying the presence of various dragonflies and tracking the dates of their first and subsequent sightings. In addition, we identify the larvae of dragonflies and seek to maintain the biotope to increase their populations. We also engage in educational activities for ecological conservation by lecturing about organisms in the water and offering programs for parents and children of the community.

The Eco Road Proposal

In the Hanshin-Kan region, an axis of water flow from the mountains in the north to the plains and seaside in the south crosses a transportation axis of roads and railways that run primarily east and west. During the reconstruction after the earthquake, about one hundred landscape architects, both practitioners and academics, started the "Hanshin Green Net," and I worked as its secretariat. The members of this Hanshin Green Net have since conducted activities to provide

Fig.13 Eco-Road Town proposal.

Fig.14 Sumiyoshi River.

communities with greenery and water. We considered the waterways of mountain areas as places for habitats for various plants and animals and proposed linking water and vegetation, including the reconstruction of rivers and the construction of biotopes. We had proposed an "Eco Road Town" as an ecological intersection of the east-west transportation axis and the north-south water axis. This was to be created through the cooperation of citizens, professionals and government representatives working together (Fig.13 & 14).

Land meets Water: The formation of waterfront landscapes in Kobe City

The views from the waterfront to the mountains and from the mountains to the waterfront have been reconsidered in discussions about the formation of new waterfront landscapes in Kobe City. In views from the waterfront, the foot of the mountains and the urban area are visible, and the mountainous landscape of Kobe has been evaluated positively again. In the view from the city and the mountains, the seashore in balance with buildings and urban greenery has also been evaluated highly. At the same time, community design plans using historically important buildings that stand along the seashore, along with a shopping center as new waterfront development are being promoted to create important landscape points (Fig.15). These valuable waterfronts are divided into several areas. One is from around Sannomiya, which is at the center of Kobe, to Meriken Park, which is a relaxing place for citizen, another is Harbor Land, which is a commercial area. Harbor Land has many historical buildings, including well-kept brick warehouses that are still being used although they had suffered damage from the earthquake (fig. 16). Based on a proposal by the Kobe City Landscape

Fig.15 Axis's on the map of the waterfront area.

Fig.16 The waterfront landscape.

Fig.17 Mountain, city area and the sea.

Fig.18 Location of the Hyogo Canal Regatta.

Fig.19 The area of Hyogo Canal and the place for the Regatta (Kobe City Council).

Fig.20 Second Hyogo Canal Regatta in 2006 (Kobe City Council).

Fig.21 Third Hyogo Canal Regatta in 2007 (Kobe City Council).

Council, of which I was a member, a competition was held to decide the style of development. The council made using the brick warehouses a design condition and asked the public for redevelopment plans. Through this process, the historical area of Harbor Land has been reborn as a new commercial area.

The Hyogo Canal and community design using water

The artificial stream from Matsumoto flows into the nearby Hyogo Canal. This canal was built gradually from the early 19th century, but it had not been used in recent years, and the water in the abandoned canal had become very dirty. I will describe how this canal has recently been revived by citizens below (Fg.17 & 18). Hyogo Canal is the biggest canal in Japan and had been used for the storage of timber. As the use of foreign timber increased, use of the canal declined. The canal had been cluttered with illegally docked private boats and garbage that made water dirty. In response to these conditions, the Kobe City Council, seeking new ways to use the Hyogo Canal, asked the general public for ideas as part of a "Gathering of Ideas for Vibrant Community Design" program in 2003. The proposal of a competitive boating group, entitled "Promotion of a Kobe Citizen Regatta in Hyogo Canal" and a proposal for the "Foundation of General Community Sports Clubs," were selected as useful ideas to make the canal into an attractive waterscape. The Hyogo Ward Office became the secretariat for the community and cooperated with the competitive boating group to realize the proposal. Through these activities, the value of the Hyogo Canal as a community property has been realized and motivation to vitalize the canal had increased. The Kobe City Council tried to move abandoned timbers and build handrails at landing places to improve security.

In the community, they also prepared to establish a general community sports club at Hamayama Primary School. Then, this sports club and the boating group joined together and founded a committee for regatta training. In 2005, the first regatta was held. In 2006, the boating group left this organization and the general community sports clubs of the three communities (Hamayama, Wadamisaki, and Meishi) along the canal organized and managed the event. The canal has been restored with cleaner water, and it now hosts a canoe regatta and supports a pearl producing industry. Activities have been expanded to include not only elderly people, but also young students and children who enjoy the competitions and their preparation. This trial restoration has been publicized in other areas as a successful example

Fig.22 Third Hyogo Canal Regatta in 2007 (Kobe City Council).

Fig.23 Third Hyogo Canal Regatta in 2007 (Kobe City Council).

of community design using a waterfront to improve the landscape. We are now conducting community design using water in many places through cooperation between citizens and government agencies. We highly evaluated these canal regatta efforts as successful examples of community design and recommended it for an award for community design in western Japan from the Japan Institute of City Planning. Although the earthquake was a tragic experience, it did have a positive impact on activating community design using water through the cooperation of citizens and governments in many places.

Conclusion

The area called Hanshin-Kan, including the city of Kobe, is blessed with many rivers flowing from the Rokko Mountains and abundant underground water and springs that flow into the Pacific Ocean. Since the Great Hanshin Awaji Earthquake, citizens have cooperated in various kinds of activities as volunteers with government representatives and professionals for community design using water and green. This expansion of citizen activities and increased consciousness about water and plants has brought the communities of the Hanshin-Kan and Kobe region into a new era.

Fig.24 Poster for the Third Hyogo Canal Regatta (Kobe City Council).

Recapturing a Waterfront

Panama City, Panama

~ **Ken McCown** ~ Urban Designer, Arizona State University and Design Workshop, US ~ Abstract

This paper will describe a project designed for the Panamanian Government and their World Heritage Office. This project is the redesign of the waterfront in the El Chorrillo-district, a typical barrio in Panama City, Panama. The context of the project led the designers to ask; How can water unite cultural and natural systems, and global and local organizations?

El Chorrillo is a fascinating area. It is the former stronghold of Manuel Noriega. As the United States Armed Forces forcibly removed him from power with a beachfront invasion; they demolished this neighborhood, creating a hole in the urban fabric. El Chorrillo lies immediately below Cerro Ancon, the freedom hill symbolic to the Panamanians. A World Heritage Site, Casco Viejo, borders El Chorrillo to the East and to the west border contains the Bridge of the Americas over the Panama Canal. It is next to the Smithsonian Institution's Tropical Research Center, and the Amador Peninsula where Frank Gehry's Museum of Biodiversity is currently under construction.

The invasion left this neighborhood damaged and destitute, devaluing the

resources bordering it. This dangerous area limited the free mobility of citizens and tourists as El Chorrillo is at the center of these places of interest. The government realized it must improve the area, but simultaneously, work to keep the existing residents, bringing them along into the prosperity rehabilitation will create.

The El Chorrillo waterfront became the place to restore the function of the urban systems to connect the Canal, Cerro Ancon, the Amador Peninsula, and Casco Viejo. The barrio is renewed as an activity center of the city. The redesign of the place provides opportunities to tell the intricate cultural stories of the people and to rehabilitate natural systems. The project shows the power of the meeting of a city to a unique waterfront where tidal differences extend to a quarter of a mile. When the water retreats, the local citizens use the land for its resources. Therefore, the connection between water and land are critical to the people of El Chorrillo.

This design addresses ecological issues, such as water quality. In this plan, the Smithsonian Institution's research center would set up a water cleansing and research wetland. This provides an opportunity for a global institution to interact with a low-income community by working with local organizations. These interactions can create opportunities for scientific education and employment in environmental engineering for the youth of El Chorrillo. Additional ecological issues this design addresses include the restoration of the mangroves, a plant community devastated by cultural and military activity, and the creation of islands to improve the health of the tidally exposed ocean floor. The islands restore destroyed channel flows that mix seawater from the ocean and the freshwater running off from the rainforest to balance a proper estuarine mixture in the mangrove areas.

Culturally, the design provides opportunities for a civic space that allows for the expression of the Panamanian's complex history. A timeline running along the waterfront denotes the intricate colonial histories of a nation at the center of global trade. Especially noted is the invasion. Poorly documented, more people died in the United States invasion of Panama in El Chorrillo, than in the World Trade Center Bombings in New York City. Yes, this story is rarely told. The design includes a civic space for the documentation, research and interpretation of this event that links water and land, tracing the path of the invasion.

The new design for the waterfront in El Chorrillo shows how water may be the thread that unites a narrative of cultural and natural histories, global and local institutions, and the weaving of human and natural systems. This occurs in the shadow of the Panama Canal, at the nexus of global trade, adding an international element to the design. How will the United Nations, the Panamanian Government and Canal Authority and the Smithsonian Institution come together to manage and direct the rehabilitation of the El Chorrillo Waterfront for its citizens and global tourism and trade?

2.2 Land meets Water – Talkshops

Building with Nature

The Strength, Weakness, Opportunity, and Threat (SWOT) Analysis of Mangrove Forests in the Coastal Areas of the Tropics and Sub-tropics
~ Nik Ismail Azlan

(Abstract) Stradling Both Sides of the Coast
~ Katherine Dunster

(Abstract) Natural Storm Water Management with Green Roofs
~ Wolfgang Ansel

(Abstract) Topotypes: Ground as Design Material for Coastal Projects
~ Thierry Kandjee, Sebastien Penfornis

Urban Waterfronts

(Abstract) Water in Ghent: dumped, filled in, embraced – The EU-project 'Water in Historic City Centres'
~ Philip De Roo, Yves Deckmyn

Urban River fronts along the Rhine
~ Cornelia Redeker

(Abstract) Reflections in the Moscow River
~ Anna Kurbatova

Building with Nature

The Strength, Weakness, Opportunity, and Threat (SWOT) Analysis

Mangrove Forests in the Coastal Areas of the Tropics and Sub-tropics

~ Nik Ismail Azlan ~ Dept of Landscape Architecture, UiTM Shah Alam,

Malaysia

Mangrove is unique inter-tidal wetland ecosystem found in sheltered tropical and subtropical shores and riverine areas. It is characterized by high temperature, fluctuating salinity, alternating oxygen and low oxygen conditions, periodically wet and dry, unstable and shifting substratum. The characteristics of mangrove forest varied regionally and locally among fringe, riverine, and basin zones. Nevertheless these mangrove forest ecosystem play an important role in providing sources of tropical fish products and bore the brunt of coastal erosion and sedimentation. This paper will discuss the S.W.O.T. analysis of the mangrove forests to provide information for the significant contribution it brings to 50% of the population along the coastal areas of the tropics and sub tropics. Hopefully there is considerable scope to improve public understanding and appreciation of the value of mangrove resources and of the benefits to be obtained from their existence.

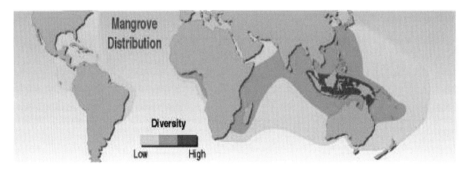

Figure 1. Mangrove distribution in the world.

Introduction

Mangroves may not be found or able to survive in temperate countries such as the Netherlands, the Scandinavian and other European countries but their importance and contributions to human population within the coastal waters of the tropics and subtropics have been immensely valuable. The tsunami of 2004 in the coastal areas of Asia has emphasized the need to view the mangroves in terms of natural protection, physical barrier, economic benefits and alternative tourism activities.

The Origins of the Mangroves

The mangrove vegetation of the world can be divided into two broad groups (Figure 1). The first is mangroves occurring in the Indo-Pacific region extending from the east coast of Africa, India, Indonesia Malaysia to Samoa in the South Pacific.

The second group, occurs along the west coast of Africa between Mauritania and Angola, in the Americas on the east coast between Barbados and Brazil and on the west coast between Mexico and northern Peru. Indonesia has the largest total area of mangrove forest while the Sundarbans swamp region in Bangladesh and India is the largest single chunk of mangrove forest in the world. The mangrove ecosystem in Malaysia is more diverse than in tropical Australia, the Red Sea, tropical Africa and the Americas. Diversity of mangrove plant species tends to increase with precipitation, and decreases with increasing latitude.

The Characteristics of the Mangroves

Mangrove trees grow where no tree has grown before. They are able to survive inundation by salt water twice a day, and in "soil" which is unstable and poor in oxygen (Figure 2).

They also have to deal with swollen rivers carrying silt during the wet season,

Figure 2. Mangrove survive in salt water and in soil which is unstable and poor in oxygen.

as well as violent storms that hit the coasts. To deal with salt, all mangrove trees exclude some salt at the root level, and all can tolerate more salt in their tissues than "normal" plants, often in quantities that would kill other plants. But some have more effective ultrafiltration at the root level to exclude more salt. Any salt that gets through are believed to be stored in old leaves which are later shed. These include Bruguiera, Sonneratia and Rhizophora. A few can tolerate high levels of salt in their tissues and their sap can be up to one-tenth as salty as sea water. They then secrete the excess salt through special cells on their leaves. Although mangrove trees are adapted to grow in salt water, they require regular flushing with freshwater. They will die if immersed in saltwater all the time. Many mangrove trees have special adaptations to give their offspring the best chance in their harsh habitat. Many provide their seedlings with a good store of food and floatation devices. In some, the fruit does not fall away when it ripens. Instead, the seed within the fruit starts to germinate while it is still on the mother tree, and the mother tree channels nutrients to the growing seedling (vivipary). In some plants, the growing seed does not break through the fruit wall while the seed is on the mother plant but only after the fruit falls off (crypto-vivipary). This is the case with Avicennia and the seed coat of its fruits drops away more quickly in water of the right warmth and salinity, usually in a spot best suited for an Avicennia seedling (Figure 3).

Mangroves also help in soil stabilization and erosion protection. The stability mangroves provide is essential for preventing shoreline erosion. By acting as buffers catching materials washed downstream, they help stabilize land elevation by sediment accretion, thereby balancing sediment loss. In regions where these coastal fringe forests have been cleared, tremendous problems of erosion and sil-

Figure 3. Vivipary of the specie Avicennia that will drop to the mudflat below to regenerate.

Figure 4. Rhizophoraceae species of mangrove ecosystem.

tation have arisen. The World Conservation Union's report on the global status of mangroves (IUCN, 1983) lists 61 species. Major mangrove species belong to less than 15 families but the most frequently occurring mangroves belong to the Rhizophoraceae (Figure 4), Sonneratiaceae and Avicenniaceae.

The most important species is Rhizophora (Figure 5) with arch formed supporting roots, and Avicennia or Sonneratia, which both have breathing roots propping them up from the mud. Mangroves occur in areas where strong wave actions are absent. The most extensive growth of mangroves can be seen in estuaries of rivers and protected lagoons and coastal lakes. Mangroves occur in areas of high humidity and their luxuriant growth is often associated with a high rainfall. Minimum air temperature and seasonal variations in temperature are important in the growth of mangroves. As cited by Chapman (1975; 1977), the best mangrove growth and development occurs where the seasonal temperature variation does not exceed 10°C and where the air temperature in the coldest month is higher then 10°C. Mangrove ecosystems thrives in riverine (river dominated areas), fringe (tide dominated areas) and basin (intermediate interior areas) mangroves. Fringe mangroves receive the brunt of tidal actions, and basin mangroves have the greatest diversity in tree species. The mangrove vegetation is characterized by low tree diversity, almost exclusively mangroves, with a low broken canopy. Mangrove plants have a number of highly specialised adaptations to regular tidal inundation by saline waters. These include (i) breathing roots which allow them to survive in anaerobic sediments, (ii) supporting structures such as buttresses and above-ground roots which enable them to grow in unstable substrate, (iii) low water holding potentials and high intracellular salt concentrations to maintain favourable water relations in saline environments, (iv) foliage salt-

Figure 5. Arch forming roots of Rhizophora species.

excretion to remove excess salt from the sap (Figure 6), (v) xerophytic (water – conserving) leaves to cope with periods of high salinity stress, and (vi) buoyant viviparous propagules for dispersal and establishment in new areas.

The Benefits of Mangrove

The coastline where mangrove thrives is protected because the roots of mangroves act to trap sediments that would otherwise be washed back out by the waves. Moreover, mangroves provide a habitat for many different species of animals, including bats, lobsters, manatees, and birds. 75% of all tropical commercial fish species pass part of their lives in the mangroves, where they encounter nursery grounds, shelter and food. Other ecosystem services provided by mangroves include protection from strong winds and waves. Mangroves' protective buffer zone helps shield coastlines from storm damage and wave action, minimizing damage to property and losses of life from hurricanes and storms.

The strangest creature living in the swamps are little fish called mudskippers Figure 7). During low tide, these fish walk around the mud looking for prey. Some species have suckers on their undersides that help them to climb rocks and mangrove trees. Their prey consists of small crabs, mollusks, worms, and insects. The mangrove swamps are also nurseries for many coral fish. The swamps provide a protective area for the coral fish to develop to the point where they can travel further out into the ocean to the coral reefs.

There are many species of birds that live in the mangrove areas. This is an ideal area for these birds to live in due to the easy access to both food and resting area. Many birds have developed special characteristics to their beaks and feet to help

Figure 6. Salt crystals formed on grey mangrove leaf.

them adapt to this environment living off of certain prey. Pelicans and other seabirds live in the canopies of the mangrove swamps. During the breeding season, they form large nesting assemblages of adult birds and their offspring called large rookeries. "Other animals that find shelter in the branches and are adapted to mangroves include bats, Proboscis Monkeys, snakes, otters, the Fishing Cat. As many as 200,000 fruit bats may roost in a mangrove. Some small fruit bats roost in mangroves on offshore islands where it's safe from predators and commute daily to the mainland to feed. The bats also contribute to the mangrove: Short-nosed Fruit Bat (Cynopterus sphinx) is believed to be the only pollinator of key mangrove trees (Sonneratia).

The roots and branches of mangroves provide an ideal site for animals to feed, mate, and give birth. A symbiotic relationship exists between many animals and the mangrove; for example, crabs feeds on the mangrove leaves, as well as other nutrients and then recycle minerals into the mangrove forest. In addition to controlling coastal erosion the mangroves can expand into the sea, a process known as accretion; this results in an increase in area of mangroves – a sort of natural land reclamation. To understand better the impact of mangroves to the coastal ecosystem it is best to describe them in terms of S.W.O.T. analysis. The analysis is to provide information for the significant contribution it brings to 50% of the population along the coastal areas of the tropics and sub tropics.

Figure 7. A typical mudskipper within the mangrove forest environment.

The Strength of the Mangroves

Mangroves protect the coast from erosion, surge storms especially during hurricanes, and tsunamis. Their massive root system is efficient at dissipating wave energy. Likewise, they slow down tidal water enough that its sediment is deposited as the tide comes in and is not re-suspended when the tide leaves, except for fine particles. As a result, mangroves build their own environment. Despite their benefits, the protective value of mangroves is sometimes overstated. Wave energy is typically low in areas where mangroves grow, so their effect on erosion can only be measured in the long-term (Figure 8).

Their capacity to limit high-energy wave erosion is limited to events like storm surges and tsunamis. Erosion often still occurs on the outer sides of bends in river channels that wind through mangroves, just as new stands of mangroves are appearing on the inner sides where sediment is accreting. The amount of protection afforded by mangroves depends upon the width of the forest. A very narrow fringe of mangroves offers limited protection, while a wide fringe can considerably reduce wave and flood damage to landward areas by enabling overflowing water to be absorbed into the expanse of forest. Mangroves help to filter water and maintain water quality and clarity.

Red mangroves (family Rhizoporaceae), which can live in the most inundated areas, prop themselves up above the water level with stilt roots and can then take in air through pores in their bark or lenticels. Black mangroves live on higher ground and make many pneumatophores (specialised root-like structures which stick up out of the soil like straws for breathing) which are covered in lenticels. These "breathing tubes" typically reach heights of up to thirty centime-

Figure 8. Mangrove forest to some extent can reduce wave energy.

ters, and in some species, over three meters. There are four types of pneu-matophore—stilt or prop type, snorkel or peg type, knee type, and ribbon or plank type. Knee and ribbon types may be combined with buttress roots at the base of the tree. The roots also contain wide aerenchyma to facilitate oxygen transport within the plant.

The Weakness of the Mangrove

Despite their benefits, the protective value of mangroves is sometimes overstat-ed. Mangrove cannot largely withstand large erosion process on its own. Mangrove trees are constantly being uprooted significantly in areas where large number of ocean going ships passed through along the Straits of Malacca, Malaysia where 90,000 ships passed through annually, hence exposing the shore-line (Figure 9).

Wave energy is typically low in areas where mangroves grow, so their effect on erosion can only be measured in the long-term. Their capacity to limit high-ener-gy wave erosion is limited. Erosion often still occurs on the outer sides of bends in river channels that wind through mangroves, just as new stands of mangroves are appearing on the inner sides where sediment is accreting.

Figure 9. Felled mangrove trees as a result of waves from ocean going ships.

The Opportunities in Mangrove Ecosystems

In a mangrove swamp, one cannot simply walk about without getting soiled and dirty, unless special boardwalks have been built, and even then, the walk has to follow a set trail. There is no scenic beauty there unless one is a mangrove specialist or a forester or a botanist trying to identify tree and plant species; the tide has to be right before a boat ride can be arranged. Yes, one can listen to sounds of birds and insects, but it is difficult to actually see large birds that are often pictured in the brochures. These birds must be very shy of people or easily frightened. Eco-tourism activities within the mangrove ecosystem are one of the opportunities that should be considered. It would be possible and enjoyable to construct limited infrastructure facilities such as: boardwalks, automatic listening devices, an interpretative center, jetty, clearing the streams of broken branches, building landing places along the boating route, etc (Figure 10).

Touring activities such as bringing tourists to the various spots of interest, providing trained guides and giving a running commentary as they pass interesting spots along the guided tour would be examples of selected eco-tourism. Walking through the boardwalk during high tide, visitors can see small fishes darting from the jagged, twisted roots of one mangrove tree to another. The tangle of roots serves as a hiding place for young fish from larger predators. Tree climbing crabs and sea snails also avoid predators by climbing the aerial roots of mangroves. Mangrove forests provide not only refuge and nursery grounds but also food to young marine species. The fallen leaves and branches nurture the marine environment. Accommodation near the site and collecting entrance fees can be built into the cost of the tour package. Presentable eateries and souvenir shops

Figure 10. A boardwalk in the mangrove forest that provides and opportunity for eco-tourism activities.

outside the mangrove areas, serving locally available food and crafts, preferably from the brackish water where the mangrove thrives can provide added income to the local community. The opportunities presented above should benefit three main entities – the environment, local community and the visitors' enjoyment of the mangroves.

The Threats to Mangrove

Unfortunately, mangrove forests are some of the most threatened ecosystems on the planet because of their proximity to the ocean (prime resort/development property) and the tendency to see them as useless swamps full of all sorts of threatening creatures. Over the past twenty years, great swaths of mangrove forest throughout Southeast Asia have been cleared to create commercial shrimp and prawn hatcheries (Figure 11).

Ironically this form of aquaculture has come at the expense of the natural fish and shrimp hatchery. Changing coastal landscapes such as coastal development, aquaculture production and mangrove felling will contribute to the loss of ecological integrity and environmental sustainability. Once mangrove forests are damaged, recovery can be very slow. Despite replanting programs over 50% of the World's mangroves have been lost. It is often stated that mangroves provide significant value in the coastal zone as a buffer against erosion, storm surge and tsunamis. While there is some attentuation of wave heights and energy as seawater passes through mangrove stands, it must be recognised that these trees typically inhabit areas of coastline where low wave energies are the norm. Therefore their capacity to ameliorate high energy events like storm surge and tsunamis is

Figure 11. Large areas of mangrove forest being turned into shrimp farming.

limited. Their long term impact on rates of erosion is also likely to be limited. Many river channels that wind through mangrove areas are actively eroding stands of mangroves on the outer sides of all the river bends, just as new stands of mangroves are appearing on the inner sides of these same bends where sediment is accreting. They also provide habitats for wildlife, including several commercially important species of fish and crustacea and in at least some cases export of carbon fixed in mangroves is important in coastal foodwebs.

Conclusion

Mangroves are an integral part of the coastal ecosystem within the tropics and the sub-tropics. Mangroves provide habitat for many marine and terrestrial animals, birds, and insects. They also provide shoreline stabilization with their extensive root structure and build islands through a process of sedimentation. Dense mangrove stands protect shorelines from storms and surges damage and increase coastal stability. In addition to onshore provisions, mangroves also protect oceanic ecosystems. By trapping sediment, mangroves allow seagrass beds to flourish. They also filter water washed over the land that could carry harmful sediment and debris that could threaten fragile coral reefs. Mangroves therefore are necessary elements of the coastal ecosystem. They provide several ecological, socio-economical, and physical functions that are essential in maintaining biodiversity and protecting human populations along the coastal areas. The role of mangroves is very important, both economically and ecologically – as a natural resource and as protection to the environment – and both aspects cannot be separated without causing damage to the area. Mangrove tree formations contribute to the marine food web through their production of detritus, and several commercially important species of marine animals are known to spend at least part of their life cycle here. For this reason, mangroves should not only be considered as forests, but also as producers of food in the form of crabs, fish and shrimp. Their complex architecture, combined with their location on the edge of land and sea, makes mangrove forests strategic greenbelts that have a doubly protective function. They protect seaward habitats against influences from land, and they protect the landward coastal zone against influences from the ocean. The Asian tsunami that occurred on December 26, 2004, revealed the valuable buffering functions of mangroves. After the tsunami, there is considerable scope to improve public understanding and appreciation of the value of mangrove resources and of the benefits to be obtained from their sustainable management. The explanation of sustainable management systems needs to be undertaken within the formal educational systems, but must also be offered to the general public and to particular sectors within the population such as decision makers and local people. There is a need to improve the communication and flow of knowledge between scientists, managers, holders of traditional knowledge and the wider public.

Stradling Both Sides of the Coast

~ Katherine **Dunster, CSLA** ~ R.P. Bio. Unfolding Landscapes, Canada ~

Abstract

The majority of the world's population now lives in high-density urban areas close to coastlines. Eight of the ten largest cities in the world are located in coastal areas. And, according to the Global Rural Urban Mapping Project at Columbia University, rural populations in coastal areas are much denser than in other rural landscapes. Many major cities were initially located on or near estuaries and harbours that allowed people to take advantage of abundant marine food resources and water transportation, to develop sea borne trade with other nations, and later to exploit scenic beauty and shoreline resources for recreation and tourism. Marine waters play a crucial role in maintaining the health of the planet's ecosystems, including the provision of food for humankind. Coastal waters provide the only means of subsistence for many communities around the world, particularly for rapidly expanding coastal populations. Of the 13,200 known species of marine fish, almost 80% inhabit coastal areas, and most begin their lives in food-rich seagrass meadow habitats. Seagrasses provide important and valuable ecological contributions to coastal ecosystems worldwide. Vast underwater and inter-tidal seagrass meadows edge the coasts of every continent except Antarctica. They provide habitat and nearshore nursery areas for fish and shellfish, and perform important ecosystem functions such as filtering coastal waters, dissipating wave energy, and stabilizing marine sediments. Seagrasses often occur in proximity to, and are ecologically linked with, coral reefs, mangroves, salt marshes, estuaries, bivalve beds, and other marine habitats. Seagrasses are the primary food of species such as manatees and green sea turtles, other marine mammals such as Orcas feed on fish that begin life in seagrass nurseries. All are species of great public interest; all have direct links to the human food chain, to economic opportunities, and most critically, to ecosystem health.

As the world's human population continues to expand and live disproportion-

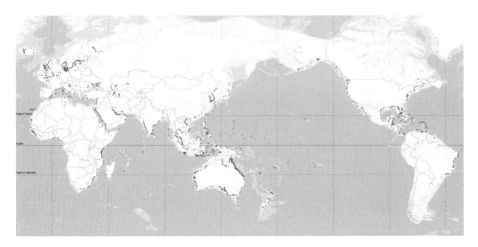

Figure 1. Global Seagrass Distribution Map (UNEP).

ately in coastal areas, natural habitats are altered, damaged, diminished, and destroyed both on land, and in the sea. Lagoons and coastal waters are "reclaimed", filled, and developed; floodplains around estuaries are built over and reduced; seagrass meadows are scoured, dunes are leveled, mangroves and other coastal forests are cut down. Channel flow, tidal inundation, and freshwater discharges are disrupted by construction of seawalls, jetties, docks, dikes, groins, and onshore structures. The physical and chemical qualities of these habitats are degraded by the discharge of municipal, industrial, and agricultural effluents. Plant and animal community composition and functions are altered by domestic and agricultural runoff of pesticides, herbicides, and fertilizers. Coastal food fisheries are often overexploited and depleted, at great social, economic, and ecological cost.

Seagrasses are vulnerable to many threats, both anthropogenic and natural. Runoff of nutrients and sediments from land-based human activities has major impacts in marine environments where seagrasses usually thrive. These types of indirect human impacts, while difficult to measure, are cumulative and considered the greatest worldwide threat to seagrasses. Both nutrient and sediment loading affect turbidity and water clarity. Seagrasses require sunlight for photosynthesis; without clean and clear water, seagrasses decline quickly. Direct impacts to seagrass meadows occur from boating, land reclamation, construction in the coastal zone, dredge-and-fill activities, and destructive fisheries practices.

Given these scenarios, coastal areas now face many environmental challenges related to increased population demands, including human-induced global climate change. Rising sea levels and severe storms will require many changes to the way humans live, work, and interact within coastal areas. At the same time, coastal areas offer many interdependent social, economic, and environmental opportunities that require sensitive planning, greater coordination of decisions at all scales, and effective linkage of management actions across all disciplines working within the land-sea interface.

Traditionally, landscape architects have assumed responsibility for the planning, design, and management of sites firmly grounded on the terrestrial side of coastal areas. Often, the marine environment is treated merely as a pleasant backdrop to residential, commercial, and tourism development along coastlines.

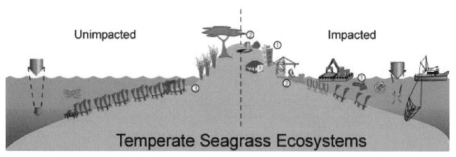

Figure 2: Temperate Seagrass Ecosystem Habitat Summary, (Integration & Application Network, Image & Video Library, University of Maryland Centre for Environmental Science, http://ian.umces.edu/imagelibrary/displayimage-784.html).

While landscape architecture is practiced above high water, the impacts of landscape architects working in coastal areas can reach to inter-tidal areas and the bottom of the sea where seagrasses thrive. Within the land-sea interface, landscape architects fueled by new knowledge and design tools, and best practices, can become the critical professional linkage that connects science, design, planning, engineering, and management disciplines together to meet the multifaceted challenges confronting coastal areas. With one foot on land and the other in the water, landscape architects can gain a better understanding of ecosystem needs in coastal areas, which in turn will lead to better design and planning as well as the chance to become coastal conservation leaders.

The purpose of this paper and presentation is to raise awareness of the critical role that landscape architects must play in coastal conservation, planning and management. Particular attention will be given to nearshore and inter-tidal marine ecosystems where landscape architects have not traditionally practiced their profession. Using examples from coastal British Columbia, such as the new Green Shores Project, I will present a number of best practices that will help landscape architects working in coastal terrestrial areas to avoid contributing to degradation or destruction of adjacent marine environments and seagrass habitat.

Figure 3: Where Dry Land Meets Wet Sea: Coastal dune ecosystems filter essential freshwater into adjacent inter-tidal seagrass habitat (K. Dunster).

Figure 4: A Coastal Planning and Land-Sea Interface Mistake (K. Dunster).

Natural Storm Water

Management with Green Roofs

~ **Wolfgang Ansel** ~ Director IGRA Head Office, Germany ~ Abstract

In recent years flood disasters have become "an inconvenient truth" for many people. On a local scale this problem is very often homemade by paving of open, undisturbed land. As a result, the natural water cycle is annulled and most of the precipitation during a rainstorm is immediately routed into overloaded storm-sewer pipes. Moreover, the impacts of global warming and the attendant stronger storms with more rainfall have tightened the situation. So, at present, public water authorities are at the crossroads. They can try to solve the problem conventionally by costly end-of-pipe interventions, e.g. the extension of stormwater collection, storage and treatment facilities. However, these efforts fail to address the source of the problem – impervious surface. Therefore, modern stormwater management policies go upstream and manage the problem in a sustainable way by using green roofs for temporary water storage.

Within the array of preventive stormwater management techniques, green roofs play an outstanding part. This is not only due to the fact that 40-50 % of sealed surfaces in urban agglomerations represent roofs. In fact green roofs are real all-rounders in an economical and ecological sense. The immediate water runoff from vegetated roofs can be reduced by 50-90%, depending on the roof system build-up and substrate. A large part of the water returns into the natural water cycle by transpiration of the plants and evaporation from the substrate. The accompanying cooling effect of this process contributes to a better microclimate and a decrease of the "urban heat island effect".

The remaining excess rainwater drains from green roofs with a substantial lag in time: so the peak flow rates are reduced. Due to the natural drainage pattern of green roofs, less or smaller dimensioned sewerage systems can be installed on new development areas or large projects. Innovative stormwater masterplans include the combination of green roofs with cisterns, so the roof water, that is not absorbed by the green roof build-up, will be captured and provide grey water for other uses (e.g. irrigation, flushing toilets). As stormwater volume reduction benefits the budgets of the municipalities many water authorities promote the opening of scaled surfaces by financial incentives. In Germany, e.g. property owners receive a special discount on the annual stormwater taxes for areas which are covered by green roofs.

The installation of a green roof transfers hostile impervious places into a field of activity for landscape architects. The possibilities are nearly unlimited and range from wildlife habitats for plants, insects and birds to wonderful roof gardens or parks with lawns, perennials and trees.

Case Studies:

Stuttgart, Germany: The new trade fair, which was opened in October 2007, is covered by 70.000 m^2 of extensive and intensive green roofs. Excess water from the roofs and squares is collected and used for irrigation and water cascades. As a result there is rarely any surface run off from the site.

London, United Kingdom: The public "Jubilee Park" (22.000 m^2) above an underground shopping mall and an underground station creates a counterpole to the dense constructions in the surrounding area. In the design, trees, lawn, and fountains are especially eye catching.

Zaragoza, Spain: The slogan of the Expo 2008 in Zaragoza is "Water and Sustainable Development". It´s not surprising, that the green roof of the participants pavilion is accessible for the visitors with wonderful views over the landscape and the Ebro river.

Istanbul, Turkey: The shopping centre "Meydan" in Istanbul stands for a new generation of commercial premises. Due to the accessible green roofs it combines consumption and the beauty of nature. The central square features a fountain in summer and an ice rink in winter times.

Apart from the stormwater features green roofs provide usable landscape, preserve the roof membrane, improve the building's energy balance and interrupt the monotony of grey dismal city centres. No other measure provides so many positive effects for the environment, buildings and the living quality of the urban population at the same time. Green roofs are able to combine both – ecology and economy.

Topotypes

Ground as Design Material for Coastal Projects

~ **Thierry Kandjee, Sebastien Penfornis** ~ Taktyk [landscape+urbanism]

France, Spain ~ Abstract

Introduction – landscape resources

How can landscape architects engage with the contemporary city and react upon the challenging task of climate change? Can the notion of resources help to formulate performative landscape scenarios?

'Topotypes: ground as design material' is a current research which focuses on landscape as urban strategy through manipulation of the earth and the use of its resources. It acknowledges landscape as primarily being infrastructural. Ground and water form the base for scenarios of territorial transformation which take place in different parts of the European Coast.

Project 1 – SHOREs

As the Rotterdam Port mutates into a deep sea port, and moves westward towards the sea, the old city-based harbour is simultaneously a very attractive

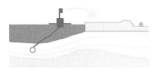

Fig 1. Can a dyke 'welcome' water?

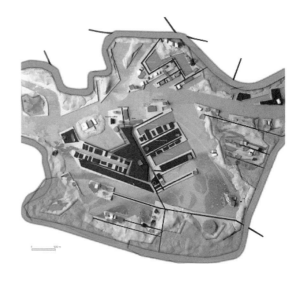

Fig 2.

spot for the city expansion, but also threatened by flood risks. Dike protection and mind sets need to change.

How can a new interface between city and port be defined?

The redefinition of the dyke deal with real estimated risk of flooding from the Maas River, due to expected high drainage peaks and rise of sea water level within the next 50 years, estimated around + 1m (see Fig. 1 and Fig. 2).

The area of the project was Heijplaat, which means literally sandy bed. Old geology maps reveal the pre-condition of the river as a more than 30 meter deep sandy bed. In SHOREs' scenario, it is literally proposed to use the enormous amount of sand material available to strengthen and widen the existing dike as protection around the left-over port basin in order to deal with overflow water. In contrast to the existing flat urban ground, the project proposes an exaggerated hilly sandy landscape, not merely a surface but a thickness – a giant river dune, able to support multiplicity and to create diverse urban situations.

The dyke as an autonomous infrastructural device becomes relational rather than oppositional:

In this scenario, movements of grounds replace movements of boats. This process marks the birth of a new landscape related to a new ecology made of substrates and movements. The sand replaces container, as the raw material of a new landscape.

The 'dune and water city' reflects upon possible new living conditions where leisure could prevail. The transformation of the port area into a place for recreation marks a shift with the original maritime activities while, at the same time, does not deny shipping and transportation of goods on the river. It proposes a new public realm in the form of a contrasting landscape, where nature, city and industry coexist.

The project investigates the possibility of landscape as a foundation for the city, and, as in a photo-negative, the possibility of the city as an imprint and memory of the river bed.

Project 2 – Liquid Sky

The spectacle of Venice

Venice is a museum, a contemporary universal know how heritage, so far preserved.

For how long? For whom? Inhabitants are leaving, while tourism increases. Climate changes, threats directly the foundation of the city. What if (a certain idea of) Venice would sink?...

What's the main idea of the project? Realize the encounter of tourism WITH the lagoon ecosystem.

How is it achieved? First , by looking at the present conditions: We need to handle sediments and tourists, lets try to do it in a symbiotic manner. Second, we propose a tourist map and invent the liquid sky as poetic destination.

And this is why you developed theses machines?

The machines serve 3 purposes: maintenance, living and enjoying. They formulate a clear index for the future map of the lagoon.

Is there any architectural concept behind your project? We design reactive process that produces a form of mechanical beauty. The machines generates experience, energy and shape the land. They built the future image of Venice as innovative water city.

Is your concept utopian or did you pay any attention to its realisation? Both. It is utopian because we propose a powerful long term vision for this territory. It is practical because simply, everything is there and can start tomorrow.

Venetian Index: animating the liquid sky

Our proposals transform the battle between sea and land, erosion / deposit, local / tourist flows into a dynamic system built around chains reactions where ecological and urban system are integrated in spectacular forms.

• Erosion, sedimentation, flow: The lagoon has a natural tendency to silt up. Its water suffers atrophy and pollution. 3 driving forces are recognized to transform the lagoon: natural sedimentation and artificial erosion are balanced in order to sustain the emerging ecological zone and create land to inhabit the lagoon.

• Wave energy garden: From the airport to Sacca San Mattia, the wave garden as the entry gate of the lagoon represents its main landmark. Tidal movements and waves created by transport boats generate EROSION dynamics and ENERGETIC pulsations. As such we can no longer oppose human presence and lagoon protection, both are symbiotic. The energy created by water movements is used for all the lagoon activities. Fig. 3.

• Inhabiting the lagoon: The lagoon as spectacle concerns both the local and the global scale. In order to enjoy it we reinterpret the Venetian Gondola into 3 typologies that offers a wide free range of programs and uses.

- Maintenance Machines for the lagoon ecosystem.

wave energy garden

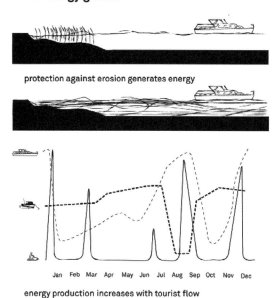

protection against erosion generates energy

Jan Feb Mar Apr May Jun Jul Aug Sep Oct Nov Dec

energy production increases with tourist flow

Fig. 3

- Temporary Venetian Housing units as refuge in the Lagoon.
- Entertainment typologies for the Lagoon. Fig. 4.
• Dredge park: drop and play: The core of the lagoon transit is the Murano Dredge Park, an energy station to reload all the electric boat system, an observatory where tourists meet sediments, and learn about the very condition of the lagoon ecosystem, and an event space in the city scale for large manifestation. Fig. 5.

Conclusion: Articulating the inhabited with the territorial

Climate change and the rise of an ecological agenda are challenging issues to engage through innovative visions and designs. If the vision defines the prospective, the infrastructural landscape project articulates the conditions and the moments of its realization.The subject of landscape design is a matter of dealing with resources, primarily ground and water: the articulation of the inhabited with the territorial.

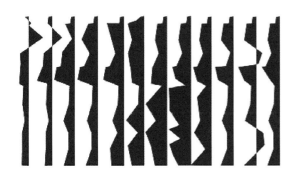

Jan Feb Mar Apr May Jun Jul Aug Sep Oct Nov Dec

Fig. 4

Fig. 5

Talkshops

Urban Waterfronts

Water in Ghent: dumped, filled in, embraced

The EU-project 'Water in Historic City Centres'

~ **Philip De Roo** ~ Landscape Architect and Urban Planner, Department of Spatial Planning, Mobility and Public Spaces ~ **Yves Deckmyn** ~ Program Communicator, Urban Renovation and Local Action, City of Ghent ~ **Abstract**

During history, water has always played a prominent role in a lot of European cities. Many of them even historically evolved at the confluence of rivers. An important reason for that was a military one; natural borders, such as rivers, have always been extremely important as a means of defense. Later on, water also became a big asset for trade activities and transport.

Filled-in

A century ago though, the vision towards water in the city started to change. Filling in water and canals became an everyday affair. Diseases were encouraged by the canals that in those days functioned as open sewers. Water was a threat to public health. The danger was not only pollution, but also its unpredictability. In the 19th and early 20th century, water was a regular menace to the city as a result of high water levels. Moreover, after the Second World War, the number of cars rose spectacularly. 'Abolished' watercourses were filled in or vaulted to make place for new traffic roads or parking lots.

Embraced

From the mid 1970s on, attitudes were changing and respect for the role of water in the city was only growing. One started to realize that city watercourses had a tourist- and an economic value, and might have a sustainable significance for the historical city, which could help improve the quality of life. In short: the water could render the public space more attractive, thereby enhancing the economic position.

Water in Historic City Centres

In 2003 six European cities joined hands for the transnational project 'Water in Historic City Centres'. This title reflects the central role that water is increasingly playing in the structural intensification of old city centres which have a historical relationship with water. All participants (Breda, The Netherlands; Chester, UK; Ghent, Belgium;
's Hertogenbosch, The Netherlands; Limerick, Ireland, and Mechelen, Belgium) are giving water an import role (again) in their city centres.

The various scopes cover a broad range of topical themes. A very important one is 'effective water management', which relies on a balance between input and output, with in some seasons an abundance of water and in others a shortage. Creating room within city centres will restore this balance. In terms of ecology, the reopening of former canals and waterways should lead towards a revitalised and more varied habitat. Further, the renewed respect for the 'recreational value' of water cannot be underestimated. Tourism also benefits from the investments in water projects. Also 'mobility' is influenced by this rediscovery of water. Excavating former canals, waterways or ports enriches the historic city centre in aesthetic terms, but it also has practical consequences: new bridges have to be built to link neighbourhoods. On the other hand, by rethinking the mobility aspect, most of the cities have started to restructure embankments and quays into promenades for slow moving traffic.

All of this proves that water certainly gives an extra dimension to historic cities. They become much more attractive and enjoyable, they receive an economic boost, and most of all: the water provides the city with fresh oxygen...

Urban River fronts along the Rhine

~ **Cornelia Redeker** ~ Architect and Researcher, Department of Urbanism,

Delft University of Technology, The Netherlands

Introduction

Agglomerations along the Rhine today are challenged by competition for location factors on a global scale. Their river front transformations currently taking place due to new boundary conditions set by climate change and industrial conversions offer the chance to reintroduce spatial complexity on a local scale. However, spatial stakes on trans-industrial urban water fronts along the Rhine are threefold and oblige a certain hierarchy: the constraints set by the Rhine as a primary navigation channel and flood management are managed on the scale of the river while urban development remains a local activity. Nonetheless, the question may be posed how these claims can be orchestrated to produce spatial qualities. Constraints set by navigation and flooding are hereby considered capable of promoting urban development beyond aesthetic conceptions. Lessons learned from the major floods in 1993 and 1995 and prospective climatic developments have lead to a paradigm change in flood management. An expected rise of water levels and consequently larger areas at risk and an increase in economic damage potential push for new urban typologies in order to enable building development on these highly attractive sites.

This research assumes three scales of relevance:
   • The River: Navigable from Basel to Rotterdam, the Rhine is one of the most dominant economic development corridors in Europe. Due to its industrial use and flood impact, it has been subject to severe anthropogenic manipulations (see fig.1) which have neglected the typological differences and qualities of its segments. A study on the specificity of the different river typologies based on their

Fig. 1 Channeled river with agglomerations.

Fig. 2 Karlsruhe.

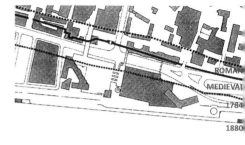

Fig. 3 Waterfront Mainz (Rahmenplan Mainz, 2005).

original state was published by the ICPR only in 2004 (Halle 2004).

• The City: For the most part Roman left bank foundations, the cities along the Rhine have developed into heterogeneous urbanized landscapes with a predominant modernist heritage of separated functions. According to UN definition all investigated cities are part of or constitute an agglomeration, yet, they hardly perform as urban entities on a regional scale.

• The urban river front as the border between River and City: The constellation between river bed morphology, water level variations and water front profile and location define the spatial parameters which negotiate the dynamic border between city and river.

Spatial flood management strategies on the scale of the river

The Rhine segments differ severely also in terms of risk. While the Upper Rhine has a much larger surface at risk, the number of persons affected is much lower. The Mid-Rhine settlements at risk are the highest due to the cities built on the narrow banks of the Rhine in the middle ages. The Lower Rhine surfaces at high risk (flood depth above 2m) are mainly those protected by dikes, but the height and maintenance of dikes and the alleged security sensed by the inhabitants of the hinterland are currently being questioned. Most threatened is the Delta Rhine Basin (ICPR flood map 2001)

The Channeling – Industrializing the river

The Channelling of the Upper Rhine in the 19th century was the first anthropogenic transformation of the river on the scale of an entire river segment and severely changed its hydraulic and morphological state. It can be considered as the industrialization of the river and severely influenced the flood regime of the Rhine. Naturally, the area downriver of the Upper Rhine is most affected by its consequences (ICPR flood map 2001) Within the past 150 years, urbanization processes and river channelling have reduced the flood plain surfaces of the Rhine branches by 65% (IRMA sponge project 2001). Retention projects along the Upper Rhine today aim to compensate for loss due to channelling and reach capacities comparable to the state before rectification.

The Expansion – increasing the number of stakeholders

The second major paradigm change was evoked by the ecological movement in the 1970s. It made the Rhine river, as other habitats, a self-organized public concern. In 2000, the European Water Framework Directive (WFD), which mainly addresses ecological aspects of water protection was legislated and recently complemented by the EU Flood Directive. The directive focuses on the coherent flood approach of member states aiming to reduce and manage the risks of floods (Proceedings Flood Conference Vienna, May 17 2006) A legal norm for boundary conditions in the Netherlands for a river dike breach lies at 1:1250 while for sea dikes it is 1:1000 (Vrijling 2004). The boundary conditions in Germany vary between 1:50 along the Mid-Rhine and 1:500 in extremely threatened cities as Cologne (Hochwasserschutzkonzept Köln). More room for the river, as a flood mitigation strategy, is already being applied on a European level for many rural areas in the Rhine catchment. Bucolic landscapes – the idyll of river expansion failing to consider the hydraulic and economic problems within given time spans are some of the arguments brought forth by hydraulic experts (Vrijling 2004). From an urban design point of view the often conservative differentiation between city and landscape seems anachronistic. A more intense combination of programs may be a key strategy for the contemporary condition of the urbanized landscape. Within urbanized areas, local river expansion strategies towards flood mitigation are still not very common due to the lack of space, higher land prices and existing building structures.

Urban Flood Management

Minimizing damage potential is the most cost-effective flood risk management measure. In awareness of the risk of extreme floods rising, total control is economically not feasible. This leads to the need to accept more risk and to develop more mitigation and adaptability in the future. By widening the river within urban areas, the water front can be expanded, while producing retention capacities on site as a possibility of incorporating more resilient techniques of flood management and possibly flood reduction on a local scale. The limited capacities of inner cities demand for local flood alleviation measures. Building a defence line is – due to scale, land scarcity, and value of a specific site – often the only possible intervention in order to protect the endangered area. Between these two extremes lies a third option, the adaptation of the endangered objects, for example when planning outside of the dikes.

Another aspect which justifies a multifunctional approach is the frequency of occurrence and duration. As floods occur annually in the Rhine catchment with a maximum duration of only several days, the existing defence structures are obsolete for most of the year. For the actual event the improved forecasting technology with flood predictions of up to 72 hours before the actual occurrence has already freed the event from being life threatening in the Rhine catchment.

Fig. 4 Innenhafen Duisburg; design Sir Norman Foster and associates and Kayser Bautechnik (Google Earth).

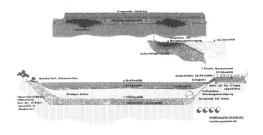

Fig. 5 Section dammed basin (Innenhafen Duisburg Enwticklungsgesellschaft).

From Basel to Rotterdam – Riverfront Developments

Historical Cities – Defensive Measures

Examples of defensive elements either temporal or integrated can be found all along the river being either temporal as in Klein Basel, in Mainz by integrating defensive elements with the historical waterfront structures by Kreysig, in Cologne by combining sheet pile walls and temporal elements or in Nijmegen with stop logs in and between the existing houses. These defensive systems are either temporal with the demand for regular practice or extremely discrete, yet subject to height limitations. Recently, research the multifunctional capacities of such systems is being investigated (Stalenberg and Redeker 2007)

Inner City Harbour Conversions – Adaptive Measures

Due to their historical position, inner city harbours are located outside of the protected areas. This implies the development of adaptive building typologies in the process of their conversion. currently different design studies are being developed for the Zollhafen project in Mainz, typologies have been developed for the Rheinauhafen in Cologne and within the UFM research project in Dordrecht different possibilities of adaptive building structures are being studied. These measures are for the most part reduced to adaptations of the ground floor. In some cases, such as the 1.5km long parking garage in the Rheinauhafen in Cologne and also due to demanded compensation capacities momentarily studied for the Zollhafen in Mainz temporal floodings are part of the strategy, but rarely offer solutions regarding the objects restoration. Maybe the most interesting harbour project, already installed in 1999, chooses a more radical approach by working with water levels and new water surfaces as a design element is the Innenhafen project in Duisburg. On site of the historical main course of the Rhine, this harbour basin has been protected from floods via a flood gate at its entrance since the beginning of the 20the century. The approach to urbanize this former harbour area implied the implementation of canals to store rain water for the newly developed neighboring housing area and a permanent rise of water levels of the harbour basin to attain a direct relationship between the buildings and the water surface. Due to channeling the height difference along the Rhine between average water levels and quay walls can reach up to 8m.

Retention Areas in Urban Landscapes

Karlsruhe, as a city along the Upper Rhine, is characterized by its meandering and originally shifting river bed and built at a safe distance to the river on a terrace 10m above the river bed. Only at the beginning of the 20th century did industry and harbour facilities began to evolve in the flood plain (Baron 2007). Today, the nature reserves and the cultural heritage of the derelict Tulla dikes, the harbour and refineries and the modernist public pool located at a side arm of the river form the hybrid landscape which is lacking a connection to the city. A retention polder for strategic flooding with 510 ha and 14 million m? will be implemented in 2014 which will be purposely flooded every 20-25 years for ecological reasons by opening its 5 gates. The city applied for the Bundesgartenschau in the Rhine meadow with a proposal to connect the city to the river (Adomat 2007). This area could serve as a potential testing site for developing a more synergetic concept between the logistics harbour, industries, landscape and landscape heritage, large scale traffic infrastructures and the technical structures related to the retention area.

Bypasses – Expanding Urban Waterfronts

• Nijmegen (Netherlands): The impact urban flood management may have on urban development along the Rhine and its branching rivers in the Netherlands may be explained via the Dutch city of Nijmegen. Located on the Waal, where river and city form a bottleneck due to the urban development along the water front and the existing defence line on the opposite bank, it is affected by slack flows during high water levels, as was the case during the floods in 1993 and 1995. Due to climate change and the inherent rise of sea levels and an increase of the normative Rhine discharge from 15.000 m?/s to 16.000 m?/s at Lobith (NL), water levels are predicted to rise about 100 cm in total along the Dutch Rhine branches if no measures are taken. Plan Brokx (www.dijkteruglegginglent.nl), a dike relocation at Lent, on the opposite bank of Nijmegen, is one of the 40 projects of the Dutch national strategy of 'Ruimte voor de Rivier' along the Dutch Rhine branches and the downstream area of the Maas to increase the discharge capacity to the North sea. The measures imply a three-step strategy – accommodating water in the region, retention measures along the river and, as a final measure, safe discharge towards sea. The intervention is financed by the ministry. The dike setback in combination with the previously envisioned urban extension plan on the opposite bank of the city can be considered the most

Fig. 6 Plan Brokx, dike relocation Lent, Nijmegen (Nijmegen urban planning department).

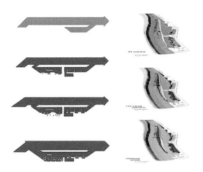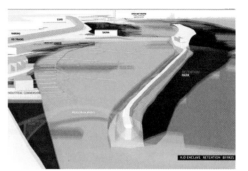

Fig. 7 K2O Urban bypass Cologne (graphics by author).

expansive within the urban realm. As a left bank Roman foundation, Nijmegen decided to cross the Waal (one of the three Dutch Rhine branches carrying 2/3 of the water) in order to extend the city in a more centralized way than growth on the left bank would allow. The setback of the dike by 350m in combination with the excavation of a side channel will give the river Waal more space. It will also create the island Veur-Lent during flooding, which will remain accessible via a new bridge. Most of the existing houses on the riverside of the existing Oosterhoutse dike can remain. The new dike in the further inland position will be constructed as a quay with buildings. The new side channel will lower the water levels during extreme floods by 35cm. The side channel will accommodate a boat stop, beaches and an interesting environment for new housing typologies. The project is currently being developed with implementation planned between 2012 and 2015.

• Cologne (Germany): The expansion of a derelict harbour basin in the city centre of Cologne creates a bypass on the right river bank. By excavating parts of an existing park and meandering the water front of an industrial conversion area a side channel is developed which is capable of diversifying the more or less monofunctional role of the river as the space necessary to create a panoramic view. To redirect the current, the existing open air theatre is remodelled into an amphitheatre. During average water levels this feature enables a velocity reduced water exchange making it accessible for other functions. As the water level rises, the theatre is flooded and as the water level exceeds a certain level, it transforms into a water slide, activating the bypass function of the new side arm. This may produce flood relief upriver on the opposite bank where the historical city lies, one of the areas with the highest economic damage potential, annually affected by flooding. The necessity to adapt buildings to the dynamic condition of this site has led to the development of floating piers which, over a fixed maximum angle, can accommodate house boats or yachts. They can not only adapt vertically to the change of water levels, but also horizontally to the increase of current once the bypass function is activated. According to first estimations, the bypass will not have negative effects on water levels downstream due to the width and slope of the Rhine at the height of Cologne. This project was the master thesis project

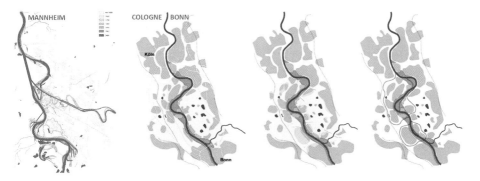

Fig. 8 Flood endangered areas   Fig. 9 Restructuring sprawl via river expansion (Jorg Sieweke, Stadträume am
and parks in old Rhine arms   Rhein, workshop 2007, Regionale 2010).
(Lohrberg
Landschaftsarchitekten).

of the author at the Berlage-Institute in 2003 and served as a basis for further explorations of river expansion within the urban realm.

• Mannheim and Cologne (Germany): An approach towards locating potential sites for bypasses may be to map the palimpsest of former Rhine arms in relation to momentary urban footprints. Blau Mannheim Blau, a study to investigate the position of the city of Mannheim between Rhine and Neckar delta, shows often former Rhine arms are todays urban green areas. A projection of new side channels may serve as a measure not only to structure developments on a regional scale, but also to create additional waterfront sites. The project (Fig. 9) shows this approach as a measure to steer development for the sprawl condition between Cologne and Bonn in the Lower Rhine basin.

Groyne City – Parasite Structures

• Hitdorf North of Cologne: To ensure the depth of the navigation channel, groyne structures are typical water front profiles along the broad river bed of the Lower Rhine. Buoyant parasites emerging along them may show urban potentials yet to be discovered. Sedimentation processes between the groynes cause problems for buoyant structures. At the same time, river expansion measures include the lowering of groynes and may imply an erosion of the groyne fields (Yossef 2005). If these highly attractive water front sites could be developed by combining flood management, navigation and urban development this could become a new urban waterfront prototype along the Lower Rhine.

Relevance of Projects for Landscape Architects, Designers and Planners

The capability of producing visions / communicating ideas as well as developing interdisciplinary design strategies which incorporate different time scales and spatial interdependencies are the architectural tasks in the field of future urban river front developments. The number of currently developed design guide lines help to develop adaptive architectural typologies. However, how expansive measures can help to restructure the regionalized condition of Central European city today are only beginning to evolve.

For both adaptive and mitigative approaches a high degree of uncertainty applies. Due to the much vaster time scale of expansive approaches which imply morphological changes of the water front, it will only find its way into practice if the advantages of synergetic design strategies will become more evident. They are dependent on research into synergetic effects regarding technical processes (inlet / outlet structures, technical infrastructure), material studies (surfaces, sponge qualities..), climatic factors (expansion of flood periods beyond the winter flood period, extremely low water tables as in 2003) to inform economical models beyond qualitative aspects.

Reflections in the Moscow River

~ **Anna Kurbatova** ~ First Deputy Urban Environment Research &

Development Institute (UERDI), Moscow, Russia ~ Abstract

Moscow is an ancient city with centuries-old history. Since 1147 when it was built, it has been rebuilt a lot of times and this process is still going on. Generations were coming after generations, and one social structure was superseding another one. The city of Moscow was granted functions of metropolis a few times, and each time except the last the city lost them. The capital went through the period of total liquidation of historical heritage buildings and construction of futuristic buildings designed by an architect Le Corbusier. Nowadays it is the biggest northern megalopolis and capital with grandiose plans for reconstruction activity.

The main objective of ecological policy enhancement when developing Moscow architecture design is arrangement of conditions required for restructuring city territories and decreasing negative anthropogenic influence on environment down to ecologically admissible rates. The most important objective of this kind of restructuring is transforming the Moscow-river valley landscape system into an architectural structure that could be valued as effective, stable, sustainable, functional and environmental.

The beauty and picturesqueness of the Moscow landscape is to a great extent owing to the Moscow-river with its lateral tributaries. The historical and business centers of the city, main industrial zones, sports-facilities and recreational zones are located on the river banks. During the recent decades the streamside landscapes potential was underestimated in the architectural policy. This caused degradation of water and riverside urban ecosystems on the area up to 1/3rd of the whole territory of the urban valley systems. The exploitation of river water areas was even more irrational. During summer time only 1/5th of its territory was used for tourist's navigation.

Today the waterside on the both banks of the Moscow-river, including most significant insular and peninsular sites makes up to 185km. A thorough analysis of the functional structure showed that the dominant types of usage are: Natural, Natural & Industrial, Public, Residential, Industrial & Transport, Idle. (Diagram 1)

The maximum length (about 60km) belongs to the sites with industrial and transport function 32,4 % (2 and 3). And 58,3 % of their total length belongs to the South Administrative District of Moscow. The minimum length of the industrial area sites, which is about 15%, belongs to Northwest Administrative District.

Idle sites located alongside the Moscow-river streamside take the second place and their length comes up to 47km (25,2%), and the maximum length (27km) belongs to the Northwest Administrative District. As to the Central and Southwest Administrative Districts there are no idle sites over there. At present time the majority of waterside in the Central Administrative District belongs to the sites with public function (about 40% in the District), and taking into consideration the lack of idle sites and insignificant length of sites with industrial function (about 9km), there is practically no potential over there for developing new recreation zones.

Taking into account the existing development of the Moscow-river streamside, the following groups of areas can be distinguished according to direction of the planned transformations. First group covers the Districts with existing residential housing, industrial and public development. Second group covers the recreational natural areas of nature (recreational zones, parks, gardens, squares, boulevards, recreational centers within specially preserved natural area).

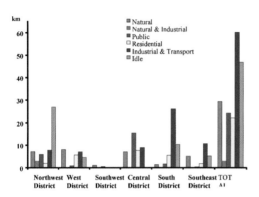

Diagram 1. The length of sites with different function alongside of the Moscow-river.

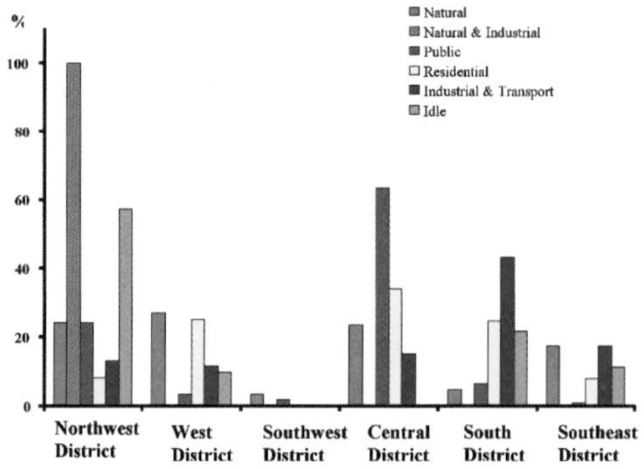

Diagram 2. Ratio of sites with different functionality located alongside of the Moscow-river (% in each District).

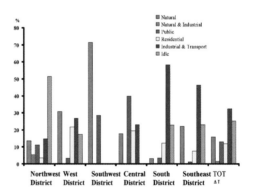

Diagram 3. Ratio of sites with different functionality located alongside of the Moscow-river (% in functional group):

In the first case the main factor for forming and improving the urban landscape environment is the application of ways and methods for comprehensive accomplishment. In the second case the main objective is ecological rehabilitation and restoration of territories of nature areas, sites of specially protected natural areas in accordance with legislative regulations for architectural activity & functional destination, specially protected natural areas belonging to the historical and cultural heritage: historical parks, gardens, manors.

The selection of objects for comprehensive landscape accomplishment on the Moscow-river streamside will be done according to the certain architectural situation, such as:
• Location of the object in the city: in the historical center, in the middle of the city, at the periphery;
  • Location of the object in relation to a certain functional zone of the city;
  • Historical, cultural and natural characteristics of the streamside;
  • City-planning role of the streamside;
  • Position in prospective architectural and spatial organization of the city.

Ecological rehabilitation and landscape accomplishment of the stream-side areas will make it possible to enlarge their capitalization, change the structure and profitability of residential and recreational building activities in Moscow. This will allow putting an end to the conflicts on a topic of land tenure concerning the territories, located at a boundary of different functional zones.

Day Three, July 2, 2008

3

Flow of Water

The source of our water is snow and rain. It collects in streams, rivers, and aquifers that bring needed water, sometimes too much for us to use, or not enough at all. As landscape architects we see rivers as the life line in a landscape, structuring our settlement and trade. Rivers become lines of communication, cultures develop along their flow. Water captures the imagination, therefore it is no surprise to find so many different perceptions of water in many civilizations. It opens our mind to another understanding of water. It is no surprise to find various philosophic arenas that deal with water in the landscape as a theme.

Water brings perceptions of landscape. Of course, these are culturally predisposed, and seem to be of only local importance. But a careful study may reveal more globally valid lessons.

Current trends in landscape urbanism are explored as a new model for urban design allied with Deleuze's "waterscape urbanism" taking Bangkok as a case.

The past intimacy between nature and landscape in the old districts of Dubai's Creek, remains a valuable source of authenticity for the booming, luxurious, Arabian novel ambiance.

The edge of Hindu's most holy river the Ganges has been sacralized in Varanasi as a vibrant and memorable city landscape for people in harmonious collaboration with nature, however vulnerable it may be.

Ancient planning strategies have proved their validity for thousands of years in Beijing. Now they pose a compelling warning for imminent, irreversible problems - although, superficially, they seem to be irrelevant for modern society.

Rivers flowing through our human landscapes provide rich opportunities for identity and sustainability of cities, communities, and the human landscape.

Rehabilitation of the riverfront in Shiraz proves an exceptional opportunity to fulfill ecological and recreational needs of the residents, promising a more sustainable community in the long run.

Spectacular redevelopments along the Han River in Seoul are good for city marketing, but need to be reconsidered with respect to locality and place identity.

3.1 Flow of Water – Papers of Morning Sessions

Bangkok Liquid Perception: the Chao Phraya river delta and the city of Bangkok
~ Brian McGrath, Associate Professor of Urban Design, Department of Architecture, Parson the New School for Design New York, US; Co-author: Danai Thaitakoo. lecturer at the Department of Landscape Architecture, Chulalongkorn University, Bangkok, Thailand

Place-telling at Dubai Creek: Encoded Visions
~ Tim Kennedy, Assistant Professor, Architecture Department, School of Architecture + Design, American University of Sharjah, United Arabic Emirates

Sacralizing the Water's Edge: the Landscape of the Ghats at Varanasi
~ Amitabh Verma, Assistant Professor, University of Georgia, US

The Drying Beijing, The Rethinking of Fengshui
~ Fu Fan and Zhao Caijun, Phd candidates Beijing Forestry University, Beijing, China

Urban Riverfront Rehabilitation, Recalling Nature to the Public Realm
~ Sareh Moosavi, Kamyar Abbassi, and Mehdi Sheibani, Authors (MLA), Shahid Beheshty University, School of Architecture and Urban Planning, Landscape Architecture Department, Tehran, Iran

Critical Reflection on Han River Renaissance Project in Seoul
~ Kyung-Jin Zoh, Professor Ph.D. Seoul National University, Department of Landscape Architecture, Graduate School of Environmental Studies, Korea

Room for Rivers
~ Regina Collignon, Program Director Room for Rivers, Ministry of Transport and Infrastructure, Netherlands

Bangkok Liquid Perception

The Chao Phraya river delta and the city of Bangkok

~ **Brian McGrath** ~ Associate Professor of Urban Design, Department of

Architecture, Parson the New School for Design New York, US ~ **Danai**

Thaitakoo ~ lecturer at the Department of Landscape Architecture,

Chulalongkorn University, Bangkok, Thailand

Liquid perception, according to the cinema theories of Gilles Deleuze, is the promise or implication of another state of perception: "…a more than human perception, a perception which no longer has the solid as object, condition or

Figure 1: The watery Chao Phraya Delta with Bangkok sprawling into rice fields to the east and fruit orchards on the west bank.

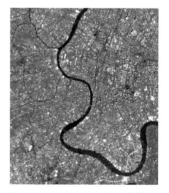

Figure 2: Bangkok circa 1890 (left) and 2004 (right) The two views show how the Bangkok urban morphology follows the pattern of water-based rice and fruit framing.

milieu. It is a more delicate and vaster perception, a molecular perception, peculiar to a 'cine-eye'" (Deleuze, 1986). This paper explores a radical shifting in emphasis from the current trend in landscape urbanism, towards a more systemic approach to urban ecosystem understanding in urban design – a waterscape urbanism inspired by the concept of liquid perception.

Much of contemporary ecology is conceived around measuring ecosystem performance through a watershed framework. In the Hubbard Brook Experimental Forest, ecologists developed a working ecosystem model by measuring the inputs and outputs in a hydrologically defined small experimental watershed in the White Mountains of New Hampshire (Bormann and Likens, 1981). In the Baltimore Ecosystem Study, experimental models derived from Hubbard Brook are being tested for the first time in urban, suburban and exurban sites (www.beslter.org). The social science model for this study, the Human Ecosystem Framework, links critical biophysical resources to social systems through the flows of individuals, energy, nutrients, materials, information and capital. In urban ecosystem science, both urban and rural patterns are recognized as recombinations of vegetative and built patches structured by watersheds identified as Patch Dynamics (Shane, 2005). Urban ecological structure and performance is understood through measuring inputs and outputs of flows through relatively small, bounded patches over time. The discipline of Urban Design is now being added to this framework in order to create new dynamic design models of urban ecosystems. Much of the work points to a reassessment of the way rivers and waterflows have been engineered to pass around and under cities rather than through them. This paper will examine contemporary Bangkok in the context of Siamese waterscape urbanism. A pre-modern, locally controlled, human ecosystem watershed model structured and sustained Siamese cities for centuries. An animist tradition combined with an inherited Hindu-Buddhist cosmological framework created a tributary culture for a forest and agricultural production society, locally managed, with a Dhamma King, as the symbolic Lord of Life symbolized through water.

Figure 3: The Chao Phraya River and the city skyline of Bangkok.

Figure 4: The Bangkok Noi canal crossed by new expressway creating two levels of the city, one land and another water based.

Along the 14th parallel, day and night oscillate neatly between predictable twelve hour divisions and months pass with little change in temperature barely affected by the earth's axial tilt. However between May and October, a slight shift in atmospheric currents brings monsoon rains from the Indonesian archipelago north to the mountain ranges ringing northern Thailand whose runoff feeds the Mae Nam Chao Phraya River Basin - and Bangkok sprawling across its flat, silted tidal delta. Seasonal cycles of precipitation, rather than temperature extremes of winter and summer, bring rhythm to life just above the equator, putting into motion human cycles of planting, harvest and migration, as well as shaping Siamese beliefs and rituals. The mountain rainforests release a sacred mixture of rain and nutrients which follows the historical geography of the capital cities of the Kingdom of Siam through the alluvial valleys at Sukhothai (13th century); terraced floodplains converging at Ayutthaya (14th-18th centuries) before finally depositing in deltaic Bangkok (18th to present). Siamese urbanity and domesticity evolved from intimate association with climatic, topographic and hydraulic conditions. River, canal and lagoon based garden cities retained six months of rainwater for the following six dry ones, staging ceremonies and rituals in sync with attentive observation of hydrological cycles and variations.

The Siamese fluvial geography was overcoded by a feudal tributary power system. Up-stream vassals and lesser kings sent annual gifts to the royal houses in the successively downstream capitals, from which auratic power was reflected back to village hinterlands (Thongchai, 1994). Honorific space materialized a layered Buddhist cosmology of distant Kings and river valley kingdoms comprising distinct watersheds. Power was primarily symbolic, as villages made decisions about land and water management locally. Contemporary life in a newly industrialized country follows the less predictable flows and fluctuations of global capital. Thailand's strategic Cold War alliance with America catapulted the Kingdom's economy to a world stage, and new ideas and fantasies from abroad now freely mix with ancient myths and rites. When rice prices fall and word of jobs in Bangkok reaches small subsistence agricultural settlements, economic migrations trickle and then flood the capital city. Now, media flows in a reverse direction of the watershed, and television broadcasts from Bangkok infiltrate nearly every household in the Kingdom. Modern Bangkok disseminates images and messages much more rapidly and viscerally to the rural majority's village TV screens, than news and laws from the distant Kings of the past, producing more impulsive and less predictable human responses.

Today, the Chao Phraya River Basin is managed by a vast network of hydro-electrical and draught control dams and reservoirs by ministries in Bangkok rather than tributary kingdoms. Modern dams and huge reservoirs replaced cities as locally controlled and maintained water retention systems modeled on the Tennessee Valley Authority with World Bank and American assistance during the Cold War. Water and floods were thought to be technologically controllable and manageable in a system that is more ideologically aligned with techno-rational models than with the complexities of indigenous Thai socio-hydrology and urbanism. Contemporary urban ecosystem science and Siamese urbanism both point to the creation of cities as water retention systems not dams – for socio-cultural as well environmental reasons.

Encoded Visions

Place-telling at Dubai Creek

~ **Tim Kennedy** ~ Assistant Professor, Architecture Department, School of
Architecture + Design, American University of Sharjah, United Arabic
Emirates

Dubai, one of the world's fastest growing cities, has created at breathtaking
speed one of the world's largest waterfront developments. Much to the detriment
of its ecology, multi-billion dollar projects, enormous human-made islands, are
forming off its coast. The city's tourism trade is one of the largest sectors of its
economy and has garnered international attention among travelers wishing to
partake of luxurious Arabian ambience. At the heart of old Dubai are the districts
that straddle the original creek; they harbor the original context of the city's
ancient reputation as the most notorious port on the Arabian Sea. The contrast
between the old and new Dubai is what attracts many of the tourists to its port
center. Yet the new modernist narratives being set in place are at odds with the
sustainability of the authentic experience that the Dubai Creek has to offer. An
exploration of the place names around the creek points to a past intimacy
between landscape and culture and tells a story that could inform how these
tourist sites can retain their valuable resource of authenticity.

Walking the Ruined Map of Dubai Creek

"The past is not dead, it is not even past." – said William Faulkner.
The Dubai Creek has continuously been an important harbor for ships sailing

Figure 1 : Dhows and ferries crossing Dubai Creek.

to various ports to the Arabian Gulf and countries of the Indian subcontinent and the east coast of Africa (see figure 1). Walking the map of streets and public alleyways of the old districts that straddle the Dubai Creek, one finds place names embedded like fossils in a map. Names derived from other unseen places that form an intertext, a locus of intersecting histories and place. In part because of the people of the United Arabic Emirates (UAE) are from a culture of the spoken word, the records and history books of the region lack definite historical names and dates. Place names are sometimes found in poetry and song without a geographical dictionary of reference. A case in point would be the myths that surround the origin of Dubai.

Some scholars maintain that the origin of the name Dubai has Arabic roots while others contend the name's origin is Persian. Many stories abound including one that says that the Arabic root word Daba is derived from the word Yadub, which means to creep. This word refers to the process by which the creek creeps from the sea into the dry land and is likened to the movement of a snake across the sand. Another story states that Dubai has a Persian etymology which translates the word's meaning as "having two sides". This story logistically refers to the settlement being defined by the two sides of the creek. Neither of the various origin stories can be verified through evidence but the city's moniker dates back to the 6th century as a name of the location.

The Bastakiya district, which fronts the Creek with its multiple textile souks, is clearly a derivative of the province of Bastak on the southern shore of Iran and denotes the immigration and settlement of those Iranian merchants who traveled from across the gulf waters.

A palimpsest in ancient times denoted writing material (as a parchment or tablet) used one or more times after earlier writing has been erased. Reading Dubai's rich palimpsest of the built environment bordering the creek, involves

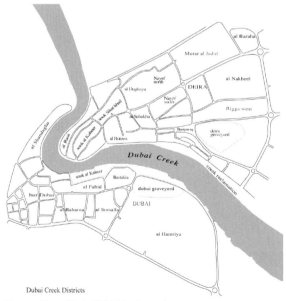

Figure 2: Map of Dubai Districts circa 1965.

unearthing the temporal depth of names as well as mapping their spatial narratives. The district on the north side of the creek is named Deira whose root meaning comes from the Arab word for circle and, as such, refers to the area as the home circle or home place. The Al Ras district in Deira means the head of land that defines the promontory that juts out into the creek. Following the line of the creek's edge from the head is Al Buteen, which akin to the belly (or its diminutive sense of tummy) because it is where water is collected and is situated in relation to the description of the profile of land as a body form. Naming the land according to human anatomy reflects an intimacy and assumed reverence for the localized ecology.

Place names model local topos

Naming is a fundamental strategy for making places. The named site becomes a storied place. Each name carries its own inception, the story of how it got its name (Johnston, 1999). There are untold possibilities when landscape narratives are seen as entwined through lived experience. It's not so much that the places remind us of stories, but rather, they exist because of the stories associated with them (Johnston, 1990). The stories encoded in the collage of place names require an act of recovery to make them intelligible to the tourist. Incorporating place narratives into the built fabric of the historic districts along the Dubai Creek could be designed as a pattern of way-finding for tourists seeking to penetrate the exuberant diversity of its streets and alleyways (see figure 2). Little known, the labyrinthine network of pedestrian alleyways set off of the vehicular streets offers the peripatetic traveler a view of daily life hidden from the thoroughfare. The courtyards that exist where the alleys converge are the sites of a condition of the public domain that doesn't know its name. Atmospheric of a past time, the public alleys create a system of open space that inhabits and connects a pedestrian web of commercial and social interactions (see figure 3).

Contrary to wilderness places, such as the Empty Quarter that are unknown as places, the sites of old Dubai are saturated with meaning. They resist being turned into the typical tabula rasa of the modernized site cleaned of all local associations. A multitude of stories compete for attention and do so with conflicting interpretations and story lines. A palimpsest in ancient times was used one or more times after earlier writing has been erased. It can also be used as a metaphor of the traces of diverse layers apparent beneath the surface of the built environment. The districts that straddle the Dubai Creek reveal through their place names a palimpsest linked to the narrative between Landscape and Culture. With assistance by Dr. Amer Moustafa with the translation from Arabic to English, the following list of place names of the districts on both sides of the creek evidence this connection:

1. Al Rigga district – refers to a landscape pattern where a shallow water table precipitates the ease of digging water well.
2. Muraqqabat district – named because of the design of its water wells. Muraqqabat means "those of the long neck" and describes the tall stone collars that ringed the wells' openings.

3. Nakheel district: Nakheel is the plural (like fish) meaning a group of Palm trees and described the vegetative pattern of the area.
4. Dhaghaya district: named for its close proximity to the sea and its inhabitants of fisherman.
5. Al Wuhelda district: named for a single landmark Palm tree that distinguished this place.
6. Al Barsha district: named after the planting of trees in groups, which looked like a decorated landscape.
7. Al Muteena district: named as the land of mud.
8. Umm Rumool district: named after sand dunes consisting of soft sand, which has certain characteristics.
9. Abu Hail district – named after the well of potable water that marked this place.
10. Al Qusais district – one legend has this historic area named after the rag roog plant in the Al Uthnien family group of trees.

Opposing this congruency between 'genus loci' and place name are many of the modern tourist sites in Dubai: Dubailand, Internet City, Media City, International City, The Greens, and The Meadows often evoke their own versions of narrative topos but with reference to other mythologies and imaginative literature outside the historic context of the UAE. The place names along the Dubai Creek provide a framework map as palimpsest, a temporal collage marking various episodes of origin, settlement and change. The persistence and accumulation of names create important juxtapositions of different times and their stories.

Archetypal Identity of Place

The differentiations of the modern world have the same structure as the tourist attractions: elements dislodged from the original natural, historical, and cultured context, fit together with other such displaced and modernist things and people. The differentiations are the attractions where an ancient weathered dhow is berthed next to a modern yacht; an old world souk is housed across the street from a multi-storied commercial mall. This juxtaposition simultaneously separates these things from those originally figured cultural elements and brings the people liberated from traditional attachments into the modern world where as tourists they may attempt to discover or reconstruct a cultural history or identity (MacCannell, 1999). Dubai famously offers a wide spectrum of tourist scenarios that range from expansive white sand beaches, elaborately franchised desert oases to man-made snow-covered ski slopes.

Honorific names were not foreign to the native emirati. The Umm Hurair district next to the Bastakiya district was so named for a legendary lady who had many, many cats. On the Deira side of the creek the Naif district was named by a legendary poet after "the Tall One"; Naif being a proper noun. This tall archetypal figure was the guardian of the district. The Hor Al Anz district was named after a legendary racehorse whose owner, having retired his favored steed, allowed her to roam this area of Deira. She was later buried in this lowland (Hoor) district. Baniyas Square in the Al Buteen district of Deira was named for the members of the Baniyas tribe who would gather in the square's open space to begin their return caravan back to Abu Dhabi. The same square was supposed to be named as a memorial for the Egyptian president Gamal Abdel Nasser but the absence of signage in the square indicates political erasure. This square and several other sites in the area will soon be affected by the proposed Dubai Metro system scheduled to run underground through the district. While this new system is expected to relieve ground traffic, it will also create a new means of conveyance for tourists to the area.

Names figure in the narrative plots surrounding questions of identity; giving presence to unknown, taking possession of space, interpreting and remembering the past, and reclaiming connections to place, history and nature (Potteiger, 2000). Currently under construction, in close proximity to the Burj Dubai, whose final height will give it the distinction of the world's tallest building, the developers Emaar UAE are advertising properties for "The Old Town". As Emaar's website states: "The development ranges from low-rise three storey apartment buildings to a number of exclusive mid-rise buildings with Penthouses. Architectural cues are taken from traditional buildings, including the Al-Bastakia neighbourhood of Bur Dubai and the residences of Sheikh Saeed Al-Maktoum and Mohammed Shareef Boukash – with textures that reflect the gypsum, clay or sarjool plastering used in the early twentieth century" ("Old Town", 2007). With its unrelenting economic growth, Deira's future development could well follow a narrative that includes the abandonment of the city's historic port for the world of high finance. The area could devolve into a state of no identity except a "poly-identity" suitable for whatever is projected into it... a faceless place blurred into one (Beauregard, 2005). At the end of the central axis of the nearly completed man-made island "Palm Jumeirah" the 2,000 room Atlantis Hotel is scheduled for completion in 2008. Based on the mythical lost continent of Atlantis, the hotel will be similar to its twin Atlantis Hotel in the Bahamas. Adjacent to the hotel is a proposed archeological attraction entitled "The Dig" where tourists can search among faux ruins and extract imbedded "specimens" as keepsakes. The tourist ensconced in his destination resort is sold a fabricated replica of the past (presumably manufactured in a distant Third World country) as a substitute for the authentic encounter with the place-telling of Dubai. Adjacent to the existing

Figure 3: Where alleyways lead to Dubai's rare occasion of public space.

Figure 4: Dhow workers along the tourist's path at the creek.

waterfront, the proposed "Palm Deira" will be twice the size of the "Palm Jumeriah" drastically changing the character of Deira's "Old Town".

Place is directly aligned with memory and how individuals remember a space. Mark Turner, in his book Literary Mind, wrote, "Narrative imagining – story – is the fundamental instrument of thought. It is our chief means of looking into the future, of predicting, of planning, of explaining. Most of our experience, our knowledge, and our thinking are organized as stories" (Turner, 1998). Erasure of the collective memory and place identity can be appraised by a sustainable approach to the local identity of the creek. Foregrounding the cultural narratives would inform those tourists desirous of experiencing what makes Dubai different from the other destination resorts they would have the opportunity to visit. Sustaining this cultural resource would also tell the tale of lived experience to a current population and provide them with an immediate connection between their environment and their self-interest. One of the basic strategies of any sustainable approach must be to avoid the risk of irreversible losses of our sustainable resources. Learning to read the complex spatial narrative of a map goes beyond the curious names. While physical forms of early settlement may have vanished, the names that persist still speak of the symbolic life of generational community.

Conclusion

The place names, coding place-telling into stories, are evidence of the past inhabitants, sustainable integration with the surrounding environs. As Kristina Hill writes, "they support, a vision of sustainability with messages suggesting: 1) cultivation of insight into the sustainable challenges that we face; 2) avoid the human tendency towards ideological and technological hubris; and 3) perceive the patterns in our landscapes that have implications for ecological processes and human health"(Hill, 2000). The districts that border both sides of the Dubai Creek are framed by re-presentations of the past functions of public and private life. The old creek makes visible for the ephemeral tourist a tangible view of its society and its works. This framed habitat is in stark contrast to the destination resorts and franchised bubbles that house the flux of tourists.

The past nature of the creek is made part of the present, not in the form of some reflected spirit of the place, but as revealed in the objects on view as tourist attractions. The work activities that continue the commercial operations along the creek are front-staged as a work-display tableau for the tourist's leisurely perusal (see figure 4). Authenticity of experience remains the tourist's coin of the realm and is measured against the familiar franchise conglomerate fantasies manufactured for their consumption. The ongoing activity of dhows docking from the sub-continent to unload their cargo destined for the nearby souks is not a costumed drama staged for visitors benefit but a timeless activity that continues to serve the creek-side settlement. The ongoing narrative along the creek reaches back to ancient times and the accumulation of its stories staggers the imagination to understand the depth of its history. One constant that keeps the past from overwhelming the present is the constant flow of water that washes away the past and keeps both its shores in an eternal present.

Sacralizing the Water's Edge

The Landscape of the Ghats at Varanasi

~ **Amitabh Verma** ~ Assistant Professor, University of Georgia, US

Introduction

As the holiest city in Hinduism, Varanasi occupies a place of unparalleled prominence in Indian culture and history. Considered the axis mundi by Hindus, it is the chosen city of one of the most significant deities in Hindu cosmology, Lord Shiva, and has always been a pivotal subject of religious mythology and hagiography. Its many names hint at its position of prestige – it is called Kashi, The City of Light, Brahmapuri, The Microcosm of the Universe, and Avimukteshwari, the City which Lord Shiva shall never forsake (Rani 2001). In addition to its association with Lord Shiva, the fundamental source of the city's sanctity is its location on the banks of the Ganges, the most sacred of all rivers in the Hindu pantheon. Accorded the stature of a goddess, the river is worshipped as a nurturing mother and purifying sacred stream, offering salvation to human souls by washing away their sins. This search for redemption forms the central tenet of Hinduism, and Varanasi continues to be a destination for Hindus who believe that they will attain salvation or nirvana by dying there and being cremated on the banks of the holy Ganges. The city shares a reciprocal divinity with the river – just as the city is sanctified by its location on the sacred Ganges, the Ganges is also considered holiest when it passes by Varanasi.

The original settlement was associated with two other sacred rivers. On the western bank were two tributaries of the Ganges, and it was between them that Varanasi was built. The city limits were demarcated by the river Varana to the north and the Assi to the south, and it is from their names that the city's name derives.

Historical Antecedents

Varanasi is one of the oldest continually-inhabited human settlements in the world (Eck 1982), with roots going back to the initial days of the Vedic civilization, which established the culture and identity of India. This period, from 1000 BCE to 500 BCE, saw the evolution and propagation of Vedic culture throughout the Gangetic plains (the plains of northern India along the path of the Ganges). The previous system of small and individual tribes was supplanted by a more cohesive political structure, and by 1000 BCE there existed 16 kingdoms in the area, one of them called Kashi, of which Varanasi was the capital city. By 500 BCE, the political arena was dominated by four of the original kingdoms, Kashi being one of them (Ching et al. 2007, 93). Because of its unique religious identity, Varanasi became a city of wealth and power, emerging as a spiritual center as well as a place renowned for learning, art, culture, literature and music, a reputation it retains even after several millennia.

Vedic civilization possessed a strong ecological sentiment, with its underlying ethos of environmental responsibility and stewardship. The Vedic perception of the universe was that of a pure and sacred system, in which each element was assigned a degree of divinity. In this scenario, man was viewed as the transgressor, and minimizing human influence on pristine nature was emphasized in all aspects of social conduct. This view of the human-nature relationship saw nature as the dominant partner, with man subservient to it. Correspondingly, Vedic literature consisted of hymns composed in praise of these divine entities, whose benediction was considered essential for the well-being of the human race.

Vedic culture and religion were oriented around the veneration of Mother Nature, in all her manifest forms of landscapes and natural phenomena. This translated into viewing all aspects of the surrounding natural environment as sacred. Rivers, caves, mountains and forests, weather phenomena such as rain, thunder and storms, and in particular the elements of nature – fire, sun, light, wind, earth, water and space – were all "personified, deified and worshipped" (Chattopadhyaya 2003, 148). Of these, the significance of water "surpasses that of other natural elements" (Sinha 2006, 192).

Figure 1: Steps at Assi Ghat.

Figure 2: Temple at Assi Ghat.

Figure 3: Manmandir Palace.

Figure 4: Steps below Manmandir Palace.

Varanasi's Built History

Throughout history, Varanasi has been a destination for travelers from around the world, including students, monks, pilgrims, artists and philosophers, along with workers in search of a livelihood. It also included a significant number of royalty and other wealthy nobility wishing to spend time in the holy city along the sacred Ganges. Notable amongst them was the Buddha, who made his way to the city in the 6th century BC after attaining enlightenment (Ching et al. 2007) and preached his first sermon at Sarnath, a town located on the outskirts of Varanasi. The venue of his premier declaration, a deer park located along a river, became a site of significance in Buddhist hagiography, and this event consequently made Varanasi a place of pilgrimage for two of the most important religions in India.

Varanasi's prestige greatly enriched its built form and transformed it into a city of remarkable grandeur. In addition to structures built by local residents, there were significant contributions made by non-residents over the millennia. As expressions of piety and charity, several building projects, including temples, rest shelters, and public wells were financed by royalty and nobility from around the country. Structures were also built as private residences or as places for residence during prolonged or frequent visits to Varanasi. Cumulatively, this process led to the creation of a remarkable architectural ensemble, reflecting not only local architectural tradition but also the building idioms of other parts of India from which the visitors came. Although some of this heritage has been lost over time, a significant amount still remains and hints at the grandeur of Varanasi's past.

Much of this building activity was concentrated along the riverfront, since the desire to interface with the river was the primary impetus for this construction.

Figure 5: View of the Ganges from Manmandir.

Figure 6: Ganga Mahal Ghat.

Buildings on the banks facilitated access to the river for ceremonies and daily worship, while providing continuous views of it throughout the day. Additionally, due to their location on the western bank of the river, the east-facing buildings provided an uninterrupted view of the rising sun, the worship of which ensured the commencement of an auspicious day. The ceremonial viewing, or darshan, of the rising sun, accompanied by the morning prayer, or surya namaskar, represents another manifestation of Hindu nature veneration and one which, although several thousand years old, is still dutifully observed by millions of Hindus around the country.

The Landscape of the Riverfront

The Ghats are the most distinctive features of Varanasi's built form, and have become the iconic image of the city familiar to viewers around the globe. Stretching along the entire length of the city, they form an edge of continuous interface with the water, creating a prolonged yet intimate connection between the static buildings and the moving water. In effect, the Ghats collectively function as a city-long, riverside park, composed of numerous individual plazas, each with a distinctive form, context, history and meaning.

The term *Ghat* is the Hindi word for bank or landing, and signifies the heightened value of the transitional space where the land meets the river, especially in context of its religious or ceremonial function. In this city where all of its parts are holy, the Ghats constitute "the most sacred geography" (Ching et al. 2007, 94). The banks of the Ganges at Varanasi possess a highly symbolic meaning as a place for performing sacred and religiously-ordained rituals, and were formalized and converted into clearly-defined and ordered spaces to reflect their symbolism as well as for enhanced functionality. This transformation took the form of the construction of open plateaus or plazas at varying elevations above the water, from which a series of linear but irregular steps cascade down to the water, in some instances continuing past the waterline and into the river for quite some distance. The size and configuration of the individual Ghats are not consistent but respond to local conditions of topography and architectural delineation.

As spaces intended to facilitate engagement with the river, the Ghats are extremely successful urban designs. The level plazas allow the congregation of large groups of people, while the steps moderate the number of devotees interacting with the water and further control the number entering into the river. They also allow for a multidimensional relationship with the water, enabling three vantage points for the worshipper: on the plaza above the water and removed from it, actively engaging the water and touching it, or in the water and surrounded by it. This choice lends itself well to the diverse array of ceremonies that are conducted by devotees, some of which require merely the presence of water, while others require an active and tactile engagement with it. The Ghats serve as a theater for the continuous performance of rituals and ceremonies at all hours of the day. The intense activity begins before dawn, when innumerable worshippers gather to perform the surya namaskar. During the day, devotees arrive to bathe, conduct ceremonies, perform cremation rites, consecrate a new marriage, perform yoga or simply offer prayers to the Ganges. Around these religious activities, others continue with the mundane tasks of everyday living – bathing, washing clothes, strolling along the water or taking a boat ride.

Architectural character of the Ghats

The Ghats are an unbroken architectural vista, reflecting the landscape as the building facades curve in response to the bend in the river, and rise in elevation with the steep topography of the hill. The result of a long process of accretion, the buildings encompass a multitude of architectural styles, colors, shapes, materials, textures and details. The built character of the riverfront is remarkably composed and organized, while retaining spontaneity and diversity. The assemblage presents a record of building traditions as they have evolved over the ages. The building typology represented, includes temples, modest and grand mansions, pavilions, plazas and terraces. Although most of the structures are religious, a number of secular buildings are included among them as well. Altogether, the Ghats present a spectacular six-kilometer long panorama whose collective visual impact is enhanced when viewed from across the river.

The Ghats include some of the most prominent historical and religious sites in Varanasi. Primary among them is Lolarka Kund, believed to be one of the oldest sacred sites in the city (Eck 1982). Located at Assi Ghat, it is a stepped well that descends 15 meters to the water. Its name, meaning the Well of the Trembling Sun, hints at its function as a sacred site for the tribal solar cults that existed in the region before the founding of Varanasi. Some of the religious traditions of these aboriginal tribes were later consolidated into Hindu beliefs, and so Lolarka Kund was appropriated as a site of sanctity by Hinduism. It has lost some of its importance to other sites along the ghats, however, and is not used by many on an average day. But on Sundays (which is the Day of the Sun in Hindu tradition) and on other festivals associated with the sun, it attracts large crowds of worshippers (Pathak and Humes 1993, 212).

Further north is the remarkable Manmandir palace, one of the most architecturally significant buildings in Varanasi. Built originally as a palace for his family by Raja Mansingh in 1600 CE, the sandstone building reflects the sophisticated

Figure 7: View of the Ghats looking south.

Figure 8: Sunken temple.

architectural tradition of the king's native desert state of Rajasthan, with exposed stone courses, crenellations, and the projecting balconies, or jharokhas, which characterize this style. The individual balconies are treated as intricate pieces of sculpture and the construction shows a masterful treatment of stone to create aesthetic features of great delicacy. The building also demonstrates the adaptation of design principles to a local context, as the jharokhas, employed in the desert to facilitate the flow of cooling breezes, here serve to provide sweeping views of the holy river and the rising sun.

The palace was modified by one of the king's later descendants, Sawai Raja Jaisingh, when he built an observatory on the terrace of the original palace in 1710 CE (Rani 2007, 29). An individual with a keen interest in astronomy, he built a chain of observatories across India, including this one at Varanasi. Consisting of a series of oversized instruments to track and measure celestial objects, the observatory was one of the earliest scientific structures in India. Today, it serves as a museum and is a reminder of one of the most interesting episodes in India's architectural history.

The cremation grounds at Manikarnika Ghat and Harishchandra Ghat embody the most symbolic, emotional and spiritual connection between the city and the river. Here, the salvation promised by Varanasi is delivered by the cremation of the human body and the immersion of its ashes into the Ganges. The sanctity and solemnity of the cremation grounds preclude an examination of them as urban spaces, but they are nevertheless significant and meaningful components of the Ghats. It is noteworthy that while in other Indian cities the cremation ground is considered an inauspicious place, in Varanasi the opposite holds true, and it is viewed as "the most auspicious of places" (Eck 1982, 33).

As the Ghats are the focus of the city, Dasashwamedha Ghat serves as the focus of the Ghats themselves, and is the epicenter of social interchange in the city. Unlike the other ghats, the building façade at Dasashwamedha Ghat is held back from the waterfront, thus creating a large open space which enables the congregation of sizeable groups of people and the conduction of public ceremonies. Access to the Ghat is by means of a dramatic cascade of steps leading down to the river from the street, with expansive views of the Ganges from the top. On auspicious holidays and festivals, the extensive edge of contact with the water

Figure 9: Access Steps to Dasashwamedha Ghat.

Figure 10: View from Dasashwamedha Ghat.

allows several devotees the opportunity to approach the water simultaneously.

In addition to its religious dimension, Dasashwamedha Ghat also plays a significant secular role as the preeminent urban space in Varanasi, with sizable traffic even on days of no particular significance. It is utilized at all hours of the day, and in addition to people arriving with a religious motivation, it is also a destination for visitors with recreation in mind. Large numbers of people access the space to take advantage of the vistas. The steps leading to the water are popular for the way they enhance the spatial character of the space and provide unusual vantage points for observation. In this space is evident the entire spectrum of daily life in Varanasi, in all its incarnations – worshippers, tourists, recreational visitors, souvenir and food vendors, boatmen, trinket sellers, etc. In addition, the other remarkable characteristic of Indian cities – animals roaming freely – is evident in great abundance, here in Hinduism's holy city, an illustration of the Hindu veneration of life in all its forms, both human and non-human. Since this plaza has become an essential attraction for foreign tourists to the city, it is one of the few places where visitors can get to know the locals, and vice versa.

Dasashwamedha Ghat is also the setting for the most symbolic communal ceremony in all of Varanasi, and one which is a remarkable manifestation of the fundamental philosophy behind Varanasi's birth, history and continued existence. Here, the veneration of the Ganges, formalized in the Vedic worldview of many millennia ago, is affirmed by the performance of a daily ritual at dusk, attended by an audience of several thousand spectators. Every evening, seven priests representing different temples from around the city conduct a group prayer in an elaborate and choreographed ceremony as an act of thanksgiving. The object of their veneration is the Mother Ganges, and prayers are offered to the river in gratitude for the patronage that it continues to show towards Varanasi. The traditional Hindu prayer ceremony, or aarti, is performed accompanied by music, chanting of Vedic hymns and lighting of lamps. The ceremony culminates in the offering of flowers to the river, which are released into the flowing water along with burning clay lamps. It is an act of daily acknowledgement by the city's residents of the intimate and eternal connection between the river and their city.

Figure 11: Worship ceremony at Dasashwamedha Ghat.

Figure 11: Worship ceremony at Dasashwamedha Ghat.

Conclusion

The Ghats are an invaluable repository of the sacred Indian building tradition, and constitute an unparalleled cultural landscape. They symbolize the concept of reverence for nature, rooted in the environmental ethos of Hinduism and integrated into everyday rituals. Their organizational patterns are a case study of significance for the exploration of urban spaces which are primarily related to or oriented towards water.

More importantly, however, the Ghats are an exceptional example of harmonious collaboration between human design and nature. Their form and composition are the result of an indigenous approach towards design which embodies a sensitivity towards the environment, natural features and topography. They accommodate the necessary human needs and activities while acknowledging the presence of the river, and make no attempt to dominate it, becoming a vivid illustration of development which refrains from excessive manipulation of nature. As even a superficial overview of urban development around the world indicates, the natural environment has been degraded significantly in recent years in the name of growth and progress. However, the environment and its constituent rivers, forests, mountains and lakes are all part of a fragile and irreplaceable system which cannot be easily repaired or rescued if damaged beyond limit in the course of development. The alteration of this delicate ecological balance has serious implications for communities in the future. Although humans possess the power (and the technology) to affect significant change in their surroundings, it is vital to evaluate decisions in light of implications for the environment. Nature must be valued and treated with respect, and not viewed as an obstacle to progress. It is incumbent upon all communities, but upon designers and planners in particular, to make ecologically-conscious and responsible choices that will ensure the continued protection of nature in the distant future. Nature can be protected in the process of creating vibrant and memorable cities for people, and Varanasi serves as a living illustration in support of this argument.

The Drying Beijing

The Rethinking of Fengshui

~ **Fu Fan** ~ **Zhao Caijun** ~ Phd candidates Beijing Forestry University,

Beijing, China

Fengshui Theory and its Rules

Fengshui is a set of ancient principles that the Chinese used for selection and construction of their living environment. Through the description of optimized spatial patterns, Fengshui guided people harmonizing their living environment with nature. It has a long history. The term Fengshui appeared in ancient times (for instance in the ancient Jin Dynasty 265A.D.-420A.D.), but activities of similar relevance can be found even much earlier (fig. 1). During the era when Fengshui originated, people had no power to conflict with nature, so they had to select sites with good conditions to settle down. Thus, many Fengshui principles easily accord with ecology. Even today, people still treat Fengshui as a standard to evaluate their residential environment in China, actually to evaluate surrounding ecology.

Chi, the word for 'air' in modern Chinese, is the theoretic kernel of Fengshui. Here Chi means vigor or energy. Ancient Chinese believed that Chi exists in all

Figure 1. Site Reconnaissance in Zhou Dynasty
(Kang Liang, Kang Fu, 1999).

creatures and non-creatures, and makes everything full of life. Therefore, also the living environment should be full of Chi. Whether the site has good Fengshui or not depends on whether or not the site is full of Chi and able to hold Chi. To understand this in the modern way, it means the site of good Fengshui provides healthy environment, bio-diversity, less disasters, and is easy to survive.

• Book of Cemetery by Guo Pu of Jin Dynasty says, "Chi floats with wind, stops at water. Ancient people made it accumulate, control it to move and stop, as means Fengshui."

• Book of Poetries has a poem titled Lord Liu, which describes Lord Liu, ancestor of Zhou (1106 B.C – 770 B.C.) migrated and then settled down in a good place. This poem is treated as an evidence of very early Fengshui activity.

Fengshui believes that Chi will be levitated by wind, and accumulate around water. Thus, gales need to be avoided, while breezes are welcome. For a site, it should be surrounded by mountains of lush vegetation, and the mountain in the north should be high; the site should be located on a sunny south slope and close to a river; the river should slowly flow from northwest to southeast, and the site on its north bank should have ponds and wetlands around. Physically, these requirements to the site accord with the geographic and climatic features of

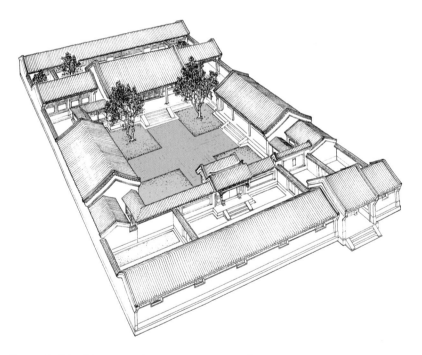

Figure 2. Traditional Court House (Kang Liang, Kang Fu, 1999).

China. China lies in the northern temperate zone, influenced by monsoons and is topographically low in the southeast and high in the northwest. In winter, extremely chill and dry monsoon winds usually blow from the northwest, and a high northern mountain can block it; in hot summer, the monsoon winds from the southeast are slowed down by low southern hills, blowing over a river, to bring humid air to the site. The site on the south slope of a hill and north bank of a river catches ample sunshine, ensures enough water supply, and avoids flooding which usually occurs on the south bank of river. The ponds and wetlands around the site guarantee pure water, and flourishing vegetation provides fresh air and rich food. We can see some similar principles in Western design theory. For instance, John O. Simons mentioned a gopher village in the preface of Landscape Architecture, "close by a creek or slough for water. ...... When these wise little critters build their towns, they search out the southeast slope of a knoll that will catch the full sweep of the sun each day to keep their dens warm and cozy. The winter blizzards that pound out of the north and west to leave the windward slopes of the rises frozen solid will only drift loose powder snow on top of their homes."

Undeniably, Fengshui is a complicated compound thought, which includes scientific contents, and plenty of superstitions caused by misunderstanding or erroneous cognition of nature. Unfortunately, people are willing to amplify the superstitious part to make it mysterious. For example, Fengshui objects any extension to the west, either for a residence or a city. The common mystic explanation is that extensions westward, the direction which represents the ancestors, will insult them, and thus cause disasters. Ironically, Fengshui traditionally treats north as the direction of the ancestors, antinomy to the above, and it does not object any extension to the north. A reasonable explanation might be that west usually is the upstream direction for rivers in China, the development in upstream area might have an adverse impact on water quality and supply to downriver area. In addition, a toilet is located in the southwest of a traditional court residence to avoid wind blowing stench into the bedrooms. When rooms are added in west, stench might be blown to this annex (fig. 2).

As the architecture technology develops and the geographic areas where Fengshui is implemented change, Fengshui principles can be adapted, and sometimes, it might be forbidden. For example, if Fengshui is applied to the Colorado River region, which flows toward the southwest, we must pay more attention to the water flow and topographic features, instead of the theoretic principles that do not fit to site conditions. Moreover, in today's peaceful world, it will be ridiculous to locate a city among mountains for security. Certainly, blocking the extremes of the monsoon is necessary. Fengshui also emphasizes separation between bedroom and toilet, because there was no toilet bout in ancient China. But nowadays, an exhaust fan and drainage facilities can solve practical problems. Fengshui commonly requests a river close to the site.

Fengshui emphasizes respect to nature and attention to the site. Its rules can be adapted or adjusted according to conditions of site. When we integrate Fengshui rules with design, we must bear in mind that the prerequisite is to satisfy the site conditions and ecological demands.

Ancient Beijing: A Paradigm of Fengshui

The earliest city settlements in the Beijing area date back to about 1027 B.C. With the advantages of Beijing's Fengshui situation, since then, many dynasties designated Beijing as their capital (Table 1).

The site-selection and construction of ancient Chinese cities enriched the principles of Fengshui theory. The rules for City Fengshui do not only consider the eco-environment, but other issues, like economy, politics, city planning, etc. as well. For example, building a city on planar field can reduce construction and building cost, and provide convenience for future city growth. The surrounding mountains and hills can block not only mistral in winter and typhoon in summer, but also an enemy's invasion. The northern mountain should be high because most of invasions in Chinese history were from the North. Close to a river, the city can flourish through river transportation, as well as enjoy convenient water supply and drainage. The mansion of a ruler should be located in the center of the city, in order to show his power. The grid road pattern makes administration more reliable and efficient, while curving roads along water are for the sake of both economy and esthetics. The water bodies inside a city can preserve water, sluice flood, adjust the microclimate, and form a pretty landscape. In City Fengshui, the importance of water is much stressed, as Guo Pu says, "Accumulating water is the prerequisite, even more important than holding wind."

Recently, Ray Huang developed the idea of the 15-inch isohyet line in his book, China: A Macro History. That is, in Chinese history, the nomadic races in the north of this line used to invade the south to pillage crops, and reverse, when food was scarce. It also proves the importance of water as sustaining livelihood.

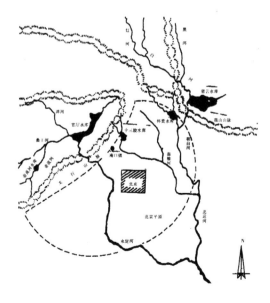

Dynasty	Time Span
Jin	1153-1213
Yuan	1264-1368
Ming	1421-1643
Qing	1644-1911
P. R. China	1949-

Table 1. Dynasties designating Beijing as capital

Figure 3. External Fengshui Pattern of Beijing (Kang Liang, Kang Fu, 1999).

Ancient Beijing is a paradigm of Fengshui, and its site-selection and construction totally accords with Fengshui rules. Zhu Xi, a scholar in Song Dynasty, said: "Beijing has good Fengshui, the northern mountain seem as if it stood in a cloud, Mount Tai is the eastern hill while Mount Hua is the western hill, Mount Song is the southern hill, and hills south to Huai River are the southern foothills." This Fengshui pattern is on the national scale. On a local scale, Beijing lies in the North China Plain, with Mount Taihang in the west; Mount Yan in the north blocks winter gales; the foothills in the east and south allow breezes to reach the city in summer, brooks lie on the site, and Yongding River flows in the south (fig. 3). The mountains and river define the external Landscape Pattern outsides Beijing. The Great Wall in the north prevented Northern enemy invasion in history. The axis of Beijing extends from the Gate DiAn to the Gate YongDing, and there are regular blocks arranged on the both sides of the axis. The Forbidden City is located in city center, and its Fengshui pattern north the JingShan (Scenic Hill), west the Front Three Seas, and south the Gold Water River (fig. 6).

Some believe that the symmetrical and grid pattern in traditional, Chinese city planning is the result of Confucianism. However, it had appeared before Confucianism and offers an easy way to administrate, so it was adopted by dominators who canonized Confucius.

The Grand Canal running North, forwarded corns and goods, and promoted the economy. Haidian in the northwest spread with ponds and wetlands, and formed a main wellhead area of Beijing for good quality water. The Long River sourcing from Haidian runs into Beijing, and carries water to the Six Seas, and then flows through the Forbidden City to the Tonghui River in the southeastern.

The large lakes inside Beijing have shaped the urban scenic areas, especially the Front Three Seas (fig. 4) and the Rear Three Seas (fig. 5). The Front Three Seas

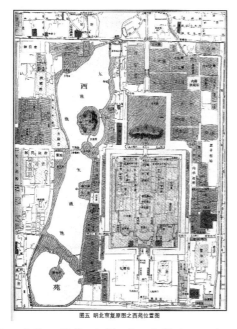

Figure 6. Map of Beijing in Ming Dynasty (Hu Jun, 1995).

and Rear Three Seas can be called Six Seas, which historically are urban scenic areas. The former, including North Sea, Middle Sea and South Sea, were royal gardens and the latter, including Front Sea, Rear Sea and West Sea, were public landscape areas. The Seas actually are a series of lakes, which are natural water bodies but artificially processed.

The Drying Beijing: The Dying Fengshui

As the environment crisis goes worse, human society has to be confronted with serious issues of climate change, resource exhaustion, and ecological deterioration. More direct impact is from water scarcity. Cities which used to be rich in water now have to struggle for the lack of water. With industrialization, population explosion and rapid urban sprawl, Beijing, once rich in water resources, has become one of the big cities in great need of water. Amount of water per people in Beijing is only 1/30 of the average of the world. According to Beijing Water Resource Bulletin 2005, "In 2005, the total surface water resources amount to 758 million cubic meters, the total groundwater resources amount to 1,846 million cubic meters, and the total water resources amount to 2,318 million cubic meters, 38% less than the perennial average value of 3739 million cubic meters." "By the end of 2005, the average depth of groundwater is 20.21 meters, decreasing 1.17 meters than that of 19.04 meters by the end of 2004, with a decrease of 600 million cubic meters of groundwater reserves." More serious, "2005 is the 7th year since 1999 when the groundwater depth continually descends" (Beijing Water Resource Bulletin 2005).

The lack of water does not only cause inconvenience of living or esthetic loss in city landscape, but also leads to ecological crisis. In principle, Beijing's Fengshui is going bad, or even drought. First, the rivers around Beijing gradually decrease, especially the Yongding River, which has had flow-breaking for many years. The vegetation of the mountains shrinks due to drying, so that the mountains are not pretty as before. Thus, the external Fengshui pattern is undermined. Secondly, surface water, the major water supply to Beijing before, cannot provide enough water to support the city operation. In order to gain more water, a great

Figure 4. The North Sea (Photo: Xue Xiaofei).

Figure 5. The Rear Sea (Photo: Zhao Caijun).

deal of groundwater has to be pumped up. However, it leads to subsidence of large area, against Fengshui theory which emphasizes the firmness of ground-work. Thirdly, the water bodies inside Beijing lose natural water resource for the lack of water. In order to match functional and visual demand, water is halted down-river, opposite to the Fengshui principle which desires flowing water. The consequence is contamination of water, and zero-flow down-river. Fourthly, dirt floats in dry air, and occasionally sandstorms takes place. The Chi (remember, the same word for 'air' in Chinese) accumulated in this way is not good, more wind is desired. Finally, the most serious problem is pollution of water, which is what Fengshui most care about. For example, in 2005, the water quality of The Six Seas was Grade V, not reach the target of Grade III; potassium permanganate and

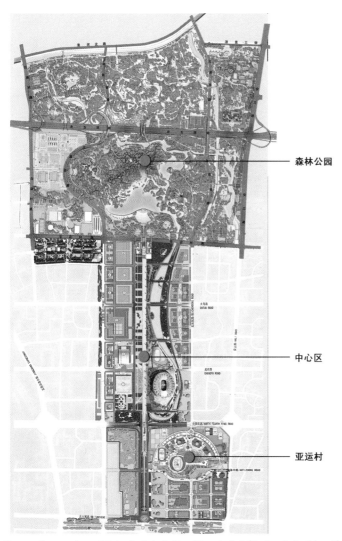

森林公园

中心区

亚运村

Figure 7. Dragon-shaped Water Body in Beijing Olympic Park (Hu Jie, et al. 06/2006).

BOD both exceeded the standards. The degree of eutrophication is medium level (Hu Jie, et al. 06/2006). In 2005 according to a report: "78 reaches of 5 surface water systems are monitored. Among them, 22 reaches come up to relevant standards of functional water quality, 28.2% of the total in quantity and 45.3% of the total in length", "21 lakes are monitored. Among them, just 1 comes up to relevant standards of functional water quality, 4.8% of the total in quantity and 35.7% of the total in area." "18 reservoirs are monitored. Among them, 11 come up to relevant standards of functional demands, 61.1% of the total in quantity and 66.1% of the total in capacity" (Beijing Environmental Statement of 2006). Currently, water supply of main water bodies in city is from reservoirs. The water capacity can just meet the minimal requirement, and ecological demand cannot be satisfied (Liu Yuxin, et al., 2007). The lack of water weakens Beijing's Fengshui. That means Beijing Fengshui pattern is dying as Beijing goes drier. Moreover, some Fengshui principles might not be used in such a situation. That is, some Fengshui rules are dying.

Worse Reality: False Implementation of Fengshui

When Beijing suffers from water crisis now, unfortunately, urban planners are not aware of the seriousness of this issue. They still introduce some inappropriate Fengshui principles into city planning. For instance, they design large-scale artificial water bodies for holding wind and gaining water or, we should say, it is just for visual enjoyment. However, it is wrong from both Fengshui and from the ecological viewpoint. Fengshui emphasizes the movement of water, and claims that flowing water will never go bad, or rot. Even man-made water bodies should have an inlet and an outlet to keep water flowing. However, current artificial water bodies does not have natural water inlets, and need water feeding. Thus, part of limited water resources has to be used to fill it, and complement it constantly because of evaporation. In order to prevent leakage, waterproof is used to hold water, which cut off the connection to soil and groundwater. Without movement, inefficiently self-cleaned by only ornamental aquatic plants, water quality will easily be deteriorated and undergo eutrophication. Pumps are used to keep water circulating and flowing. However, it will consume large quantities of power. Although the evaporation of water can increase the humidity in surrounding area to improve microclimate, in current dry situation, moisture will be quickly evaporated to the upper air, so that people on the ground will not get benefit from it. Furthermore, when water quality deteriorates, the smell with evaporation will make people sick. Things relapse into a dilemma, that is, planning and design using Fengshui theory make Beijing drier, which is not what Fengshui theory expects. The main reason to cause it is that essence of Fengshui is disobeyed, that is, respect to ecological environment.

The Olympic Park is such a case. It lies in the north axis of Beijing, with a total area of 1215 ha. An artificial water body designed in the shape of a dragon takes up more than 80 ha of this park (fig 7). It is a misunderstanding to consider the dragon shape as implementation of Fengshui. Fengshui opposes figurative shape, which is conflict with aesthetic tradition in China. Balance between similar and not similar, nonfigurative similarity is what Fengshui pursues. This kind of planning, which seems to imprint a seal on the map is very bad, and with poor scale. In Fengshui theory, headstream is required for a water body, but the park did not consider it. Therefore, water supply would be a big issue. According to a report by the designers, the Central Lake of 22 ha needs water suppleted, as much as 576 thousand cubic meters per annum (Ton Qing-yuan, et al. 08/2006) (Table 2). To this assumption, the whole water body will need about 2.3 million cubic meters water.

According to the press, 70 thousands cubic meters of water need to be filled in the water body daily (Liu Yuxin, et al. 2007). Although the former figure is much less than the latter, it is still a big proportion of Beijing municipal water supply of 100 million cubic meters. In addition, in order to keep the Central Lake clean, water has to be circulated daily during the period from March to November. 10 to 20 thousand cubic meters of water will be circulated daily, a large consumption of power (Ton Qing-yuan, et al. 08/2006). If other water bodies also need circulation by pump, the consumption would be more enormous. There were indeed some large water areas in ancient Beijing (table 3), but those were built when Beijing was rich in water. Furthermore, most of these used existing water bodies, with only minor adaptations. The existing water area in Olympic Forest Park amounts to only 16 ha. To excavate a water area of 70 ha on the site is a huge work (Hu Jie, et al. 06/2006).

However, this wrong model of planning is not corrected by governmental agencies. According to Beijing Environmental Protection and Ecological Construction Plan, the Eleventh Five-Year (Quinquennium) Plan from 2006-2010, urban waterscape system will be extended to "increase the urban water surface from existing 920 ha to 1236 ha." If the average water depth is 1.5 meter, 4.74 million cubic meters of water will be used to fill the new water areas. Estimated with the data

Month	Evaporation	Water for green lands	Central Lake pervasion	Surface runoff	Rain on water body	Total water requirement
Jan	1.4	0	0.5	0.1	0.1	1.7
Feb	1.7	0	0.5	0.2	0.2	1.8
Mar	3.4	5	0.5	0.4	0.3	8.2
Apr	5.8	5	0.5	0.9	0.7	9.8
May	7.2	5	0.5	1.5	1.1	10.2
Jun	6.8	5.8	0.5	3.4	2.5	4.9
Aug	4.9	6.2	0.5	8.1	5.8	0
Sep	4.1	6.2	0.5	7	5	0
9	3.8	5.8	0.5	2	1.4	5.5
10	3.1	5	0.5	1	0.7	7
11	1.9	5	0.5	0.3	0.2	6.9
12	1.3	0	0.5	0.1	0.1	1.6
Total	45.4	49	6	25	18.1	57.6

Table 2. Central Lake water balance (10k cubic meters), Olympic Forestry Park.

Name	Total area (ha)	Water area(ha)
Old Summer Palace	350	140
Summer Palace	290	220
North Sea Park	68.2	38.9
Beijing Olympic Forest Park	680	72.5

Table 3. Some Beijing parks with large water area.

from Olympic Park above, the water suppletion for the new water areas amounts to 9 million cubic meters per annum. It will be a big challenge to Beijing's water supply.

Another case is the Nanshui Beidiao project, part of which is to transport water from Yangtse River to Beijing through pipelines. According to Fengshui theory, water should not flow from south to north, but from north to south. However, this project is opposite to it. China is topographically low in southeast and high in northwest. Delivering water from the South to the North will lose a great deal of water on the way, as well as consume a large amount of power to pump the water up. In addition, once Beijing gets more water, the city will continue to expand, and then more water will be demanded and transported from other places. It will only create a vicious circle.

Major Recommendations

The global issue of water scarcity is complicated and hard to solve, especially for Beijing, a metropolis with a huge population. However, we are still willing to share our ideas, some of which are based on rethinking Fengshui principles of water. Main Fengshui principles of water are as follows: water is the most important element of our living environment; sites should be close to water, but away from flooded area; water should flow; water quality must be clean; water must be protected; water bodies inside the site are required.

The importance of water should be emphasized. Water is the essential element not only for creatures survival and economy growth, but living improvement. Without water, city could not exist and develop. Therefore, landscape architects should put this idea in the first place in planning and design. People should be encouraged to save water. Besides reducing and recycling industrial, agricultural and living water, unnecessary water usage should be reduced. Landscape architects should reduce water body in design, especially large water body without covered by tree shade, moreover, trees evaporating lots of water should be forbidden to use. New water resources should be discovered, especially those ignored before. Storm water drained away by pipeline before, would be a new water resource now. To encourage storm water collection, Beijing government rewards 500 RMB per square meters for effective collecting area. Although storm water collection is increasingly used, we still need to call for more practices. Beijing is doing a roof reconstruction project of millions of square meters, however, unfortunately, visual esthetics is more considered, instead of storm water collection and solar energy utilization. Grey water is another usable resource, and widely used in Beijing parks. How to effectively combine storm water collection, grey water and other new water resources with landscape is what landscape architects should research on.

Water quality management should be paid more attention. Traditionally, sewage is drained to river and purified by hydro eco-system. However, the hydro system cannot to deal with today's excessively polluted water. Government should be asked to increase sewage treatment facility, and avoid to draining sewage directly into river. Wetlands should be restored or constructed in light pollution area. However, there is undesirable chaos that constructed wetland is so over-praised that people get wrong impression that wetland can replace sewage treatment facility. Furthermore, many advocators only provide concepts, and their wetlands are not different from common ponds. Grey water and constructed wetlands will be used in Beijing Olympic Forest Park (Hu Jie, et al. 06/2006). If the system runs well, it could be a good example.

Fengshui principles, originated from Agricultural Society, should be adjusted. Even if they were completely right before, it should be adjusted now, due to the developing society and changing environment. The principles, which were right before but go wrong now, need to be adapted or discarded. For example, large water surface is not suitable for a city's lack of water, especially when water supply for the city is not enough. Perhaps underground water bodies might be a better solution, and green land could be constructed on top. Landscape architects should take responsibility in front of water and environment crisis. Not just as citizens, saving water in daily life, but also as professionals, mitigating crisis through knowledge and technique.

Conclusion

After the Industrial Revolution, rapid development in technology makes it seemingly possible that people could change nature, and control nature. Therefore, in planning and architectural design, natural setting of the site is less considered. For instance, a city can be built in bottomland with dam to block off flood; a city can be built in the desert with piping to supply water; a toilet can be designed without window for ventilation when using an exhaust fan. Everything seems reasonable before crisis comes. However, the disdain to nature is ironical, when sea level rises, water resources become scarce, and energy runs out. When we re-stress Design with Nature, Fengshui could provide some advices. We must know, Fengshui is not the only way to solve environmental issues, and Fengshui, which was originated thousands years ago, could not provide solutions for all current issues. But, Fengshui could provide a way of thinking, telling people to respect nature, protect resources. A landscape architect, whether he trusts Fengshui or not, would be successfull when he considers site conditions, designs with nature, and develops in sustainability.

Urban Riverfront Rehabilitation

Recalling Nature to the Public Realm

~ **Sareh Moosavi** ~ **Kamyar Abbassi** ~ **Mehdi Sheibani** ~ Authors (MLA),

Shahid Beheshty University, School of Architecture and Urban Planning,

Landscape Architecture Department, Tehran, Iran

Introduction

After abusing urban rivers through years of hard use and neglect, river corridors have been reassessed as important resources for the preservation of nature and habitat restoration, as they can generate a continuous natural feature within the urban landscape. Moreover, these corridors have the potential to function as healthy, appealing environments, reconciling people with nature in the midst of the industrialized urban bustle.

Shiraz, an ancient city located in the southwest of Iran, has always been renowned for its pleasurable gardens and fabulous architecture. However, like other metropolises in developing countries, it has lost much of its natural and man-made open green spaces through rapid development, resulting in a lack of natural recreational spaces and increasing environmental problems.

"Rud-khaneh-Khoshk", or Khoshk stream, is currently a dry flood channel, passing through the urban context of Shiraz and its green patches of gardens. Flowing from northwest to southeast, this river is the confluence of several seasonal flood streams of the watershed. Restoration and rehabilitation of this channel is an exceptional opportunity to fulfill both ecological and recreational needs, while improving its public image from a menacing, abandoned flood channel to a vibrant corridor. More specifically the goals are listed below:

• Control seasonal floods and decrease flood damages.
• Improve water quality and quantity.
• Create and Improve opportunities for recreation while protecting ecological resources.
• Improve access for those in urban areas to outlying natural and recreational resources.
• Preserve and protect the ancient gardens and green landscapes along the river.

Approach

The study presented here aims for restoring hydrological processes, enhancing habitats, and providing opportunities for human activities along the urban river. In this process the first step would be a quick review of literature on landscape ecology for the riverfronts followed by major ecological principles of riverfront design, developed from worldwide frameworks, concepts, and guidelines. Each principle then would be juxtaposed with the current situation of the river, leading to creative local solutions and ideas supported by relevant sketches and illustrations.

Shiraz, history and characteristics

Shiraz is the capital of Fars Province and the sixth most populated city in Iran, and is located in the southwest of the country; it is is renowned for its poets, architecture, wine, and flowers. It is also regarded by many Persians to be the city of gardens, due to several fabulous gardens and orchards that can be seen throughout the city. Shiraz was founded in the 7th century and was the capital of Iran during several periods of its history. Shiraz's vast plain is around the southeastern part of it, and is regarded as one of the fertile plains of the country for its rich ecological and natural resources. Since the industry sector was not developed until the late 19th century, the main structure of the economy was based on agriculture and gardening. The plain is surrounded by two mountain ranges from north and south where natural springs have emerged on their southern skirts contributing to the development of gardens and natural green fields of the region. Exponential growth of the population after the Islamic revolution, due to the influx of immigrants from rural communities to the city, led to rapid uncontrollable development of the city structures, consequently resulted in the fragmentation of agricultural land and gardens. Such valuable green patches of nature were soon replaced by several high density buildings. This was followed by the outbreak of the imposed war, leaving no chance to recover the degraded sites. Therefore citizens gradually lost their contact with nature as the city confronted the lack of sufficient green spaces.

One of the natural features which have been in the focus among the metropolitan authorities is the urban river. Shiraz already has the natural gift of The Stream. It creates a continuous corridor through the whole city, brings in spectacular vistas of the surrounding landscapes, and has a great potential in generating considerable effects on ecological qualities of the urban life.

Project Area

The stream's two main tributaries: Nahr-e-A'zam from the north-west and Chenar-Sookhteh from the west, join at the point of Hossein-Abad Bridge, ending up into a wide dry channel called "Rud-Khaneh-Khoshk" that literally means the "dry stream". The channel runs from north-west to south-east, passing 33.5 kilometers through the city and finally discharges to Maharloo Lake. The Khoshk Stream is a seasonal flood channel mostly dry from May till October, facing the loss of spring/summer flow throughout the year. However during periods of high precipitation, the river overflows and damages the urban structures along its banks. Surely the increasing invasive development on the floodplain is the main threat to the natural milieu of the river. In order to provide safety for these man-made structures, the natural channel is channelized by high stone and concrete levees. As a result, not only the river features were visually blocked, but it also has endangered the river's natural health. Most of the decisions made for river's flood control, have degraded the riverfront's sense of place: As it is made impossible to access and enjoy the landscape, the river is turned into a lost, forgotten

Figure 1. Map of Iran and location of Shiraz.

Figure 2. General Map of Shiraz.

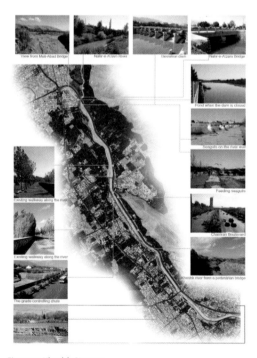

Figure 3. Khoshk Stream.

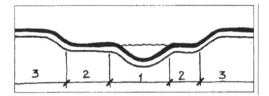

Figure 4. Landscape units of rivers.

flood channel. As long as these seasonal rivers are treated as mere flood-channels, their public image is unconsciously degraded into a destructive element.

The gardens along the river at the north-western part of the city and on the southern side of Chamran Boulevard, form an important part of Shiraz current green spaces. The absence of proper planning management to optimize the use of water resources for irrigating the gardens along the river bank, has also threatened the life of these valuable greeneries. The part of the channel passing through the green vicinities, has turned into a lifeless corridor creating a gap between two green districts: Ghasr-e-dasht private gardens located on the south of the river and Chamran gardens and a recreational linear park along Chamran Boulevard on the northern side (Fig 3). Rehabilitation of this river not only would reduce the probable threats of overflows and supply the required water sources for irrigating those gardens, but also could offer opportunities to develop recreational green spaces for the citizens and connect the separated two green zones on either side of the river, making the waterfront accessible for people's use to the greatest extent possible. But the question is: how can we make water accessible to the largest number of people and at the same time preserve its purity and the ecological milieus?

Awareness of environmental qualities has increased with the need to regenerate degraded urban areas, preserve and restore natural resources, and improve water qualities. What is now at stake are environmental issues that require a much more global approach. Therefore ecological approaches in design and planning have emerged, and a new discipline has appeared: Landscape Ecology.

Landscape ecology and the ecological components of urban river

The most recent efforts to define landscape ecology emphasize the need for integration between bio-ecological and geological perspectives (Moss 2000a, 2000b). A landscape might range in size from hectares to square kilometers in area, comprising a heterogeneous area where ecosystems are repeated in similar form and interact (Forman and Gordon 1986). Landscape ecology is the analysis of this space. The river or stream corridor as defined by Forman and Gordon (1981) is formed by the channel, the river banks, and the floodplain, surrounded or limited by hillslopes and uplands. For the purpose of this study, the river corridor is divided into three landscape units identifiable in the corridor cross section: 1) channel and river banks, 2) floodplain, and 3) hillslope and uplands (Penteado 2004).

Each landscape unit plays different roles (or has a specific function) in the corridor. For example, nutrient flow and erosion are inhibited by stream bank vegetation (Forman 1995). The stream bank provides shade, overhanging vegetation for cover, detritus in the form of leaves, and large woody debris. The floodplain, also known as the riparian zone (Tabacchi et al 2000), provides stream with organic matter. The uplands help control the input of dissolved substances, such as fertilizers, road salt, pesticides, and other organics as well as heavy metals (Forman 1995). Considering the biotic and physical components of the river corridor, as thoroughly described by Penteado in his article "The river in the urban landscape" (2004), the main ecological components of a river are defined as:

- Hydrology processes including River continuum, Floods, Ground water, Stormwater, and Drainage.
- Geomorphological structure/function including Soils, Erosion, Slopes.
- Particle flow including Sediments, Pollutants, Nutrients.
- Biological structure/function including Vegetation, Seed propagation, Habitats, Wildlife (birds, terrestrial, insects), Fish population.

Principles for Ecologically Sound Riverfront Design

This section provides an overview of principles for planning and designing Khoshk Stream renewal and discusses the comprehensive, holistic, and regionally specific approaches needed to improve the ecological and economic health of this urban riverfront. The principals are divided into three categories based on the approach scale: General Principles, Planning Principles, and Design Principles

General Principles

Ecological goals and economic development goals are mutually beneficial: Turning the dry channel into a healthy, running river with natural efficient environment, would be appealing to visitors and residents. An engaged public that enjoys riverfront features and activities also would care about the river's long-term health - which in turn builds a sense of connection and stewardship for the river. Beyond supporting tourism, these benefits also include cost-effective flood control, improved water quality, reduced infrastructure costs, and increased property values.

Protect and restore natural river features and functions: Fortunately the natural morphology of the Khoshk Stream has been maintained in most parts while passing through the city (Fig 5). The current cross-section of the channel also matches the average volume of flood water passing through without spilling over the banks.

Among factors which has interfered the natural dynamism of the flow is the Nahr-e-A'zam deviation dam and the grade-controlling chute (Fig 6) in the project area. Designing eco-structures to support the natural flow and preserve natural features of the environment is necessary. For instance in designing grade-control structures, the natural patterns of the breaks in river bank slope – as observed in the untouched suburban landscapes - could be adopted to form a terraced bank made up of the existing bed stone strips.

Figure 5. Aerial image of the river passing through the urban context.

Regenerate the riverfront as a human realm: The Khoshk Stream has not always been a peaceful neighbor for the urban residents, mostly remembered as a menacing flood channel. As a result its vibrant potentials have been neglected through times: surrounded by concrete and stone levees, making it inaccessible and out of sight for the citizens, eventually omitted from the daily flow of urban life. Although sociable people of Shiraz are renowned for their great tendency in attending pleasurable natural places and public recreational events, the negligence of the organizations in charge, has ultimately deprived these outgoing citizens from experiencing the presence of a unique natural corridor. As a result people mostly retreat to the private gardens located in the suburbs in times of vacations and the poor section of the society are compelled to pass their days off among the greenery of the boulevard medians and squares. Rehabilitation of this lifeless corridor could be a unique opportunity to meet the recreational needs of the citizens while bestowing a new identity on this forsaken urban milieu.

Planning Principles

Planning for riverfront revival must consider regional development patterns, natural and cultural history, flood control, public access, recreation, and education. The following principles should be integrated into a master plan of the river and implemented through zoning and building codes, engineering standards, and site plan and design.

• Demonstrate characteristics of the city's unique relationship to the river. Every river city has a unique relationship and history interwoven with its river. Even though research in historic texts reveals it, one can barely find specific remarks upon the historic/cultural role of the Khoshk Stream in Shiraz, but the most important aspect which makes the river vital to the city is its generosity in supplying the water requirements for the gardens, agricultural lands and few water-mills: the fabulous cultural landscapes which the ancient city is renowned for. From this point of view the riverfront could be treated as a platform on which the essence of life and healthy interactions with nature could be grasped

Figure 6. Man-made Chute.

Figure 7. Construction of bypasses within the river flood-plain.

by the weary but eager citizen.

• Minimize new floodplain development, because rivers are dynamic. The construction of new traffic by-passes within the river banks, to solve the heavy traffic problems, is regarded as one of the main threats to the riverfront health (Fig 7). While such improper development would block the pedestrian-friendly access and disconnects the riverfront from its neighborhoods, it also increases the amount of impervious surface and the risk of costly flood damage. As undeveloped, connected floodplains are essential to river health, new development on the riverfront, including trails and parks, should be designed to minimize floodplain intrusions.

• Provide for public access, connections, and recreational uses. Easy access to riversides is vital to draw people to the riverfront. Visual connections to the river from nearby commercial and residential areas also are important (Otto, McCormick and Leccese 2004). Current economic revitalization along riverfront, such as the new mixed-use development of a linear park on the northern side of the boulevard and riverbank (Fig 8), with trails, restaurants or cafes, sitting areas and open spaces, can work in a more successful way when visual and physical access to the water is included.

The experience of walking along the river will be enriched by several design elements, including steps and ramps on the southern side of the river along the Saheli Street, pedestrian and bicycle trails along the river, pedestrian bridges to provide the access to the northern side. Adequate seating and benches for resting and observing the natural life of the river, particularly for watching and feeding birds will also be installed along the walkways.

• Celebrate the river's environmental and cultural history. Riverfronts are rich in both human and natural history. Educational and cultural programs, performances, and public art entice people to the riverfront. Educating the public about the river and its natural systems will generate a sense of stewardship and a connection to the river's history (Otto, et al 2004). Holding interactive programs to illustrate the cultural history of the site (such as the ancient water-mills and traditional approaches in using water for irrigation in the past), introducing wildlife and different ecosystems of the river and providing proper fields for traditional ceremonies should be considered along the riverfront. Celebrating spring is

Figure 8. Chamran Linear Park.

another example.

• Sizdah-Beh-Dar: Water and Nature celebration day in Iran. Unlike most people of the world, Iranians celebrate the New Year in Spring with the resurrection of nature: The holiday consist of a thirteen-day period which starts right at the beginning of the season. Sizdah-Be-Dar -the last day of these holidays- is a very common celebration among Persians as it is the day of celebrating water and nature in Persian mythic culture. On this day people avoid sadness and despair as a sign of gratitude for the nature's gifts, taking refuge in nature. As an old tradition, people throw their thirteen-day hand-made verdures into water as a sign of prosperity and as a gift to "Anahid (Nahid)" - the goddess of water.

Shiraz hosts many tourists during holidays every year. Thus rehabilitation of the river gives the city an opportunity to attract even more tourists and visitors to enjoy the holidays and to revive the old traditions by encouraging people to respect the sanctity of nature and water.

Design Principles

The principles presented in this study are based on the landscape scale and will be used to develop recommendations as well as design solutions (strategies) to enhance ecological function at the site scale for rehabilitation of the Khoshk Stream.

• River Continuum and Connectivity. Rivers have been discontinued by dams, locks, and weirs in order to control floods and make navigation possible. In general, dams should be avoided as they can severely alter natural flows, raise water temperatures, trap beneficial sediment and other materials, and create impassable barriers to fish (American Rivers 2003). The flood control programs presented for the river by the municipality experts in charge include construction of a new dam with the height of 70 meters which is now under development. Also a deviation dam is already constructed at the point where Nahr-e-A'zam river joins the main flow. Figure 9 and 10 show that retention of water by weirs interrupts the river continuum while creating sedimentation on its upper portion and changes habitat.

Fig 9. Deviation dam of Nahre-A'zam and sedimentation after the dam is opened.

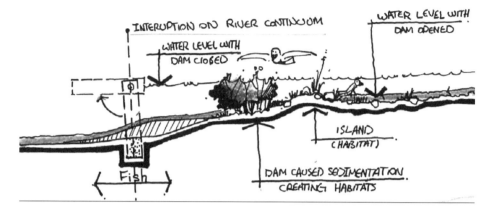

Figure 10. Longitudinal section of the River with the deviation dam, islands created by sedimentation after lowering of water.

Figure 11. The loss of spring/summer flow, represents a negative impact on the life of the river.

Figure 12. Channelizing the river to avoid flood damage!

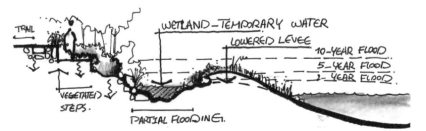

Figure 13. Lowering of levee to allow partial flooding and vegetated steps.

Although construction of such engineering structures may force negative impacts on the river's natural dynamics and continuum, the loss of spring/summer flow, represents a much more negative impact on the presence and hydrological life of the river (Figure 11). Keeping such engineering works, requires proposing alternative structures and solutions to allow function, such as steps for fish migration in dams.

• Floods. Although important for natural processes, floods are usually undesired in urban areas (Bechtol 2008). Traditional approaches to flood control in most cities like Shiraz, have relied on structural works, such as widening, raising the levee's height, lining with concrete, or straightening by cutting through channel meanders to shorten the flow distance (Fig 12). Indeed, despite the noticeable cost spent for engineering works built on the river bed and on the floodplain, flood damages continue to escalate in parts because of intensified floodplain development and engineered river corridors. Minimizing such development and creating wetlands can reduce flooding threats besides filtering stormwater. Construction of the new dam can also help control flooding.

There are some ecological solutions, such as lowering portions of existing levees or river banks where ever it is possible to create areas of sediment deposition, where wetlands could form (Fig 13). These measures could increase biodiversity and ecological function in areas where homogeneous plantings or highly managed areas occur (Penteado 2004).

Another alternative to hard engineering is bio-engineering (also known as soft engineering) which has gained acceptance among civil engineers and public works departments. Bio-engineering uses plants and other natural materials to simulate natural forces that, in turn, control floods, maintain water quality, provide access to recreation, reduce erosion, and create wildlife habitat (Riley 1998). In extremely urban situations with a narrow floodplain, where naturalized bank slopes and wetlands are not possible, using hybrid engineering methods such as ripraps, vegetated slopes and gabion walls that are packed with soil and planted is suggested (Fig 14).

• Groundwater. Groundwater in the city is affected by built structures (buildings and roads, for instance) that diminish its quality, divert its flow, or pollute it. Existence of high buildings near streams can directly interrupt the flow of water; it also compresses or lowers portions of bed rock, expelling water. The flow of water between land and stream is also an issue: adoption of retaining walls might represent a barrier that might cause lowering of the water level in a channel (Penteado 2004). Possible solutions for the flow of the groundwater between channel and floodplain can include revegetation of the riverbanks and adoption of pervious materials such as gabions and porous materials (Fig 15). Considering buffer zones can also filter polluted runoff before reaching the main flow.

• Stormwater and Drainage. Traditional drainage systems facilitate fast conveyance of water. The ideal drainage occurs when runoff flows as sheets of water on low slopes and pervious surfaces, reducing speed and allowing infiltration and filtration (Penteado 2004). Stormwater can only be controlled, treated, and used as a resource in the landscape if decisions extend beyond the limits of the river-front. For example, the use of gabions to stabilize riverbanks, allows the flow of groundwater. However, if actions are not taken to allow water to infiltrate, instead of flowing inside pipes, the river will lose water to its surroundings instead of receiving groundwater and reaching equilibrium (Fig 15). As example of structures, trenches, swales, retention and detention ponds can be used to postpone water discharge, delay runoff, and be the base for sedimentation and filtration.

• Pollutants, Nutrients, and Sediments. Nutrients and pollutants originate mostly on the matrix and are carried by runoff toward rivers. The floodplain has the potential to function as a buffer for much of the occurrences on the urban matrix. Water pollution is considered as one of the most important problems in case of Khoshk Stream as the urban channel and its surrounding landscapes has been turned into a place for dumping waste and discharge of raw industrial, agricultural and urban sewage while the industrial pollutants from the factories covers the highest level (Bidokhti and Monajjemi 1996). Besides the need for displacement of such industries out of the restricted zones and the necessity for organizational supervision over the discharge of such pollutants, developing buffer zones is highly required for urban-runoff filtration and pollutant absorption before such detrimental factors reach the water body of the river. But riverfronts are exceptionally difficult areas in which to create vegetated buffers because of the need for water views and access, recreation, park management, safety, crime prevention, and flood protection. Features that can work as buffers are swales, filter strips, and setbacks. Reduction in use of pesticides, fertilizers, road salt and other pollutants is also suggested (Fig 16 and 17).

.As seen in figure 18 there have been efforts in planting rows of Black Poplars (Populus nigra) alongside the channel as a means of creating a buffer zone, carried out by the city's Parks and Green Space Organization. Such green strips contribute to riverbank stabilization and absorption of nutrients and filtration of few pollutants, but block the access and views from the road and residences towards the river. Planting lower plants and shrubs –instead of trees- is suggested in places, while complying with the appropriate planting patterns along the flood-

Figure 14. Sample for Vegetated Gabions.

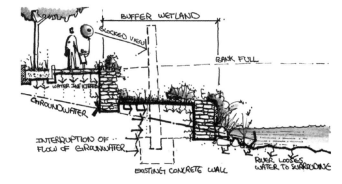

Figure 15. Existing concrete walls substitute natural banks. Walls impede ground-water to flow between land and channel in both directions. Vegetated gabions and permeable paving allow water infiltration to maintain continuous flow.

plain slopes.

• Riverbank and Stabilization. The stability of river banks and the flow of groundwater both can be achieved with the use of gabions. However, if not integrated with native vegetation, gabions might facilitate the flow of pesticides and other chemicals to the river. Ideally, riverbanks should be restored with native riparian vegetation that stabilizes (Fig 19) while absorbing water, pollutants and nutrients (Penteado 2004). In biotechnical engineering, native plants are interspersed with an engineered erosion-control system, such as geotextile fabrics. Plantings are not expected to hold the soil, but they do provide habitat. For example, riprap can be naturalized by interplanting live stakes of Willows or other native species. Within a year, live staking can provide shade, habitat, and erosion control (Sotir and Nunnally 1995). Restoring the river's natural features in parts of highly altered environment of the Khoshk Stream is somehow impossible. Yet there are numerous strategies to "soften" the concrete retaining walls and other hardscape features which suggest several techniques to add native plantings to the wall where substitution of stepped gabions, native plants and piles of vegetated rocks is not impossible. One calls for the installation of a "timber grid," a latticework that extends beneath the waterline on the wall and supports aquatic plant species. The grid creates new habitat by providing cover for

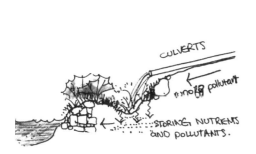

Fig 16. Culverts should be moved away from the bank

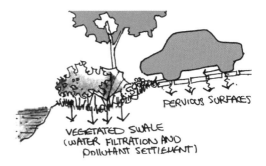

Fig 17. Road pollutants are filtered through vegetation swale.

Figure 18. Planting Poplars along the bank.

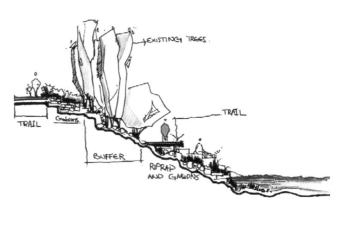

Figure 19. Strip of vegetation to stabilize riverbanks and function as buffer.

young fish. Other strategies include attaching root wads to timber pier pilings and creating "floating planters" for native upper-shore plants.

• Soil and erosion. Geological structures with high erosion sensitivity and the destruction of beds of vegetation, result in erosion and sedimentation. In times of floods, large amounts of eroded sediments are carried by the flow and deposit behind the bridges and dams. While such sedimentations decrease the functionality of the bridges and result in the river overflow, at the same time they are considered as a fertile bed of soil which must be stored and used for planting, although mainly flushed away by the flow (Fig 20). Water surges have also caused in-stream and lateral erosion in some spots like the Ma'aali-Abad Bridge vicinities leading to destruction of the solid levees. Stability of river banks through vegetated gentle slopes or terraced fields and use of permeable pavements also reduces erosion and natural transport and deposition of sediments.

• Vegetation. Native vegetation helps filter runoff, controls flooding, and reduces or eliminates erosion and keeps the bank stable which means preserving river depth and width. Native plants provide shelter and food for wildlife. Canopy trees, shading creeks help lower the water temperature and therefore create more favorable conditions for native fish. As stated before, one of the two main tributaries from the Stream of Nehr-e-A'zam joins the main channel of the Khoshk Stream right where "Chamran" boulevard starts. This branch has a more natural character than the main channel. Urban development had less impact on this part of the watershed and its riverbanks. As seen in figure 21 various types of hydrophilic plants and shrubs such as Willows (Salix babylonica and Salix excelsa) and Oriental plane trees (Platanus orientalis), growing in several private gardens, present a spectacular scene along the river, forming the natural greenway of the region.

Figure 20. Erosion on the bank.

The native species which would be chosen for the new riparian zone are listed as: Salix babylonia, Salix excelsa, Platanus orientalis, Nerium indicum, Populus nigra, Eucalyptus species, Punica granatum, Ficus carica, Tamarix L., Pyracantha Roemer, Citrus aurantium, Berberis integerrima Bunge, Cupressus sempervirens.

• Habitats and wildlife. Wildlife presence in the city has been a controversial topic and many times desired in the overall matrix. Disturbance of habitats by urbanization alters the natural dynamics of wildlife populations (Penteado 2004). In Shiraz at the end of winter, The Dried-up River's natural environment turns into a desirable habitat for seagulls and other migrating birds from the south. These birds are mostly seen at the confluence of the Nahr-e-A'zam Stream and the Khoshk Stream, behind the Nahr-e-A'zam Deviation Dam. Storing the water behind this dam in spring and summer times results in sedimentation of rich soil particles and deposition of plants seeds. As the dam opens, rich islands of sediments are formed making appropriate spots for these birds to rest and feed and for visitors who enjoy watching them (Fig 9 and 22).

• Fish population and habitats. Fish populations in the channel are rarely formed. Habitat is lost because of unsteady flow of water, pollutants, alterations in temperature, low rate of dissolved oxygen, loss of vegetation cover and shade, and discontinuation of the river continuum which blocks fish migration. After providing a steady flow of water throughout the year, factors such as riparian vegetation, pollution control at the watershed scale and the creation of artificially built structures or natural habitats (trunks, rocks, stepped gabions) play a definitive role in recovering fish population.

Figure 21. A'zam Stream flowing in a more natural context, Fall and Summer scenes.

Conclusion

For at least the past three decades, cities have been rediscovering their rivers as valuable ecologic, economic, and community assets. The trend appears to be continuing and perhaps even accelerating as the environmental issues – mainly the climate change and accessibility to healthy quality water – beside the psychological needs of citizens for more open natural green spaces are rising each day. The riverfront rehabilitation in Shiraz is an exceptional opportunity to fulfill both ecological and recreational needs of the residents while promising a more sustainable community for the current and next generations. As integrating ecological considerations in riverfront redevelopment practices have proved much more sustainable social and economic achievements, the prominent aspect of this project is the presence of relevant ecological principles from the first stages of general planning to the design strategies proposed for creating recreational opportunities. It is hoped that such approaches would be adopted in relevant projects through integrating all the required expertise simultaneously to assure an entire fulfillment for the society as well as ensuring respect for the nature.

Acknowledgements: We thank professors: Dr. Jahaanshah Pakzad and Dr. Niloofar Razavi.

Figure 22. Seagulls migrate to the city to rest and feed along the River.

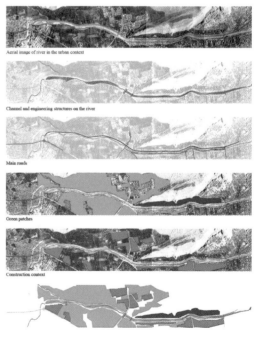

Figure 23. Analysis plans.

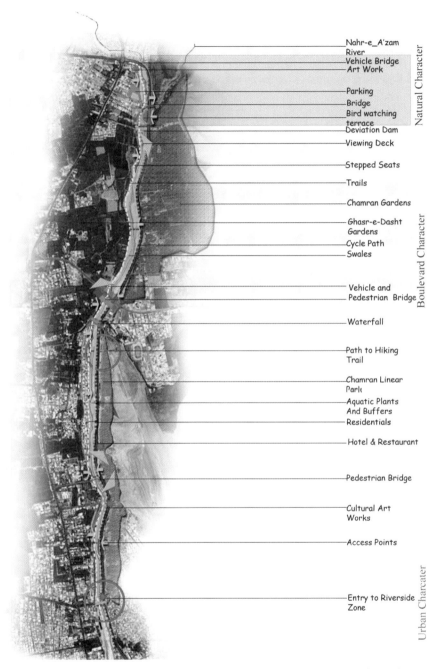

Nahr-e_A'zam River
Vehicle Bridge
Art Work

Parking
Bridge
Bird watching terrace
Deviation Dam

Viewing Deck

Stepped Seats

Trails

Chamran Gardens

Ghasr-e-Dasht Gardens

Cycle Path
Swales

Vehicle and Pedestrian Bridge

Waterfall

Path to Hiking Trail

Chamran Linear Park

Aquatic Plants And Buffers
Residentials

Hotel & Restaurant

Pedestrian Bridge

Cultural Art Works

Access Points

Entry to Riverside Zone

Natural Character

Boulevard Character

Urban Charcater

Figure 24. The conceptual plan proposes three zones along the stream: Natural character, Boulevard character and Urban character

Toward a Spectacle City

Critical Synopsis of the Han River Renaissance Project in Seoul

~ **Kyung-Jin Zoh** ~ Prof. Ph.D., Seoul National University, Department of

Landscape Architecture, Graduate School of Environmental Studies, Seoul,

Korea

The Han River Renaissance Project is one of the most effective tools for urban regeneration and city marketing in Seoul. The project can be understood as a comprehensive development, encompassing cultural planning, urban planning, landscape architecture, and engineering. The city of Seoul has launched the project to attract visitors and to give a new identity to the city, as well as restructure the existing urban space and city life pattern. In this essay, the background of the entire project process will be discussed while focusing on four riverside park designs. This essay aims at constructing a critical overview of the Han River Renaissance Project and suggesting an alternative vision. I suspect the present trend in various riverside park designs pursue the idea of an image of a spectacle. Taking into account the inevitable condition of the city, we need to reconsider the excessive use of strong image making with respect to the locality and place identity

Introduction

Transformations involving water have been one of the most effective tools for urban revitalization and city marketing in many cities in the world. The city of Seoul is not the exception. The Cheonggyecheon Restoration Project has been one of the most successful recent pubic projects, in terms of seeking a balance of environmental values and economic interests at the same time. As the project has often been regarded as the main accomplishment of former mayor (now the President of Korea) Lee Myoung Bak, a new urban public project called the Han River Renaissance Project was launched by the new mayor of Seoul last year. Interestingly, both landmark projects utilize water as a catalyst for enhancing the quality of city life and urban regeneration. The Han River Renaissance Project aims at upgrading the quality of the urban landscape together with connecting the land with water in various modes. It is a comprehensive planning strategy which encompasses social and economic sectors, including a development plan around the Han River, improvement of the landscape, and adoption of water transportation, etc.

In this essay, the concise story of the Han River Renaissance Project, including four riverside park design processes will be dealt with. Finally, this paper casts the essential questions on the Han River Renaissance project, and postulates an alternative vision in the urban waterfront project. My argument concerning the on-going trend of spectacle development in the Han River Project will be discussed. I suspect some Han River Renaissance projects, including the construction of four riverside parks, rely heavily on creating a city spectacle. Given this phenomenon as an inevitable characteristic of a postmodern city, we need to reconsider the strategy that we will adopt in urban projects related to water.

Turbulent History of the Han River

In to the official information, introducing the Han River Renaissance Project, the Han River is portrayed as the symbolic locus of life and history for Koreans. "Since the days of Joseon Dynasty, the Han River has been a gateway to Seoul, a logistics hub, and a recreational center for leisure activities" (Seoul Metropolitan Government, 2008b, no page number). Seoul has been the capital city since the foundation of Joseon Dynasty in 1392. In siting the city location, the landscape of mountains seemed to be important, and the role of a river was relatively minimal. The Han River ran outside the city wall. At that time, the river was too wide for practical use and flooding was a commonplace. The riverside area was not a suitable place for residential living and was not an important factor in people's everyday life. The Han River was perceived as, and functioned as, the border of the city. In the Joseon Dynasty, the Han River was used mainly as a water transportation way. Through several ports along the river, the goods were delivered from the West Sea (Yellow Sea). There were many pavilions and villas for sightseeing and retreats in the riverside area. On the other hand, the riverside area was used in diverse ways such as the King's hunting ground, a place for military exercises, and a place for punishment of rebels. Anthropologist Song Do Young maintains that Han River was a marginal space for people outside the city wall rather than a place to be utilized for everyday life (Song 2000, pp. 63-65). After opening the port to foreigners in the 19th century, the Han River was a main venue for importing foreign culture and products. In the age of Japanese imperialism, heavy flooding of the river caused severe problems such as destroying residential living and agricultural products. In the 1920s, major bank revetments were constructed to mitigate the flooding problems. In the 1960s, several island such as Jamsil and Yoiudo along the river were transformed to accommodate the rising population of the city. Since the 1970s, Kang-nam ("South of the river") started to build large scale residential developments. The relative significance of the river has changed into the main spine for urban landscape between Kang-buk ("North of the river") and Kang-nam. Seoul has experienced breathtaking changes over the last few decades, and the slogan 'The miracle on the Han River' has been used as a theme to denote the rapid industrial and economic development, crediting the idea of function and efficiency. Massive civil engineering projects, such as constructing an embankment and flood plain, were undertaken to control the river flooding. In the 1980s, the comprehensive Han River Development Plan was executed. It was "an epochal construction project which decisively changed the landscape of Seoul" (Seoul Development Institute, 2000, Seoul). Intercity highways were built along the river and new riverside parks were constructed on the flood plain. Since then, citizens have used the riverside parks for diverse leisure and recreational activities such as cycling, jogging, gathering, and resting. However, the way of connecting land with water was neither sustainable nor strategic. Development of cultural spaces in the waterfront area has been scarce, as it has mainly been occupied by privately owned residential buildings. A monotonous landscape, such as apartment complexes and hard edge revetment, dominated the banks along the river of Seoul. Since the 1990s, there have been some minor changes, shifting the planning paradigm toward the river. Due to the enhancement of ecological concerns, an ecological park was created along a minor stream adjacent to the river. On the other hand, the urban nightscape has drastically changed over the last ten years through lighting up bridges and infra-structures. The turbulent history of urban development in Seoul is reflected in the Han River and its waterfront. The shadows of a development oriented para-digm are embedded in the landscape along the Han River

Visions and Strategies of the Han River Renaissance Project

Concerns of the Han River as a political agenda reemerged in the 2006 mayoral election campaign. The former mayor received favorable responses by imple-menting the Cheonggyecheon Restoration Project. The candidates for the mayor initiated the innovative urban project and the Han River project was the winning candidate's major campaign agenda. Oh Se-Hoon, mayor of Seoul Metropolitan Government, took up this endeavor after his inauguration. The Han River Renaissance Project as an on-going development is currently the highest profile project in Seoul. Present problems in the Han River can be summarized as the monotonous landscape along the river, a concrete embankment treatment lack-ing ecological concerns, and the dominance of ordinary parks lacking place iden-tity and cultural facilities. The project was promoted to facilitate urban innova-tion with a view to ecological restoration, cultural diversity and economic devel-opment. It also aims at restoring intrinsic functions of natural and cultural ecolo-gy around the river, and it pursues the creation of a new identity of the water-front as a growth engine. Inherent problems with the Han River can be summa-rized as disconnection, disappearance, and absence. There are spatial disconnec-tions and regional disparity between Kang-buk and Kang-nam. Diverse leisure activities, which are culturally significant at the riverside area, have disappeared. The naturally sound condition of the river has been deteriorated in the last few decades to control natural disasters and exploit the land nearby the river effec-tively. In order to improve the present situation of the Han River, two guiding planning ideas can be adopted as restoration and creation. As planning ideas indicate, the project intends to rejuvenate the fragile relationship between man and nature by enhancing the connections with the surrounding environment and creating a new icon of Seoul by discovering the potential values around the Han River. Under the motto of restoration and creation, eight themes of the planning agenda were established. These are as follows: restructuring the urban space along the Han River; creation of a waterfront town; improvement of the cityscape along the river; creation of a waterway connecting the Yellow Sea to the river; restoration of the ecological network around; improved accessibility to the river; strengthened linkages to historical sites along the river; and remodeling the riverside parks with a theme (Seoul Metropolitan Government, 2008a, no page number).

The planning agenda was specified as the action plan through a series of meetings with a diverse group of consultants. Various consecutive projects based on this comprehensive plan are closely related with the fields of landscape architecture and urban design. Several waterfront towns such as Magok and Yongsan will be new multi-complex hub towns where the issues of sustainability might be critical. Infrastructure landscape will be a significant task, related to upgrading the cityscape and improving the accessibility to the river. In the case of ecological engineering such as restoring the artificial river bank into a natural one, various specialists such as ecologists, engineers, and designers are needed to incorporate this. In remodeling riverside parks, landscape architects did a leading role, working with various other design specialists. In preparing and developing this comprehensive plan, landscape architects served in coordinator roles in both the public and private sector. The Han River Renaissance Project is a test bed for future landscape architecture and it is a typical example for landscape urbanism which is currently used as a buzz word in both the United States and the Europe.

Brand Design, New Identity: Diverse Spectrum of Riverside Park Design Proposals

Among various projects under the umbrella of the Han River Renaissance Project, remodeling of several riverside parks is ranked as the highest priority in terms of budget and project schedule. In the long term, twelve riverside parks are about to be redesigned, but only four riverside parks will be implemented at

Fig 1. Yeouido Riverside Park, now.

this planning stage. Four riverside parks are selected at the strategic locations such as Yeouido, Banpo, Nanji, and Ttukseom areas.

In the case of Yeouido Riverside Park, an international design competition was held in 2007. Eight teams, including domestic and oversees offices, were invited. Foreign Office Architect in UK, EMBT in Spain, Jones and Jones, and EDAW in USA, Dongsimwon, Seoahn Total Landscape, Shynwha Consulting, and Beyond Landscape Design Group in Korea. Yeouido riverside is currently the most crowded riverside park along the Han River because the park is located adjacent to the international finance and commerce district (Fig. 1). The main premises for the plan are to provide a high quality cultural and leisure space and facilities while connecting the park with the city and the surrounding ecological network. The technical aspect of the plan is to "create permanent cultural space which is safe from flooding by piling up the earth generated from cutting the ground of reservoir revetments in the embankment" (Seoul Metropolitan Government, 2007a, p.1). A selection process was held by a jury in November 2007. The ten jury members were: George Hargreaves (Hargreave Associates), Julia Czerniak (Syracuse University), Kathryn Moore (University of Central England in Birmingham), Dennis Pierprz (Sasaki Associates), Rob Adams (City of Melbourne), Seungbin Lim (Seoul National Univ.), Yoo-il Kim (Sung Kyun Kwan Univ.), Sung-Joong Cho (Ikun Architects and Ltd), Yong-Tae Ohn (Architecture and Urban Research Institure), and Hyo-Sub Woo (Korean Institute of Construction and Technology).

No second prize was awarded, the third prize went to EMBT, and two Korean landscape design offices were selected as the co-winners of the first prize of the competition: Synwha, and Beyond (Fig. 2, 3). It was a very extraordinary case to award two teams as co-winners, but the jury felt it would be advantageous, and wanted the two teams to collaborate in a reciprocal way. The jury's recommenda-

Fig. 2. Yeouido Riverside Park Competition, Two Winning Proposals: Synwha, above; Beyond Landscape Design Group, below.

tion is the following, "The jury has awarded joint first prize to Synwha and Beyond in order for the two proposals to complement each other. Synwha's scheme should be taken as the park framework and well designed elements of the Beyond's scheme should be adopted….The jury feels strongly that the two designers [should] work together to produce a world class park in Seoul" according to the Report of the Jury on the Winning Designs of the International Design Competition for Seoul Yeouido Riverside Park, 2007. It will be interesting to see how they develop their original plans into a single new design. After the competition, the two teams worked together to integrate each plan into one. However, looking at the new scheme at present, it seems to be very difficult to combine the different schemes into a new one while keeping the original ideas intact (Fig. 4).

The proposals of the eight other teams range from the conventional to the revolutionary. Some proposals offer to keep the present usage of the riverside park while also suggesting the stereotypical tourist destination of the wheel. Another proposal suggested traditional green space with several huge water fountains. There was also a very radical and original proposal having a band-like design structure in the riverside park inspired by Korean calligraphy. Other plans con-

Fig. 3. Yeouido Riverside Park Competition . Synwha Consulting, above; and Beyond Landscape Design Group, below.

cern recreating the riverside park as a platform for cultural locus while connecting the city fabrics and river ecology and negotiating past memories with the present life. Most of the proposals share the idea of cultural vitality driven by reshaping the urban edge. In other riverside park plans, we could see broad spectrums of different park design approaches and various design innovations. The Ttukseom Riverside Park site is mainly used for diverse recreational and leisure purposes for families. A new park plan proposes a festival theme park utilizing the history of the site as an amusement park. Artistic elements and colorful patterns are adopted to imbue new vitality into the location. Lighting strategy combined with multimedia will provide a very impressive nightscape (Fig. 5).

On the other hand, the existing Nanji Riverside Park, which is currently used as a camping site, will be re-created into an eco-friendly park. The plan for the park offers new branding as a water sports hub for activities such as yachting and a nature education site that will retain the camping site and also create natural wetlands and a natural water edge zone. The park plan emphasizes the quality of the detail design while embracing the ordinary park experience and caring for ecological recycling and regenerative energy (Fig. 6). In the case of Banpo Riverside Park, more radical solutions are suggested to give a unique brand image to the Han River. The existing park will be changed into a more urbane atmosphere, introducing strong shapes and patterns. Remodeling the Jamsoo Bridge into a bridge park will be one of the major characteristics of the proposal. The submerged bridge will be converted into a pedestrian bridge. A programmed waterfall and lighting along the bridge will be the most striking design element. Also, a floating island will be created in order to accommodate diverse cultural events and programs. If this proposal is realized, it will provide the citizens with a dazzling experience. The spectacle effect is one of main characteristics of the waterfall in this proposal.

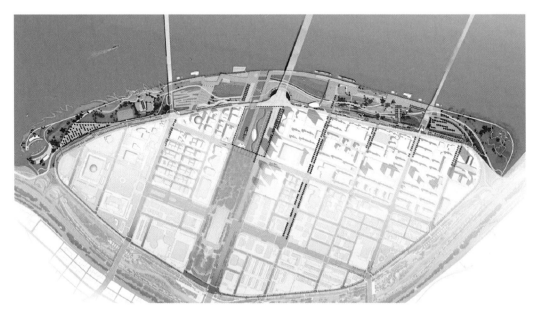

Fig 4. Revised Plan for Yeouido Riverside Park Combining Two Winning Proposal.

Fig. 5. Banpo Bride Park Waterfall Proposal.

Fig. 6. Master Plan for Nanji Riverside Park.

In summary, the proposed riverside park design can be categorized into two parts. One trend is to create a park offering a spectacle image. The other emphasizes an ordinary life experience embracing non-programmed use and ecological sensibility. However, even though the two trends pursue a contrasting value and sensibility, the underlying premise seems to be the same. The common characteristic of the two trends is a change from the current condition of the respective parks to theme-based parks, while still retaining a sense of memory and culture.

The Spectacle City: The Dark Side of Postmodern City

Among the various sub projects in the Han River Renaissance Project, the design development stage for the four riverside parks is almost finished. The revised landscape designs around the riverside parks, including lighting and infrastructure landscaping, indicate people's attitude and sentiment to the Han River. In general, transformation of the existing riverside park into the new one is mainly based on the premises of restoring and recreating cultural activities along the river. Some design elements, such as the programmed waterfall at the Banpo Bridge Park, are radical gestures for the 'wow effect' in improving the cityscape. Besides this, lighting with sound and strong design sensibility at Ttukseom and Banpo riverside parks are another example of creating the spectacle.

Is this phenomenon inevitable when world cities compete with each other? Recently, most cities are anxious to create a symbolic icon to sell the image of the city. This trend is prevalent in the various city projects such as landmarks and museum building. Recruiting world class star architects in grand urban projects is common in contemporary cities. All of these trends can be understood as creating a strong city brand. Architecture is a primary method of branding to get a strong identity of place. Anna Klingman referred to the phenomenon as brandscapes in her book Brandscapes: Architecture in the Experience Economy (2007). Flickering and colorful scenes created by light and sound are a brand image which is produced and reproduced electronically. The prevalent dominance of image culture is no exception in the city. Advertisements, digital moving screens, and architectural lighting dominate the urban landscape. Especially at night, this tendency is even worse. As David Harvey pointed out in his book, The Condition of Postmodernity (1989), the postmodern city has become more depthless and spectacular. Especially in the case of urban development driven by the private sector, this tendency seems to be strong. Quoting his own words, "an architecture spectacle, with its sense of surface glitter and transitory participatory pleasure, of display and ephemerality, of jouissance, become essential to the success of a project of sort" (Harvey 1989, p. 91.).

Seeking ephemeral beauty and surface cosmetics was clearly embedded in the present design proposals for the Han River Renaissance Project. The reason that city officials pursue a spectacle design is two-fold: first, to draw media attention, both domestically and internationally, and secondly, to satisfy Korean people's preference for spending leisure time enjoying a spectacle, rather than idling in public spaces. It would be inevitable to entice tourists and to please citizens visually. One may assert that this process of creating a spectacle can be a unique identity for Seoul in its pursuit of becoming a Mecca in information technology business. Otherwise, it may be an inherent destiny for the postmodern city.

The idea of a spectacle can not only be understood as the collection of images, but as the underlying social relation, which is mediated by images. The social relation that the new dramatized image implies means a detached stance between citizens and the river in itself. The real relationship through bodily and sensory experience does not occur in this visual image culture. We need to be cautious not to fall into the trap of the spectacle. Depending on the ephemeral stimulus and commoditized experience, it does not involve a genuine interaction with the environment. Often it failed to care adequately for the sense of place in a specified location. What we need is a reciprocal balance between the spectacle and the ordinary in making the landscape.

Conclusion

The Han River Renaissance Project might be the most ambitious urban regeneration project to restructure the way we deal with the river in the city. Through restructuring present usage of the river, it will transform the significance of the river drastically. With a broad spectrum of various projects, there is much room for the landscape architect's involvement. We examined closely the diverse design proposals for the riverside park and found that in the design proposals, our attitude toward the cityscape has been grasped clearly. Creating brands for the city is an underlying premise in the design strategy. The intention is commonly represented in the form of creating a spectacle. The spectacle strategy can be powerful in creating a strong image in a limited time span; however, it has its own limitation for sustainable development and historical continuity. As Augustin Bergue pointed out, rivers in the cities can play a critical role in the rediscovery of place. He pointed out that the present rediscovery efforts are dominated by an ecological imagery and he maintained that imaginative thinking grounded in ontological questions should be considered (Augustin Berque, 2000)

If I expand his argument further, I would say that the present effort regarding the river in Seoul is dominated by spectacle imagery along with ecological considerations. We need to look back at what we are doing in a critical way. It would be better to keep the unique identity of place and embrace everyday life's practical experiences. It is a time to reconsider the cultural significance of the design in the Han River Renaissance Project.

Fig. 7. Tuksum Riverside Park Plan.

Room for Rivers

~ **Regina Collignon** ~ Program Director Room for Rivers, Ministry of

Transport and Infrastructure, Netherlands

Because climate change is increasingly causing high water levels in the rivers, we are on the threshold of a new era in Dutch water management. In the program 'Room for the Rivers' the issue is not only approached as a technical problem, but also as a spatial and a cultural challenge. Rising the dikes will no longer be sufficient to deal with rising water levels. The new approach is as simple as it is effective: the rivers need more room. The rivers Nederrijn, IJssel, Lek, Waal, Bergsche Maas and Nieuwe Merwede, will have their forelands lowered, gullies will be dug and docks and other higher grounds will be levelled. Some areas will even be given back to the river by drawing back the dikes.

The individual natural and cultural characteristics of the different rivers and their surroundings will be the starting point of the improvement of spatial quality, enhancing each local identity. Plans have been made to extend the nature area along the IJssel and to create a river-estate. In the Biesbosch, near Dordrecht, the agricultural lands will be exposed to the influence of the river, accepting incidental flooding. The partly remaining ancient landscape will form the base of this operation, including nature development and recreational facilities.

Noordwaard, future river flood plain.

In the province of Noord-Brabant, plans have been made to give certain areas back to the river. Even though these lands will no longer be protected by dikes, they will still be suitable for sustainable agriculture. The spatial quality will be guaranteed by a carefully designed system of dwelling mounds. These plans will be further detailed by the municipality, the provincial government, the Water Boards and the Ministry of Water Management, in close co-operation with the local residents. In 2009, the plans will be finished. Six years later, the river country will be drastically altered in a positive and typically Dutch manner.

Source: *Het Landelijk Dagblad* Desgining with Water. *Het Landelijk Dagblad* is published by NVTL. Free copies available at the IFLA-congress.

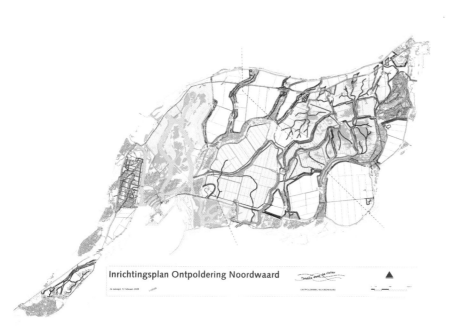

Design for the Noordwaard by Robbert de Koning.

Cross section Westenholte estate.

Design for Westenholte by Bosch + Slabbers.

3.2 Flow of Water - Talkshops

Philosophies on Water

(Abstract) Truth of Water - Aesthetics of Transformation
~ Jusuck Koh

(Abstract) Dialectics of Water
~ Mathew Davis

Culture as an Inspiration

(Abstract) Water as a Defence System in the Past - Taman Sari
~ Indra Tjahjani

(Abstract) Holiness of Water
~ Anahita Mahmoudi, Fahimeh Bahrami

(Abstract) Making the Desert Bloom
~ Ken McCown

Talkshop

Philosophies on Water

Truth of Water - Aesthetics of Transformation

~ **Jusuck Koh** ~ Chair Professor, Landscape Architecture Group Wageningen
University and Research Center, Netherlands ~ Abstract

Water bounds and shapes the land: waterscape is the other of landscape. Water
mediates and reflects; also in design and aesthetics. We cannot create water. We
can only (and must) conserve it. It is a resource to be recycled, a source for our
life. Water is community and commodity.

Not itself alive, water serves as symbol of life and indicator of life possibility.
H_2O, as science describes it, by itself, does not offer sufficient condition for life.
Only water containing minerals, nutrients and temperature begins to offer conditions and elements that allow life to develop. Such is the state of water we experience through our body. Water therefore must be grasped aesthetically and spiri-
tually as well.

Spirituality and Transformation.

To talk about water is to talk about life itself, and even the origin of life. Likewise, to talk about how to deal and live with water is also to talk about different human civilizations. Furthermore, our insightful understanding of the nature of water, and coping with water in nature, expands our understanding of the very nature of landscape and our embodied experience of it, thus of the nature of aesthetics as well as the aesthetics of nature. It also informs us of new possibilities for aesthetic languages, and design strategies and principles, for living in flux: aesthetics transcending form, and design of trans-form, or formlessness. Water is formless, transforms without compromising itself.

This paper is not about empirical scientific study of water, landscape and urban hydrology. It is deeply reflective and broadly cross-cultural, building on the author's experience with both Far Eastern and Western cultures. The reflection connects our body and land, conceptualizes land not just as being outside of our body – us being in land – but also body itself as site, or site as body. Taking an eco-poetic approach, the paper reflects the author's conviction that combining the scientific with the aesthetic access to knowing is a valuable form of knowing leading to useful, effective and affective aesthetic languages and design strategies for transformation with water.

Design of Interface.

 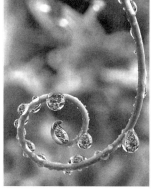

Aesthetics of Phenomena.

An excellent medium enabling various forms of life, water is also a wonderful model with which we designers can investigate the creative processes and aesthetics we encounter in nature and landscape. Water can be our instrument as well as our way. On this basis we can articulate rich aesthetic languages and design strategies for sustainable, dynamic landscape systems and inspiring human experiences of it that would lead to emotional and spiritual bondage beyond scientific understanding and ethical commitment.

Evolutionary consciousness, genetic memory, archetype, and deep structure of human consciousness, all enable us to deal with order of 'process' and 'poetics' of phenomenon, as opposed to order of form or mechanistic / rational, or organic / romantic aesthetics. Matter can become spirit through water and as such reconnects mind and body. In turn, it can expand our mind and intellect, moving our body and soul. Water tells us that body and sensuality must not be subdued by intellectual abstraction and rationalization. The seeming irrationality and chaos we find in water is only the rationality that we cannot comprehend, the order we cannot grasp. Water's own order, for too long, was seen as human disorder; while human's rigid order can be water's disorder.

The paper is structured as follows: (1) Discussion of essential 'scientific' and 'poetic' capitulation of fundamental truth about water, (2) their aesthetic implications and manifestations, and discussion about how aesthetics of nature / water and landscape (inclusive of cultural landscape) open ways to a new paradigm of aesthetics complementing static, romantic, art- and beauty-based aesthetic; (3) implications (of the attention to water) to experiential design principles for cities (and sites) leading to 'aqua-revelatory design'; and (4) summary of ten points that explain and enrich the responsible design and transformation with water as manifested in our contemporary life, in urban context.

Through understanding water, we will find a powerful way to complement formal aesthetics and to overcome egocentric design. Water enables us to connect contemporary eco-poetic design with Tao and Zen.

Aesthetics of Process.

Dialectics of Water

~ **Mathew Davis** ~ Assistant Professor of Landscape Architecture School of

Architecture Philadelphia University, US ~ Abstract

"..waters symbolize the universal sum of virtualities; they are ...'spring and origin,' the reservoir of all possibilities of existence; they precede every form and support every creation."
Mircea Eliade

This paper will explore the phenomenology of water through several authors, namely Mircea Eliade, and Gaston Bachelard through his work, Water and Matter. The reading of these authors will provide grounding for two design projects. The first, a Master's Thesis done at the University of Pennsylvania was completed in 1989. Second is a review of entries from an international design competition staged in Philadelphia to address urban blight, land vacancy, and the ageing storm water infrastructure. The lens of analysis will reflect on both the similarity and divergence of themes, namely water, and as well the process of design and representation. These projects on the one hand can be seen as systems and processes to abate the impending crisis of water infrastructure, while presenting a new strategy towards urbanism on the other hand.

Bachelard identifies a number of states of water such as clear, running, stagnant, dead, fresh, salt, reflecting, purifying, deep, and stormy. His chapters align our common metaphors of water: passivity, violence, its feminine and masculine qualities. He describes water as the only elemental substance that is found in liquid form. This aspect alone makes water enigmatic, strange, pervasive, lonely. As Stroud writes in the introduction of Bachelard's work, "Water is the most receptive of the elements, thus its strongly feminine characteristics. Water is the spring of being, motherhood. Water flows, its constant movement responding to the environment and to possibility." It is from these qualities that we derive a fundamental relation to cities, as a locus of civilization, the nurturing aspect of urban growth and development, and its relevance to future.

The modern city can be understood as a construct of denial of natural forces. The birth of the profession of landscape architecture, as well as title of "Landscape Architect" traced back to the "re-presenceing" of nature in the city. The urban grid denies topography, landform, and as presented in the Thesis work a deleterious effect when placed over existing natural water features. The work of Olmstead in New York, Boston, Buffalo and elsewhere was planned prior to full-scale development in these cities, the result would be nothing less than "opening seams" in this urban fabric, thus allowing, at least in principle, the presence of nature or natural features to persist.

The city of Philadelphia is a typical case of postindustrial urban decline that began midway in the last century, losing nearly one-third of its residents from a peak population in 1950 of 2.1 million residents, to just over 1.5 million in 2000, a number that nearly equals the population in 1910. These figures are compounded by the fact that the physical area of the city has increased by some 50% since 1910. Philadelphia is not unique in its population loss over the past 50 years. Cities such as Detroit, St. Louis, Pittsburgh and Cleveland have each lost no less than one-half of their peak population in this same period. Although the population of these comparable cities has roughly stabilized, Philadelphia continues to lose its population at an alarming rate, exhibiting the greatest net loss in population of any county in the U. S. this past decade. These figures are even more disturbing considering the economic boom the country has witnessed in the 1990s that has posted some of the lowest unemployment levels in 30 years, and an urban renaissance in Philadelphia's central urban district of a number of large scale development projects such as a nationally recognized performing arts center, new convention and exhibition facilities, new sports stadiums, entertainment and recreation facilities. In contrast to the City of Philadelphia, its suburbs have grown at a near exponential rate, posting a fourfold increase in population to approximately 4.5 million spread out over an area of some 412 square miles, translating into a 55% increase growth in land area and 48% increase in per capita land consumption. The result of the urban exodus of the past 50 years has been

Pennsylvania.

the wide scale disintegration of many inner city residential neighborhoods near what was once Philadelphia's major industrial and manufacturing districts. These areas of the city were part of a major urban expansion after 1854, annexing a number of communities and towns surrounding the historic center, which was at that time about 3 square miles. In the past five years, the City of Philadelphia has undertaken an extensive campaign to study and remediate the condition of land vacancy and urban blight. Studies have identified no less than 30,900 vacant residential lots and over 27,000 "long term" vacant residential structures, two-thirds of which are privately owned. Other estimates place the number of abandoned residential structures at over 50,000, and state that over the next five years, an additional 5000 to 7000 residential structures will be added to this figure. Plans are currently underway to demolish some 15,000 vacant residential structures, the majority classified as "eminently dangerous" and on the verge of collapse. Outside of these efforts, there has been little headway made into the planning or redesign of these communities. However, recently the City of Philadelphia, together with the Pennsylvania Horticultural Society has begun a massive campaign to integrate on-site storm water management with the demolition efforts of vacant structures, co-sponsoring and international design with these efforts in mind.

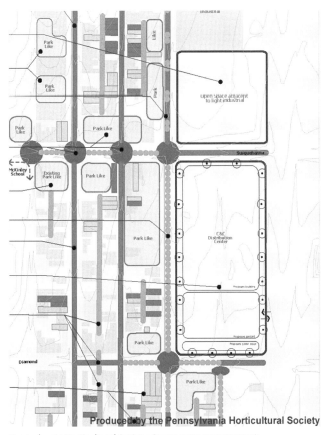

Pennsylvania Horticultural Society: Stormwater management.

Talkshop

Culture as an Inspiration

Water as a Defence System in the Past - Taman Sari

~ **Indra Tjahjani** ~ Doctor of Environmental Design University of Canberra,

Indonesia ~ Abstract

Introduction

The Republic of Indonesia is located in South-East Asia, and consists of more than 17,508 islands (Hydro Oceanography TNI-AL, November 2004). It has home to more than 300 ethnic groups. It is rich in cultures and has 731 vernacular languages (www.ethnologue.com/show_country.asp?name=indonesia, November 2004). However, the national language is Bahasa Indonesia. The Indonesian population is about 234,693,997 (July 2007 est. www.indexmundi.com/indonesia/population.html, December 2007). Java is one of

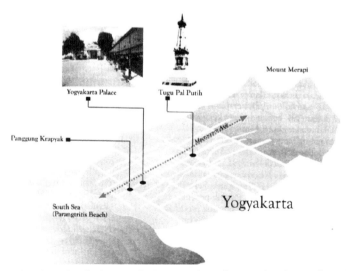

Figure 1. Imaginary Line, the Strong and Primary North-South Axis within the city of Yogyakarta (Buku Petunjuk Tilpon Yogyakarta, 2000).

the islands, and Mataram is the biggest Kingdom in Java in the past. History tells us that Mataram later on divided into two kingdoms, the Sultanate Yogyakarta and the Sunanate Surakarta.

The Sultanate Yogyakarta lies in the Special Province of Yogyakarta (or Daerah Istimewa Yogyakarta or DIY for the local name), and Yogyakarta is the capital city. The city is situated at about 30 kilometers from the south coast of central Java, covering some 3,186 square kilometers, and is located about the same distance south of the still active volcano Mount Merapi. The people of Yogyakarta still maintain the traditional Javanese cultural activities such as the wayang kulit (shadow leather puppet theater) and the music of the gamelan which are favorite activities in the pastimes.

At the center of the Yogyakarta city is established the palace or kraton of the sultan and the royal gardens. The Javanese people believe that the Kraton or the Sultan's Palace is the center of the Universe. The Palace is located in the center of an imaginary axis stretching from the north to the south, and in the secondary axis from the east to the west. The imaginary line lies between Tugu in the north to Panggung Krapyak in the south, between Code River in the east and Winongo River in the west; between the Merapi Mountain in the North and the South Sea of Indian Ocean. In this imaginary line, there is a reversed dualism linear line that tells symbolical philosophy: the direction from south to north symbolizes the birth of human being from the high place to the perishable world, and the opposite direction symbolizes the return of human being to the Dumadi (God in Javanese philosophy). Kraton is physical symbol and the King is the symbol of the real soul that presents into the physical body.

Figure 2. Map City of Yogyakarta 1895 (J. Jeakes, 1815).

The King Palace or Kraton

The Kraton or Palace was built in 1755 in the middle of a Ficus benjamina (Beringin or Waringin for the local name) forest and the first king of the Yogyakarta Kingdom was Pangeran Mangkubumi with the title Sri Sultan Hamengku Buwono I (HB I).

Starting from Mount Merapi in the North goes to the Pal Putih (white pole) passed through Malioboro Street to Beringharjo market, symbolizes women temptation and the temptation of power is symbolized by Kepatihan (now Government) building. The straight street connecting the Palace to Tugu monument symbolizes close relationship between human being and the Creator (Sangkan Paraning Dumadi); from the Palace to the South is passing through another straight street to Panggung (stage) Krapyak and ended in the South Ocean (the Indian Ocean) (figure 1.).

In short, Tugu monument is a symbol of lingga (male sex organ) and Krapyak symbolizes yoni (female sex organ) and kraton is physical blend of the two.

The Kraton or Palace consisted of several buildings in a complex that was completed with a beautiful garden. One of the complexes is the Water Castle or

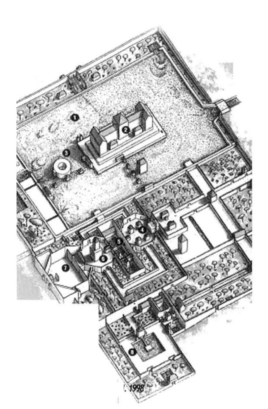

Figure 3. Bird Eye View the Water Castle 'Pulo Kenongo' within the Taman Sari Complex of Yogyakarta Palace.

Figure 4. Reconstruction of Water Palace 'Pulo Kenongo' – Taman Sari Yogyakarta surrounded by swamp (originally artificial lake) in 1881 (KITLV – Leiden).

Perfumes garden, or Taman Sari. Literally taman means beautiful garden. Formerly Taman Sari was a recreation garden, a resting house for the Sultan and the royal family, meditation place for Sultan himself, royal swimming pool and bathing pools, and canals for soldier practising; and from some research come to conclusion that Taman Sari is as a hiding place for the royal family and a camouflage place to defend against the enemy assault.

Water Castle or Perfumes garden, or Taman Sari Complex

The Water Palace 'Taman Sari' Yogyakarta complex was built around 1756 – 1758; the Old City Planning including a Pleasure Garden which has multiple functions is part of Yogyakarta City Planning since ancient times. The idea of establishing Taman Sari came from Prince Mangkubumi that was later known as Hamengku Buwono I; different sources gave different claims about who the architect or the planner and designer of Taman Sari was.

The Water Castle complex consists of Gedong Kenongo (Cananga odorata Palace) which established within an artificial Cemeti Island, Sumur Gumuling (three storey circle mosque and well), Pulo Panembung (Island for begging to God) where Sumur Gemantung (hanging well) situated and underwater passageways or tunnels; this tunnels connected the Water Castle and the Umbul Binangun Royal Swimming Pool and the Pesarean Ledok Sari Royal Cottages that has such cooling systems and the Royal Palace. The Water Castle complex was situated within an artificial lake or Segaran.

The water for the artificial lake came from Winongo River in the North that has been directed or cannalized to the Water Castle. This is a strategy of camouflage. The enemy knows that the Water Castle is a recreation place for the Royal family. Moreover, a legend speaks about secret tunnels connecting to the South Sea of Indian Ocean where Nyai Roro Kidul or the Queen of the South has her palace. The supernatural Queen becomes the wife of Yogyakarta Sultan for many generations. This secret tunnels is gateway to the world where the Sultan is meeting this supernatural wife. The setting of Taman Sari complex shows the mixture of the Hindu-Buddhist and the Islam influences, but the accessories or the motifs in each wall show the influences of Hindu-Buddhist, Islam, European, Portuguese, and Chinese. The Javanese themselves again, have their own characteristics. In Taman Sari every characteristic and motifs is used and it forms a harmonious blend.

In Conclusion

Water Castle 'Taman Sari' in Yogyakarta in particular shows how the Old City Planning which has multi functions was established in Indonesia during the ancient time, the development during the Dutch era, and the condition before 'conservation actions' and current conditions and how the future generation should take care of the place.

Holiness of Water

~ **Anahita Mahmoudi** ~ M.A in Architecture, Shiraz Azad Architecture

University ~ **Fahimeh Bahrami** ~ Landscape architects, Iran ~ Abstract

Myths are the reflections of humans' nature and have involved all men's wishes and dreams. Througout the centuries, in different nations and cultures the role of myths is different, because of differing ways of life that have always most impressive effects on the things that feature in myths. Ancient Iranians respected the Water Goddess as a powerful, but also generous God and found water an adorable element of nature. The belief in a Water Goddess made for a holiness of water that had great effects on Iranian's architectural design, especially in temples, gardens, and palaces. Only little research on ancient Iranian architecture, makes us already easily understand that water has been the basic element. It worked as a central element, that could link all the buildings having been built around it. Not only in architecture, also in urban design, water created a rich urban space by the presence of people nearby, and by the buildings that worked as an edge of urban space. Presenting the role of water in Iran's architecture and urban design is a main goal of this paper. Furthermore other purposes are:

• Research in some traditional buildings and urban spaces which have been created by the presence of water.

• To define the meaning for the different roles of water in Iranian architecture such as: the inviter element, the center point, the joint part, and the formal element.

• Finally: To reach some idea and new viewpoints that can define the Iranian garden structure and its landscape theory.

The article has two parts, the first one is related to architecture and second one is related to urban design. Two case studies illustrate the findings. Firstly, we consider the garden Dolat abad in Yazd, Iran, located in a very hot and dry climate and the role of water in gardens in this climate, and secondly we consider the Sio se pol (which means thirty three bridges) in Isfahan, Iran and the power of water in creating a splendid urban space.

Making the Desert Bloom

~ Ken McCown ~ Professor architecture and landscape architecture, Cal Poly

Pomona, US ~ Abstract

2057: Making the Desert Bloom

In 2007, the Department of Landscape Architecture at Cal Poly Pomona cele-
brated its fiftieth anniversary. As the only accredited school of landscape architecture in Los Angeles County, its graduates have shaped the landscape of
Southern California. At this celebration, its members not only looked to the past,
but also looked to the future. What might landscape architects learn from their
first 50 years of work in California to apply to the future? What could the role of
the landscape architect be in the next fifty years? How would this role affect the
appearance of the landscape in the year 2057?

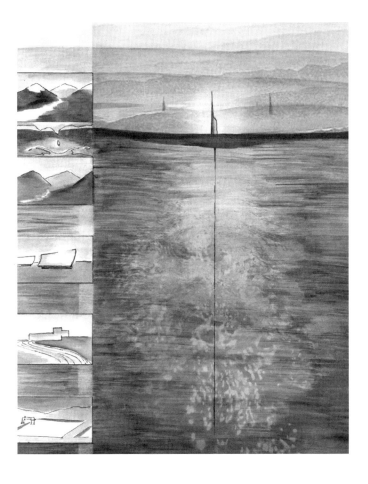

Interstate – 15 links the Ports of Los Angeles to the high desert.

A case study followed the concept of the megacity. The Los Angeles area and Las Vegas are two of the fastest growing metropolitan regions in the United States of America. Interstate – 15 links the Ports of Los Angeles and Long Beach to the Inland Empire and the high desert.

In the desert above Los Angeles lies an aquifer large enough to hold all of the water needs of the people of the United States. Could water be the future for the high desert?

This paper uses a case study for the Interstate 15 Corridor for the year 2057. It supposes a design for the next fifty years based upon resource. The largely empty aquifer and solar energy give two of the most precious resources available to modern civilization: electric power and water. While other professions design from demand, the landscape architect presupposes design and planning based upon resource availability. This project displays the important role the landscape architect can play in the coming years, and the initiative they must take to lead the environmental design and engineering professions.

This megacity study examines and proposes government management and citizen involvement, 'top down and bottom up management' as noted in Jared Diamond's 'Collapse,' for water and power resources, exploiting the vast potential for solar energy and water storage in what is now considered a waste landscape.

Global climate change models show that California will be getting less snow as years progress. A large portion of the state's water comes from snowmelt. With more rain events, and severe rain events, it will be difficult for the state to store water, due to the rapid rate of runoff. This project suggests a diversion of the aqueduct to the Mojave Basin. The large aquifer below the level of the high mountains, but still above Los Angeles, could store water for the use of one of the largest metropolitan areas of the United States.

This project suggests a diversion of the aqueduct to the Mojave Basin.

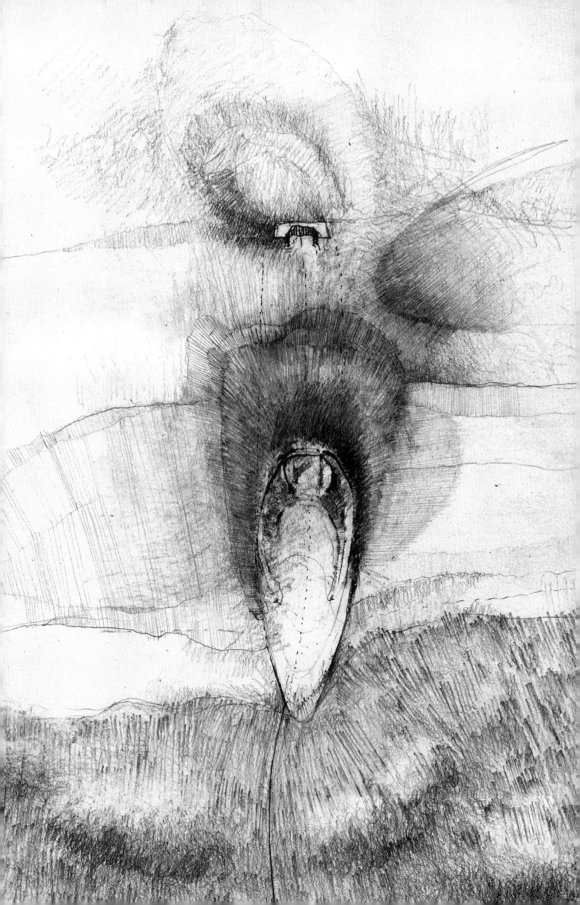

Epilogue

A personal note

~ **Wybe Kuitert** ~ editor

At a well-attended and noisy NVTL meeting in January 2006, I came up with the theme Transformations in Water and nobody actually could visualize what this would bring about. But two years later, early January this year, the success was clear: over 150 entries from almost all over the world had entered our Call for Contributions. Some were elaborate, scholarly papers, others were short and spicy abstracts. With our enthusiastic team of the Program Committee we had some happy days working ourselves through this pile of great variety and creativity in water solutions. What a wealth it was, and what a pity that we could not allow for 150 speakers!

It quickly became clear that we were touching upon a major movement in present-day landscape thinking, that is, seeing landscape as a soft process, rather than a thing that can be definitely designed and concretely built. Fine-tuning in the reviewing and programming process we managed to have some fully equipped scholarly presentations for our morning sessions, alongside abstracted and challenging statements for our afternoon talkshops. In this way we felt that it should be possible to generate a debate, to bring us further in the avant-garde of landscape planning thought.

In May, the Student Competition drew almost 400 entries, an absolute record in IFLA history, still excluding tropical Africa, though. But students clearly felt challenged by the competition theme "Transforming with Water - The Way to Paradise?". Personally, I hope that many participants took a look at the film Nausicaä of the Valley of the Winds, given as one of the sources of inspiration. This anime-film shows so pregnantly where this world is going if we as landscape architects don't stand up. Anyway, the great response at the Student Competition further convinced us of the urgency of current issues.

Just let me pick up some projects. You will find, for example, a challenging project on the Shiraz stream in Iran, which is compared to an inner city stream in Seoul, Korea, extended with a Korean contribution on the same stream and its follow-up in Seoul. And how about comparing this with some solutions that were offered for urban waterfronts along the Rhine, or some other historic water cities in Europe?

Disasters, natural or not, killing thousands of people, generate an awareness shock, as in Panama City, Kobe, Fang in Thailand, or in Holland 1953. Disasters seem to happen more and more, and the best thing we can do, is stay strong and optimistic, and use them as a challenging trigger that catapults us into new solutions. Of course, the human factor is most strongly felt in this case – pressing us to see landscape as a process also influenced by man. Which again makes us better understand how landscapes work when limitless affluence of humans is the course of the disaster: in Sao Paolo, Bangkok, or Dubai, where rivers loose their meaning because we are with so many. Dubai also shows how commercial development suffocates the meaning and identity of the vernacular landscape, which makes us wonder how important a vernacular meaning actually is.

And than there is the wisdom of ancient generations, found in the Australian desert, in old Chinese cities, and irrigation systems of the arid zones of Argentina and Iran. These show us ways to handle barely sufficient, or unpredictable resources in fragile environments.

Or, as you may also have experienced in the Congress excursions, what do you think about the finely tuned management of the abundance of water in Holland, spending huge amounts of public money? - Whereas it is rather the wise private developer under a sage government in Malaysia that makes the landscape work.

Finally, having read, reviewed, and edited for this Proceedings, many papers by the dozen, I became fascinated by the variety of meanings that landscape architecture has, as a moving force in the respective societies of various countries. From all countries presented in this book, interestingly enough, landscape architecture seems most successful in China: a crisp planning for Aksa, as demonstrated by Binyi Liu, has the potential of regaining a wasted landscape for a region larger than a quarter of whole Holland. A healthy and courageous critique on the Beijing Olympic Park is given by Fu Fan and Zhao Caijun. How is it possible to have so outspoken and easily understandable statements in a country ruled by its Communist Party? First of all, the government of the People's Republic of China is smart, and understands very well that efforts need to be made for the well-being of all People. In the landscape of China, a tradition of planting trees, and working with water, on a large scale exists, since Mao Zhedong, and actually already for many thousand years before the great leader. But in our modern and hectic consumerist society, it must be above all the sincerity of the effort of landscape architects in China that makes landscape architecture tick. They are in search for truth and for tenable positions in knowledge on landscape and its architecture. It proves the strength of the Chinese Society of Landscape Architecture (CHSLA), which is an *academic* society and not a club of professionals trying to promote, commercialize, or protect their trade, as in so many other countries. Chinese Landscape Architecture, the CHSLA journal, is rather free from policy-making and commercialism, and so far has retained its ambition in search of simply improving the quality of design and statements made. China will, without much doubt, take the lead in the coming decades to come, and I only hope we can all join in, setting up alongside IFLA, I guess, a WASLA, a World Academic Society for Landscape Architecture!

Wageningen, June, 2008

Sources, References,
and Bibliographies

To facilitate further studies Sources, References, and Bibliographies, as were received with some contributions, are given below.

Sustainable design concepts for building a Scarce-Watercity
~ Melanie Klein

• American Society of Landscape Architects, Lady Bird Johnson Wildflower Center, & the United States Botanic Garden (2007). Sustainable Sites Initiative. Retrieved November 1, 2007 from http://www.sustainablesites.org/
• Berkebile Nelson Immenschuh McDowell Architects. (2008) Sustainable Comprehensive Master Plan, Phase 1: 1-22-08 Draft. Retrieved January 23, 2008 from http://www.greensburgks.org/
• City of Greensburg, Kansas. (2007). 5 Additional Goals Added to Long Term Recovery Plan: 5 new goals adopted by the Steering Committee, Business Redevelopment Group, City Council and the Recovery Action Team. Retrieved October 20, 2007 from http://www.greensburgks.org/recoveryplanning/
• City of Greensburg, Kansas. (2007). 5- additional- goals- added- to- long- term- recovery- plan Greensburg: A City Rebuilding—Official Website of Greensburg, Kansas. Retrieved October 5, 2007 from http://www.greensburgks.org/
• Congress for the New Urbanism, Natural Resources Defense Council and the U.S. Green Building Council. (2007). Pilot Version LEED® for Neighborhood Development Rating System. Retrieved September 1, 2007 from http://www.usgbc.org/ShowFile.aspx?DocumentID=2845
• Federal Emergency Management Agency, Region VII. (2007). Long-Term Community Recovery Plan: Greensburg + Kiowa County, Kansas. Retrieved August 22, 2007, from http://www.greensburgks.org/recovery-planning/long-term-community-recovery-plan
• Kansas State University (2007). Greensburg Envisioned: Design Concepts from Kansas State University College of Architecture, Planning and Design Students in Landscape Architecture and Architecture. Unpublished booklet given by student authors to Citizens of Greensburg. December 14, 2007.
• Sorvig, K. & Thompson, J.W. (2000). Sustainable Landscape Construction: A Guide to Green Building Outdoors. Washington, DC: Island Press.
• Todd, J. & Josephson, B. (1996). "The Design of Living Machines for Wastewater Treatment." Journal of Ecological Engineering Volume 6, Issues 1-3, May 1996. Elsevier Publishing.
• U.S. Green Building Council. (2005). LEED® Green Building Rating System for New Construction & Major Renovations, Version 2.2, October 2005. Retrieved September 1, 2007 from /www.usgbc.org/ShowFile.aspx?DocumentID=1095

Water Purificative Landscapes - Constructed Ecologies and Contemporary Urbanism
~ Antje Stokman

• Ahern, J. 2007: Green infrastructure

for cities: The spatial dimension. In: Novotny, Vladimir.

• Brown, Paul (ed.): Cities of the Future: Towards Integrated Sustainable Water and Landscape Management. IWA Publishers, London, 267-283.

• Angelil, M. and Klingmann, A. 1999: Hybrid morphologies: infrastructure, architecture, landscape. Daidalos 73, 16-25.

• Allen, S. 1999: Points + Lines. Diagrams and projects for the city. New York: Princeton Architectural Press.

• Corner, J. (ed.) 1996: Recovering Landscape. Essays in contemporary Landscape Architecture. New York: Princeton Architectural Press.

• Graham, S. and Marvin, S. 2001. Splintering Urbanism. Networked infrastructures, technological mobilities and the urban condition. London and New York: Routledge.

• Hough, M. 1984: City form and natural process. Croom Helm Ltd., Sydney.

• Koziol, M. 2005: Rückbau der Infrastruktur. In: Oswalt, Philipp (Hrsg.): Schrumpfende Städte. Band 2: Handlungskonzepte. Hatje Cantz Verlag, Ostfildern-Ruit.

• Miehlke, B. 2007: WALDblick. Eine Zukunftsperspektive für die Plattenbausiedlung Mueßer Holz, Schwerin. Unpublished diploma thesis, Hanover University.

• Mossop E. 2006. Landscapes of Infrastructure. In: Waldheim C. (Ed.) The Landscape Urbanism Reader. New York, Princeton Architectural Press, 164-177.

• Mossop, E. 2005: Affordable Landscapes. In: TOPOS Nr. 50, 13-23.

• Nemcova, E. and Wust, C. 2008: Cantho Canals. Unpublished diploma thesis, Hanover University.

• Oswalt, P. and Rieniets, T. 2006: Atlas of shrinking cities. Ostfildern:

Hatje Cantz Verlag.

• Picon, A. 2005: Constructing Landscape by Engineering Water. In: Institute for Landscape Architecture, ETH Zurich (Hrsg.): Landscape Architecture in Mutation. Gta Verlag, Zurich, 99-114.

• Shannon, K. 2004: Rhetorics and Realities. Addressing Landscape Urbanism. Three Cities in Vietnam. Unpublished doctorate, KU Leuven.

• Shannon, K. and Manawadu, S. 2007: Indiginous landscape urbanism: Sri Lanka´s reservoir & tank system. In: JoLA No. 4, autumn 2007, 6-17.

• Sijmons, D. 2004: =LANDSCAPE. Architectura & Natura Press, Netherlands.

• Stokman, A. 2007: Shifting the urban Landscape Paradigm – the Ecosystem Engineering and Design Approach. In: Bunce, R.G.H. et al (ed.): 25 Years of Landscape Ecology: Scientific Principles in Practice, IALE Publication Series 4, Wageningen, 234-235.

• Tjallingii, S. 1993: Water relations in urban systems: an ecological approach to planning and design. In: Vos, Claire C.; Opdam, Paul: Landscape Ecology of a Stressed Environment. Chapman & Hall, London, 281-302.

• Van Buuren, M. and Kerkstra, K. 1993: The framework concept and the hydrological landscape structure: a new perspective in the design of multifunctional landscapes. In: Vos, Claire C.; Opdam, Paul: Landscape Ecology of a Stressed Environment. Chapman & Hall, London, 219-243

• Waldheim C. (ed.) 2006: The Landscape Urbanism Reader. New York, Princeton Architectural Press.

• Yokohari, M., et. al. 2008: Beyond greenbelts and zoning: A new planning concept for the environment of Asian mega-cities. In: Urban Ecology. An International Perspective on the

Interaction between humans and nature. New York: Springer, ´783-796

• Yu, K. and Padua, M. (ed.) 2006: The Art of Survival. Recovering Landscape Architecture. Victoria: Images Publishing Group Pty.Ltd.

• Zaitzevsky, C. 1992: Frederick Law Olmsted and the Boston park system. Cambridge, Mass.: Belknap Press of Harvard University Press.

Water in Malaysian Landscape Architecture
~ Rotina Mohd Daik and Mustafa Kamal Bin Mohd Shariff

• Department of Irrigation and Drainage, Malaysia. 2000. Malaysian Strom Water Management Manual. Percetakan Nasional Malaysia Berhad.

• Katayon, S; Fiona, M.J. Megat Mohd Noor, M.J., Abdul Halim, G., and Ahmad, J.2008. Treatment of Mild Domestic Wastewater Using Subsurface, Constructed Wetlands in Malaysia. International Journal of Environmental Studies, Vol. 65 (1) Pp. 87-102.

• Khor, C. H. 2002. The Putrajaya Wetlands Project. Technical Paper. Angkasa, GHD Engineers Sdn. Bhd.

• National Landscape Department. 2006. Landscape Master Plan of Manjung. Ministry of Housing and Local Government Publication.

• National Landscape Department. 2007. The Development of Large Scale Park in Bukit Kiara. Ministry of Housing and Local Government Publication.

• Setia Properties. 2006. Setia Eco Park Masterplan Report. SP Setia Berhad Publication.

• Shahoran Johan Ariffin. 1998. The Making of Putrajaya. Putrajaya Corporation Publication.

The Water Adaptive Landscapes in Ancient Chinese Cities

~ Kongjian Yu, Dihua Li, and Zhang Lei

• An, D. (Editor), 1990. Taikang County records: Vol.2. Photocopy from Ming dynasty Local Records Collected By "Tianyige" of Ningbo In 1524. Shanghai Bookstore Publishing House, Shanghai. (in Chinese)

• Ban, G. (Han dynasty), Yan, S.G. (Tang dynasty), 2005. "Han Shu": Geography records. Zhonghua Book Company, Beijing. (in Chinese)

• Chen, G.H., 2002. Evolution and its cultural connotation of ancient Shangqiu city. Zhongzhou Today & Yesterday, 2:26-28. (in Chinese)

• Chen. S.L. (Editor), 2004. Cao County Records, Vol.2, Vol.5, Vol.6. In: China Local Records Collection, Shandong Sub-compilation(84). Phoenix Publishing Nanjing. (in Chinese)

• Ding, S.Y., Cao, X.X., 2004. Landscape pattern dynamics of water body in Kaifeng city since the end of the Qing Dynasty (1898 A.D.-2002 A.D.), Acta Geographica Sinica, 59(6),956-963. (in Chinese)

• Han, S.X., Xiayi (Editors), 1920. County Records. Vol.2, Vol.9, Carved-stone Printed Edition. (in Chinese)

• He, J.D., Local Records Compiling Committee of Liaocheng City, Shandong Province (LRCCL), 1999. Liaocheng City Records. Qilu press, Jinan. (in Chinese)

• Heze City History and Records Compiling Committee (HZHRCC), 1993, Heze City Records. Qilu Press, Jinan. (in Chinese)

• Jiang, X.N., 1987, Xinchou He Jue Daliang Shoucheng Shu Shi, In: Tan, Q.X. Edit. Geographical Category Article Collection of Qing Dynasty, Vol.4. Zhejiang People's Press, Hangzhou. (in Chinese)

• Li, C.B., 1958, Historical Geography of Kaifeng. The Commercial Press, Beijing. (in Chinese)

• Li, G.H., Gu, J.L., 1995, Urban flood control history, actuality, problems and strategies in Kaifeng city. Water Resources Planning and Design, 3,44-47. (in Chinese)

• Li, P. (Editor), 1896. Zhecheng County Records: Vol.2. (in Chinese)

• Li, Q. (Editor), 1895, Yucheng County Records: Art and Literature(Vol.9). (in Chinese)

• Li, R.T., 1988, Influence of Yellow River to the development of Kaifeng city in history, In: Historical Geography, Vol.6:45-56.Shanghai People Press, Shanghai. (in Chinese)

• Li, S.M. (Editor), 1986, Kaocheng County Records During the Republic of China Period: Vol.3 (Important Events), In: Lankao County Records Compiling Committee (LKCRCC) edit. Lankao old records compilation. Lankao County Records Compiling committee, Lankao. (in Chinese)

• Ling, S.T. (Editor), 2004. Heze County Records: Vol.3, Vol.17, In: China Local Records Compilation, Shandong Sub-compilation (78). Phoenix Publishing Nanjing. (in Chinese)

• Liu, D.C. (Editor), 1932, Shangqiu County Records: Vol.3. Carved-stone printed edition. (in Chinese)

• Liu, T.H., 1936, Wen Shui Ji, China Water Engineering Association, Nanjing. (in Chinese)

• Liu, W.A. (Editor), 1998, Dangshan County Records, Vol.2, In: China Local Records Compilation, Anhui Sub-compilation (29). Jiangsu Ancient Books Publishing House Nanjing. (in Chinese)

• Lv, S.F. (Editor), 2002, Luyi County Records: Vol.1, In: Rare Chinese Local Records Collection. Cathay Book Shop Publishing, Beijing. (in Chinese)

• Shangqiu County Records Compiling Committee (SCRCC), 1991. Shangqiu County Records, SDX Joint Publishing Company, Beijing. (in Chinese)

• Sui County Records Compiling Committee (SCRCC), 1989, Sui County Records. Zhongzhou Ancient Book Publishing House, Zhengzhou. (in Chinese)

• Wang, M. (Editor), 1968. Suizhou Records: Vol.1, Vol.2, and Vol.9. Student Book Company, Taipei. (in Chinese)

• Wang, M.F., 1998. Re-discussion on pre-historical settlement geography in Yellow River Watershed: Case study of Henan Province. In: Historical Geography, Vol.14:79-89,. Shanghai People Press, Shanghai. (in Chinese)

• Water Conservancy Records of Heze Area Compiling Committee (WCRHCC), 1994, Water Conservancy Records of Heze Area, Hohai University Press, Nanjing. (in Chinese)

• Wu, Q.Z., 1995, Study on Flood Control of Chinese Ancient cities. China Architecture & Building Press, Beijing (in Chinese)

• Xiao, J.N. (editor), 1911, Ningling County Records: Vol.2, Vol.3, Block-printed Edition. (in Chinese)

• Xie, Y.X., 1998. Research on the origin of "Gudui" in Southwest China from the perspective of geographical factors,. In: Historical Geography, Vol.14: 51-57. Shanghai People Press, Shanghai. (in Chinese)

• Yellow River Conservancy History Summarization Compiling Committee (YRCHSCC), 2003, Yellow River Conservancy History Summarization. Yellow River Conservancy Press, Zhengzhou. (in Chinese)

• Yellow River Records Compiling Office of Heze city River Regulation Bureau (YRRCOHRRB), 1989, Yellow River Records of Heze Area. Yellow River Records Compiling Office of

Heze City River regulation Bureau (YRRCOHRRB), Heze. (in Chinese)

• Yu, K and Padua, M., 2006, The Art of Survival, The Images Publishing Group, Victoria, Australia.

• Yuan, Z. H. (Editor), 2004. Chengwu County Records: Vol.2, Vol.12. In: China local Records Collection, Shandong Sub-compilation (82). Phoenix Publishing? Nanjing. (in Chinese)

• Zhang, S.D., 2000. Study on urban form and structure, in G.W. Skinner (editor), Ye,G.T (translator), The City in Late Imperial China. Zhonghua Book Company, Beijing, pp.84-111. (in Chinese)

• Zhao, M.Q., 2000, Characteristics and origin of the overlapped ancient cities in Xuzhou city, Collections of Essays On Chinese Historical Geography.2: 129-138. (in Chinese)

• Zheng, L.D., 1985. Urban Water Engineering In Ancient Cities. China Water Power Press, Beijing. (in Chinese)

• Zheng, X. (Editor), 1963, Xiayi County Records: Vol.2. Photocopy From Ming Dynasty Local Records, Collected by Tianyige of Ningbo in 1551. Shanghai Ancient Book Publishing House, Shanghai. (in Chinese)

• Zou, Y.L.,1993, Historical Geography Study in Yellow River, Huai River and Hai River Alluvial Plain. Anhui Education Press, Hefei. (in Chinese)

Revitalizing Qanats in Post Disaster Period - The Bam Experience in Iran
~ Amir Semiari

• Salih, Abdin (2006); Qanats a unique groundwater management tool in arid regions: the case of Bam region in Iran, UNESCO Tehran cluster office.

• Haeri, Mohammad Reza (2003), Kariz (Qanat) an eternal friendly system for harvesting groundwater. New Delhi.

• Mehraby, Rahman (2007); Kariz (Qanat) in Iran, accessible at www.destinationiran.com in 25.12.07.

• http//whc.unesco.org/en/list/1208

City, Stream, and Environmental Values - Shiraz City Stream
~ Mohsen Faizi and Mehdi Khakzand

• Kaplan, R., S. Kaplan and T. Brown (1989), Environmental Preference: A Comparison of Four Domains of Predictors, Environment and Behavior, Vol. 21, No. 5, pp. 509-530.

• Eckbo, Garrett. 1998. Landscape for Living. Harvard Design Magazine. Number 6.

• Mc Harg, I. 1992. Design with Nature. Falcon press. Philadelphia.

• Poormokhtar, M. 1380. The effect of Khoshk stream in Shiraz sustainable development. M.Sc. thesis, Shiraz University.

• Hough, M. (1990). Out of Place: Restoring Identity to the Regional Landscape. New Haven: Yale University Press.

• Roshani, A. 1374. General ecology. Imam Hossein Publication. Tehran, Iran.

• Thompson, I. 2000. Ecology, Community and Delight: sources of values in landscape architecture. Spon press.

• www.City Mayors Seoul develop-ment.htm (December 2007).

• Hwang, Kee Yeon(Ph.D.). 2003. Restoring Cheonggyecheon Stream in the Downtown Seoul. Seoul Development Institute.

• www.Wikipedia,the free encyclope-dia.htm (December 2007).

• Spirn, Anne Whiston. 1998. The Language of Landscape. Yale
University Press, New Haven.

• Turner, T. 1996. City as landscape. Spon press

The Seaward March: the Pod and the Buoy
~ Cathy Soergel Marshall and Kristi M Dykema

• Bachelard, Gaston. The Poetics of Space. Trans. Maria Jolas. Boston: Beacon, 1994.

• Barras, J., S. Belville, D. Britsch, S. Hartley, S. Hawes, J. Johnston, P. Kemp, Q. Kinler, A. Martucci, J. Porthouse, D. Reed, K. Roy, S. Sapkota, and J. Suhayda. 2003. Historic and Predicted Coastal Louisiana Land Changes: 1978-2050. USGS Open File Report 03-334, 27 pp.

• Jackson, John Brinckerhoff. Discovering the Vernacular Landscape. New Haven: Yale UP, 1984.

• Penland S and Ramsey KE. 1991. Relative sea level rise in Louisiana and the Gulf of Mexico: 1908-1988. Journal of Coastal Research 6(2):323-342.

• Segal, Robert. Myth: A Very Short Introduction. Oxford: Oxford UP, 2004.

• State of Louisiana 2004. Coastal Area Ecosystem Restoration Study (Coastal 2050 Feasibility Study). Final Report, November 2004. Volume 1, Appendixes A-D.

•B ase satellite image provided by Louisiana GIS

Transforming the Gulf Coast: Rebuilding a Cultural and Ecological Infrastructure after Hurricane Katrina
~ James L. Sipes and Anne Kirn Rollings

• Dickey, G. Edward, and Leonard

Shabman. Making Tough Choices: Hurricane Protection Planning after Katrina and Rita. Based on testimony given by one of the authors, G. Edward Dickey, before the Water Resources and Environment Subcommittee, House Committee on Transportation and Infrastructure on October 27, 2005. www.house.gov/transportation/)
• Dunbar, John. Louisiana Population Rallying after Katrina, Data Shows, Evansville Courier Press, December 27, 2007.
• EDAW. TAKING A LONGER VIEW: Mapping for Sustainable Resilience. A Project of the National Consortium to Map Gulf Coast Ecological Constraints, APRIL 2006.
• Heath, Brad, Paul Overberg and Haya El Nasser. Census shows Katrina's effects on populations, USA Today, 3-22-2007. www.usatoday.com/news/nation/census/2007-03-22-new-orleans-census_N.htm
• Johnson, Kevin. "Post-Katrina Baton Rouge struggles with its identity," USA Today, updated 2/22/2007 9:40 AM ET. www.usatoday.com/news/nation/2007-02-21-baton-rouge-cover_x.htm
• Perilloux, Gary. "Jobs coming back to La. State near pre-Katrina employment," The Advocate, Oct 18, 2007.
• Steiner, Frederick, Barbara Faga, James Sipes, and Robert Yaro. "Taking a Longer View: Mapping for Sustainable Resilience," in Rebuilding Urban Places After Disaster: Lessons from Hurricane Katrina, by Eugenie Ladner Birch and Susan M. Wachter, University of Pennsylvania Press, 2006.
• Working Group for Post-Hurricane Planning for the Louisiana Coast. A New Framework for Planning the Future of Coastal Louisiana after the Hurricanes of 2005. Cambridge, MD: University of Maryland Center for Environmental Science, 2006. Available at www.umces.edu/la-restore.
• Zinn, Jeffrey A. Coastal Louisiana Ecosystem Restoration After Hurricanes Katrina and Rita, CRS Report for Congress, Received through the CRS Web, Order Code RS22276, Updated March 17, 2006.
• National Research Council. http://sites.nationalacademies.org/nrc/index.htm

Littoral machines: How Waterfronts become Coasts
~ Matthew Bradbury and Frank de Graaf

• Bush, G. W. A. (1971) Decently and in Order, Auckland, Collins Bros. and Co.
• Waldheim, Charles. (2006) The Landscape Urbanism Reader. 1st ed. New York, N.Y.: Princeton Architectural Press,.
• Dickenson, N. M. (2004) Modelling Contamination in an Urban Canal Sediment. In Wong, M. H. (Ed.) Developments in Ecosystems, Vol. one.
• Koolhaas, R. (1995) S,M,L,XL, Rotterdam, 010 Publishers.
• Morton, J. A. C., Ewen. (1993) Shore Vegetation. In Morton, J. (Ed.) A Natural History of Auckland. Auckland, David Bateman Ltd.
• Shaver, E. (2000) Low Impact Stormwater Management (TP124). Auckland, Auckland Regional Authority.

The Strength, Weakness, Opportunity, and Threat (SWOT) Analysis of Mangrove Forests in the Coastal Areas of the Tropics and Sub-tropics
~ Nik Ismail Azlan

• Brown, S. & A. E. Lugo, 1994. Rehabilitation of Tropical Lands: a key to sustaining development. Restoration Ecol. 2: 97–111.
• Chen, R. & R. R. Twilley, 1998. A gap dynamic model of mangrove forest development along gradients of soil salinity and nutrient resources. J. Ecol. 86: 37–51.
• Crewz, D. W., and R. R. Lewis. 1991. Evaluation of historical attempts to establish emergent vegetation in marine wetlands in Florida. Florida Sea Grant Technical Paper No.60. Florida Sea Grant College, Gainesville. 79 pp + append. (html)
•
http://nsgl.gso.uri.edu/flsgp/flsgpt91001/flsgpt91001index.html
• Erftemeijer, P. L. A., and R. R. Lewis III. 2000. Planting mangroves on inter-tidal mudflats: habitat restoration or habitat conversion? Pages 156-165 in Proceedings of the ECOTONE VIII Seminar "Enhancing Coastal Ecosystems Restoration for the 21st Century, Ranong, Thailand, 23-28 May 1999. Royal Forest Department of Thailand, Bangkok, Thailand.
• Field, C. D. (ed.), 1996. Restoration of Mangrove Ecosystems. International Society for Mangrove Ecosystems, Okinawa, Japan: 250 pp.
• Lewis, R. R. 1981. Economics and feasibility of mangrove restoration. Pp. 88-94 in Proceedings of the Coastal Ecosystems Workshop, U.S. Fish and Wildlife Service. FWS/OBS-80/59.
• Lewis, R. R. 1982. Mangrove Forests. Ch. 8, pp. 153-172 in R. R Lewis (ed.), Creation and Restoration of Coastal

Plant Communities. CRC Press, Boca Raton, Florida. 219pp. (pdf, 21p, 1.4MB) www.mangroverestoration.com/Lewis_1982_Mangroves_CRC.pdf
• Nik Ismail Azlan 2007, Mangrove against Tsunami: Between Myth and Reality, Unpublished Paper, Wetlands Conference, Thailand
• Nik Ismail Azlan 2008, Demographic Profile of Mangrove Eco-tourism Visitors to Kukup Island, Unpublished Paper, Wetlands Thailand .
• Stevenson, N. J., R. R. Lewis and P. R. Burbridge. 1999. Disused shrimp ponds and mangrove rehabilitation. Pages 277-297 in "An International Perspective on Wetland Rehabilitation", W. J. Streever (Ed.). Kluwer Academic Publishers, The Netherlands. 338 pp. (pdf, 21p, 1.85MB) www.mangroverestoration.com/Stevenson_et_al_1999_Disused_Shrimp_Ponds.pdf
• Turner, R. E., and R. R. Lewis. 1997. Hydrologic restoration of coastal wetlands. Wetlands Ecol. Manage. 4(2):65-72. (pdf, 8p, 2.1MB) www.mangroverestoration.com/hydrolog-ic_restoraton_of_coasta_wetlands.pdf
• Tomlinson, 1995. The Botany of Mangroves. Cambridge University Press; New Edition (March 31, 1995)

Urban River fronts along the Rhine
~ Cornelia Redeker

• Adomat,H., water management Karlsruhe, interview June 14, 2007.
• Baron H., urban planning department Karlsruhe, interviews June 13, 2007.
• Flood Conference Vienna, proceedings, May 17, 2006.
• Halle, M., Pottgiesser, T., Umweltbuero Essen. Entwicklung einer Abschnittstypologie für den natürlichen Rheinstrom. report no. 146d, ICPR.
• Hochwasserschutzkonzept Koeln, Stadt Koeln 1995.
• ICPR Rhine Atlas, 2001.
• Koridon, L., Driessen, D., Schouten, M., Dijkterruglegging Lent, municipality of Nijmegen, 2007.
• Lohrberg landscape architects, Blau Mannheim Blau, research project commissioned by the urban planning department of Mannheim, 2007.
• Sieweke, S., Stadträume am Rhein, workshop 2007 in Montagstiftung, Regionale2010, -Stromlagen, urbane Flusslanddschaften gestalten, Birkhaeuser, 2008.
• Rheindenken, Wohnen am Strom, feasibility study, Regionale2010, 2006.
• Stalenberg, Bianca & Cornelia Redeker: Urban flood protection: two strategies. p. 875-882 in: Proceedings of International Conference on Water and Flood Management; Institute of Water and Flood Management, BUET, Dhaka, Bangladesh. 2007.
• Vrijling, H. and de Boer, E., van der Hulst, Alex. Watergevecht: dijkenbrekers versus dijkenbouwers, Groene Amsterdamer No. 33, 2004.
• Yossef, M., Morphodynamics of rivers with groynes, PhD research, TU Delft, Hydraulic Engineering, 2005.
• www.dijkterruglegginglent.nl
• www.hochwasserinfo-koeln.de/
• www.icpr.org
• www.innenhafen-duisburg.de
• www.irma-sponge.org
• www.regionale2010.de
• www.ruimtevoorderivier.nl

Bangkok Liquid Perception: the Chao Phraya river delta and the city of Bangkok
~ Brian McGrath and Danai Thaitakoo

• Bormann, F.H. and G.E. Likens, Pattern and Process in a Forested Ecosystem, New York: Springer-Vertag, 1981.
• Deleuze, Gilles, Cinema 1: The Movement Image, Minneapolis, University of Minnesota Press, 1986.
• Shane, Grahame, Recombinant Urbanism, London: Wiley, 2005.

Place-telling at Dubai Creek: Encoded Visions
~ Tim Kennedy

• Beauregard, Robert A. (2005) From Place to Site: Negotiating Narrative Complexity. In Burns, Carol and Kahn, Andrea (Eds.), Site Matters (pps.39-58) London: Routledge.
• Emaar UAE Developments. (n.d.). Retrieved March 20, 2007, from http://www.emaar.com/Developments/Downtown/oldtown/Index.asp
• Hill, Kristina. (2000) On sustainable messages being coded into stories. In Benson, John and Roe, Maggie (Eds.), Landscape and Sustainability, pps 296-297, London: Spon Press.
• Johnston, Barbara (1990) Stories, Community, and Place: Narratives from Middle America, p. 120, Bloomington: Indiana Press.
• MacCannell, Dean. (1976) The Tourist: A New Theory of the Leisure Class, pps. 13-14, Berkeley: University of California Press.
• Potteiger, Matthew (1998) Landscape Narratives: Design Practices for Telling Stories, New York: John Wiley & Sons.
• Turner, Mark. (1998) The Literary Mind: The Origins of Thought and Language, pps. 4-5, Cambridge, MA: Oxford University Press.

Sacralizing the Water's Edge: the Landscape of the Ghats at Varanasi
~ Amitabh Verma

• Bhattacharya, Brajamadhava. 1999. Varanasi Rediscovered. New Delhi: Munshiram Manoharlal Publishers.
• Chattopadhyaya, D.P. 2003. Indian Perspectives on Naturalism. In Nature Across Cultures: Views of Nature and the Environment in Non-Western Cultures, ed. Helaine Selin, 147-159. Dordrecht, The Netherlands: Kluwer Academic Publishers.
• Ching, Francis D.K., Mark M. Jarzombek and Vikramaditya Prakash. 2007. A Global History of Architecture. New Jersey: John Wiley & Sons, Inc.
• Eck, Diana L. 1982. Banaras: City of Light. New York: Alfred A. Knopf.
• Kostof, Spiro. 1991. The City Shaped: Urban Patterns and Meanings Through History. New York: Bullfinch Press.
• Pathak, Ratnesh K. and Cynthia Ann Humes. 1993. Lolark Kund: Sun and Shiva Worship in the City of Light. In Living Banaras: Hindu Religion in Classical Context, ed. Bradley R. Hertel and Cynthia Ann Humes, 205-243. Albany, NY: State University of New York Press.
• Rani, Varsha. 2001. Banaras: The Eternal City. New Delhi: Prakash Book Depot.
• Sinha, Amita. 2006. Landscapes in India: Forms and Meanings. Boulder: University Press of Colorado.

The Drying Beijing, The Rethinking of Fengshui
~ Fu Fan and Zhao Caijun

• Book of Poetries, Harbin Press, 2006.
• Cheng Jianjun, Cang Feng De Shui, China Movie Press, 2005.
• Beijing Environmental Protection and Ecological Construction Plan for the Eleventh Quinquennium, Beijing Municipal Environmental Protection Bureau, 2006.
• Beijing Environmental Statement 2006, Beijing Municipal Environmental Protection Bureau, 2006.
• Beijing Water Resource Bulletin 2005, Beijing Water Authority, 2005.
• HU Jie, WU Yi-xia, LV Lu-shan, General Introduction of Beijing Olympic Forest Park Landscape Plan, Journal of Chinese Landscape Architecture, 06/2006.
• HU Jie, WU Yi-xia, LV Lu-shan, Water System Plan of Beijing Olympic Forest Park, Journal of Chinese Landscape Architecture, 06/2006.
• Hu Jun, Chinese Cities: Their Evolution and Patterns, China Architecture & Building Press, 1995.
• Kang Liang, Kang Yu, Fengshui and Architecture, Flora Literature Press, 1999.
• Kang Liang, Kang Yu, Fengshui and City, Flora Press, 1999.
• Liu Yuxin, Xuan Yongli, Reclycled Water Flow into the Dragon-shaped Waterscape of Olympic Park and will keep clean at Least 2 months, Beijing Daily, 03/28/2007.
• Ray Huang, China: A Macro History, SDX Joint Publishing Company, 2007.
• Simonds, John O., Landscape Architecture: A Manual of Site Planning and Design, Third Edition, McGraw-Hill Professional, 1997.
• Tong Qing-yuan, Zhao Dong-quan, Hu Jie, Design for Simulation & Maintainance System of Water Quality in Beijing Olympic Forest Park, Journal of Chinese Landscape Architecture, 08/2006.
• Yi Ding, Yu Lu, Hong Yong, Chinese Ancient Fengshui and Site Selection for Architecture, Heibe Science and Technology Press, 1996.

Urban Riverfront Rehabilitation, Recalling Nature to the Public Realm
~ Sareh Moosavi, Kamyar Abbassi and Mehdi Sheibani

• Afsar, K. 1965. History of the Old context of Shiraz. Melli Association.
• American Rivers. 2003. "10 Ways Dams Damage Rivers." [Accessed December 18 2008]. Available at www.americanrivers.org/damremoval/tenreasons.htm
• Bechtol V. 2008. Restoring straight-ened rivers for sustainable flood miti-gation. Disaster Prevention and Management, 4.
• Bidokhti, N., Monajjemi, P. 1996. Studies on The Khoshk River. Shahrdari Report.
• Forman, Richard T.T. 1995. Land mosaics – the ecology of landscapes and regions. Cambridge: University Press.
• Forman, Richard T.T. and Gordon, Michael. 1986. Landscape ecology. New York: John Wiley and Sons.
• Forman, Richard T.T. and Gordon, Michael. 1981. "Patches and structural components for landscape ecology". BioScience vol.31, no. 10, 733-740.
• May R. 2006. Connectivity in urban rivers: Conflict and convergence between ecology and design. Technology in Society, 28, 477-488
• Moss, Michael R. 2000a. "Interdisciplinarity, landscape ecology and the transformation of agricultur-al landscapes". Landscape Ecology 15, 303-311.
• Moss, Michael R. 2000b. "Landscape ecology: the need for a discipline?" In Richling, A. et al (editors),
• Landscape ecology – theory and applications for practical purposes. Warsaw: Pultusk School of Humanities, IALE, and Polish Association for Landscape Ecology. 172-185.

• Otto, Betsy., McCormick, Kathleen. & Leccese, Michael. 2004. Ecologica Riverfront Design: Restoring Rivers, Connecting Communities. American Planning Association (APA)

• Pakzad, J. 2005. Guidelines for Designing Urban Spaces in Iran. Ministry of Housing and Urban Development. Urban Planning And Architecture vice directorate. 393-412.

• Penteado, Homero. M. 2004. The river in the urban landscape: Landscape ecological principles for the design of riverfronts. Dissertation Abstracts International, 61 (02), 776A. (UMI No. 9963641). Retrieved October 23, 2007, from http://proquest.umi.com.ezproxy.lib.unimelb.edu.au

• Picon A. 2005. Constructing Landscape by Engineering Water: Landscape Architecture in Mutation: essays on urban landscape, 99-115.

• Pourmokhtar, M. 2002. The role of Khoshk River on Sustainable Development of Shiraz. Urban Planning Thesis.

• Riley, Ann L. 1998. Restoration streams in cities – a guide for planners, policymakers, and citizens. Washington, D.C.: Island Press.

• Tabacchi, Eric and Planty Tabacchi, Anne-Marie. 2000. "Impacts of riparian vegetation on hydrological processes". Hydrological Processes vol. 14, issue 16, 2959-2976.

Toward a Spectacle City: Critical Synopsis of the Han River Renaissance Project in Seoul
~ Kyung-Jin Zoh

• Berque, Augustin, 2000, "World cities make world rivers," Rivers in the Metropolis: Seoul Metropolitan Fora 2000, Seoul: The University of Seoul, pp. 42-61.

• Debord, Guy, 2002, The Society of the Spectacle, Canberra: Teason Press.

• Gierstberg, Frits and Warna Oosterbann, 2002, The Image Society: Essays on Visual Culture, Rotterdam: NAi Publishers.

• Harvey, David, 1989, The Condition of Postmodernity, Oxford: Basil Blackwell.

• Klingmann, Anna, 2007, Brandscapes: Architecture in the Experience Economy, Cambridge: The MIT Press.

• Seoul Development Institute, 2000, Seoul, Twentieth Century: A Photographical History of the Last 100 Years, Seoul: Seoul Development Institute.

• Seoul Metropolitan Government, 2007a, International Design Competition for Seoul Yeouido Riverside Park, Competition Guidelines, Seoul: Hangang Project Headquarters.

• Seoul Metropolitan Government, 2007b, Hangang Renaissance International Symposium: Vision of Aquapolis Seoul, Seoul: Seoul Metropolitan Government.

• Seoul Metropolitan Government, 2007c, Hangang Renaissance Masterplan, Seoul: Hangang Project Headquarters.

• Seoul Metropolitan Government, 2008a, Hangang Renaissance Project Presentation Material, Seoul: Hangang Project Headquarters.

• Seoul Metropolitan Government, 2008b, Hangang Renaissance Masterplan PR Material (English), Seoul: Hangang Project Headquarters.

• Song, Do Young, 2000, Han River and Life of Seoulites, Rivers in the Metropolis: Seoul Metropolitan Fora 2000, Seoul: The University of Seoul, pp. 63-75.

Water as a Defence Systems in the Past - Taman Sari
~ Indra Tjahjani

• Adhisakti, L.T. 1991. Conserving Planning and Urban Design of Historical Settlement. Case Study of Taman Sari Yogyakarta.

• Adhisakti, L.T. 1991. Configuration Pattern of Taman Sari Ngayogyakarta In the Relation To Its Function As A Pleasure Garden and A Defensive Area. The University of Gadjah Mada. Yogyakarta.

• Adhisakti, L.T. 1997. A Study on the Conservation Planning of Yogyakarta Historic- tourist City Based on Urban Space Heritage Conception. Thesis. Kyoto University. Japan.

• Bruggen, M.P. van and Wassing, R.S. 1998. Djokja Solo Beeld van de Vorstensteden. Asia Maior.

• Dumarcay, J. 1991. The Palaces of South-East Asia. Architecture and Customs. Oxford University Press. New York.

• Dwijasaraya,AS. 1935. Ngayogyakarta Hadiningrat. The Second. Patilasan Taman Sari. Sakti, Ngayogyakarta.

• Indonesian Heritage. 1996. Ancient History. Archipelago Press. Jakarta.

• Indonesian Heritage. 1996. Early Modern History. Archipelago Press. Jakarta.

• Indonesian Heritage. 1998. Architecture. Archipelago Press. Jakarta.

• Iriansyah, N. 1998. Strategi Penataan Kembali Pemukiman Pada Kawasan Konservasi Taman Sari Yogya. Thesis. Program Study Arsitektur. Program Pasca Sarjana Institute Teknologi Bandung.

• Iskandar, S, 2000. Istana Air (Het Water Kasteel) Jogjakarta. Translation from J. Groneman 1884. Unpublished. Bekasi.

• Ricklefs, M.C. 1974. Jogjakarta under Sultan Mangkubumi 1749 – 1792. A History of the Division of Java. Oxford University Press. London.

• Sasmito, D.I. 1983. Tinjauan Sejarah Mengenai Peranan Pesanggrahan Taman Sari Yogyakarta. Pada Masa Pemerintahan Sri Sultan Hamengku Buwono I. Fakultas Sastra - Universitas Pajajaran Bandung.

• Taylor, K. 2003. The Historical Landscape Planning. Fourth International Experts Meeting on Borobudur. Humanities Research Centre. The Australian National University. Canberra. Australia.

• Tjahjani, I. 1995. The Indonesian Landscape Heritage as an Asset of the Development of Tourist Industry. Paper on the 7th International Federation of Landscape Architects Eastern Regional Conference. The New Zealand Institute of Landscape Architects. Christchurch. New Zealand.

• Tjahjani, I. 1995. The Indonesian Culture and Landscape: A Challenge Toward the Tourist Development Industry. Paper on the 32nd on International Federation of Landscape Architects World Conference. The Thai Association of Landscape Architects and Tourist Authority of Thailand. Bangkok. Thailand.

• Tjahjani, I. 2005. "Taman Sari" Yogyakarta A Cultural Perspective in Landscape Design. University of Canberra. Canberra. Australia.

Imprint

IFLA 2008 ~ Proceedings of the 45th World Congress
of the International Federation of Landscape Architects
Transforming with Water
Apeldoorn, The Netherlands, june 30 – july 3, 2008

Edited by
Wybe Kuitert

In cooperation with
Kaspar Klap (images) and others

Lay out and production
Harry Harsema, Grafisch Atelier Wageningen / Blauwdruk Publishers

Printed by
Modern Bennekom, The Netherlands

Published by
Blauwdruk, Wageningen, The Netherlands
Techne Press, Amsterdam, The Netherlands

The IFLA 2008 World congres was jointly organized by
Stichting IFLA 2008 foundation, in cooperation with
the Netherlands Association for Landscape Architecture (NVTL)
and the International Federation of Landscape Architects (IFLA)

©June 2008
ISBN 978-90-8594-021-0

www.uitgeverijblauwdruk.nl
www.technepress.nl
www.nvtl.nl

'scape

'scape is the new international magazine for landscape architecture and urbanism. It offers a journalistic, critical and professional view of the design of landscapes and townscapes.

'scape informs, raises opinions and inspires. Richly illustrated and attractively designed, the magazine contains news, features, interviews, portraits, design criticism, essays, book reviews and commentaries.

'scape is produced and edited by the makers of Fieldwork – Landscape Architecture Europe and the Dutch magazine for landscape architecture and urbanism Blauwe Kamer .

'scape is published twice a year and distributed in collaboration with Birkhäuser Verlag AG.

The international magazine for **landscape architecture** and **urbanism**

2 x year, 92 pages, full colour individuals € 30,- students € 27,-

www scapemagazine.com

> *'ITS HERE!*

 A grand mag!

Thanks'